RUSSIAN HEROIC POETRY

Russian minstrels (*skomorokhi*) at Ladoga singing before Olearius, to the accompaniment of stringed instruments, the heroic "poem of the mighty lord and tsar Michael Theodorovich" in 1634

Russian Heroic Poetry

by

N. KERSHAW CHADWICK

*Associate of Newnham College, Cambridge; formerly
Lecturer in the University of St Andrews*

Ж

CAMBRIDGE

AT THE UNIVERSITY PRESS

1932

CAMBRIDGE
UNIVERSITY PRESS

University Printing House, Cambridge CB2 8BS, United Kingdom

Cambridge University Press is part of the University of Cambridge.

It furthers the University's mission by disseminating knowledge in the pursuit of education, learning and research at the highest international levels of excellence.

www.cambridge.org
Information on this title: www.cambridge.org/9781107431881

© Cambridge University Press 1932

First published 1932
First paperback edition 2014

A catalogue record for this publication is available from the British Library

ISBN 978-1-107-43188-1 Paperback

To

THE MEMORY OF

DAME

BERTHA SURTEES NEWALL

Уныша цвѣты жалобою,
и древо съ тугою
къ земли преклонило.
Slovo o Polky Igorevê.

CONTENTS

THE EARLY HEROES AND THE CYCLES OF
KIEV AND NOVGOROD

ILLUSTRATIONS

PREFACE

THERE is no country in Europe to-day of which we stand so much in need of knowledge as Russia. There is hardly a country of which, in its entirety, we know so little. Probably a more enlightened and sympathetic interest was felt for Russia in the reign of Queen Elizabeth than is generally felt in England to-day. It was an Englishman on a visit to Moscow in 1619 who first recorded examples of Russian *byliny*, or heroic poems.

To understand aright what is taking place in Russia to-day, it is essential to gain a perspective which even a detailed knowledge of the Soviet Republic alone cannot supply. The break with the past has been far-reaching and apparently complete, and the old is in danger of being forgotten in the new. Yet Old Russia is not dead. Her traditions linger and haunt the generation which would abrogate them. Many of the methods employed by modern democratic political machinery were employed in the past by the tsars, and for the same purposes. To mention one instance only, the colossal engineering plans, involving the transportation of whole families and villages across vast tracts of country, far from their homes, to the scenes of labour, are not a new feature. They were not new when Peter the Great constructed the Ladoga canal by similar means; and many popular laments testify to the sorrow and hardships entailed upon the individual by his enterprises, and the courage with which they were borne. The people and the nature of the country remain unchanged, and even the intelligentsia cannot wholly discard the traditional heritage of Old Russia.

Such considerations have suggested that it might be of interest to examine the oral literature current among Russian peasants in modern times in so far as it relates to the history of the country. The *byliny*, or heroic poems, are the oral records of such history. They supply a popular supplement to the more professional forms of historical record, such as the chronicles kept by religious houses, the memoirs of the lettered classes, and the royal archives. The *byliny* give us the history of Russia as viewed through the eyes of the unlettered classes—an aspect of history which, despite its paramount importance, would otherwise pass unrecorded. They bring a new factor to history by supplying what Sir Bernard Pares calls "the running chorus, so intelligent and so suggestive, of the best wisdom of the Russian peasantry". Through the *byliny* the unlettered classes have become articulate.

The events recorded in the *byliny* range over the entire period of Russian history, extending over a thousand years, from the time of Vladimir I to that of Nicholas I. The most productive periods are those in which the throne of Russia was occupied by a powerful and able ruler. The most numerous and the most ambitious of the *byliny* relate to the early period, and recount the adventures of the heroes of the court of Kiev under Vladimir I. During the period of the Tartar invasions the *byliny* are almost silent, but under Ivan IV, the great contemporary and correspondent of Queen Elizabeth, and again under Peter the Great, they burst into renewed life.

The historicity is not great for the early period, and indeed at all times these poems are apt to be unreliable as a specific record of events. The most interesting period, and from a historical point of view the most valuable, is the first half of the seventeenth century, for which the *byliny* supply us with a kind of oral chronicle. It is, in many respects, an obscure and a baffling period to historians, and these little topical contemporary commentaries are singularly welcome. At this time the bourgeoisie and the poorer classes in the towns struggle to the surface of Russian political life, and influence the course of events as at no other period; and the contemporary *byliny*, at once their manifesto and the record of their struggle, attain almost to the prestige of documentary evidence.

The literary value of the *byliny* may be said to be in in-

verse ratio to their historicity. The longest and most ambitious are those which relate to Kiev and Prince Vladimir.
Those relating to modern times are comparatively poor and
jejune. All follow a traditional heroic style which originated
in court circles, and which was already well established before
our earliest examples were recorded. This style continues,
with a few exceptions, uniform throughout. It is shared to a
great extent by the lyrics and folk-songs, on which it has, no
doubt, been imposed through the influence of heroic literature or a heroic milieu. But the *byliny* did not originate in
a peasant milieu: like the Danish ballads, they formed in the
past the entertainment of the country gentry and even the
official classes. It is only within the last hundred years that
they have become restricted to peasant circles.

Very few of the examples given below have been translated into English before, and many of them have not, so far
as I am aware, been translated into any language. Hitherto
no representative series of *byliny* have been translated into
English. Miss Hapgood's valuable little book, *The Epic
Songs of Russia*, consists of paraphrases and partial translations of composite texts from the Kiev and Novgorod cycles
only. Rambaud's work, *La Russie Épique*, includes many
translations, some complete, many abridged; but it has long
been out of print. My own work owes much to the stimulus
and information afforded by this brilliant book.

In the following pages an attempt has been made to give
a representative series of *byliny* from all periods. In selecting
from the many hundreds of examples contained in the great
Russian collections I have kept in view the two-fold aim of
illustrating the course of Russian history and the development of Russian heroic poetry. At the same time, it must be
confessed, I have often yielded to the temptation to select a
particular *bylina* because it was specially attractive in itself.
Indeed it was simply the innate attractiveness of the Russian
byliny as a whole which led me to translate them. But no one
could be more aware than I am myself how much of their
charm has been lost with the change of language.

In translating literature which has been carried on exclusively by oral tradition, and which is rich in variant versions, one is inevitably faced by the necessity of having to make a difficult choice between two alternative methods. The first is to select for translation single texts, which will inevitably be at times defective and of unequal quality. The second is to make a composite text, from all available variants, utilising the best passages and omitting none of the relevant elements. Both methods have much to recommend them, and the second method has been adopted with a large measure of success by Miss Hapgood in her treatment of the *byliny* of the Kiev and Novgorod cycles. In the present volume the first method has been adopted. The author is aware that a certain loss in the effect produced upon the reader is to be looked for in consequence. But it has been regarded as preferable in that it gives a more exact reproduction of the *byliny* as they are sung, rather than a reconstruction of hypothetical artistic forms. In the few instances where passages have been added or inserted from variants the fact is indicated in the footnotes.

The desire to reproduce the *byliny* as faithfully as possible in the form in which they are sung has also determined the method of translation. The English text corresponds line by line with the Russian text, but no attempt has been made to reproduce the metre or rhythm of the original. The translation has been made as literal as possible. Repetitions and redundant formulae have been retained as a fundamental characteristic of the *byliny*, and the static phrases and archaic poetical syntax have been reproduced as far as possible.

My warmest thanks are due to Professor Minns, who placed his library of Russian literature at my disposal, and allowed me to keep his valuable collections of Russian *byliny* for I am ashamed to reflect how long. Without his generosity it would have been impossible for me to obtain access to the collections of Gilferding and Kirêevski. I am also indebted to him for reading several of my translations in MS as well as the proofs of the Introduction, and for making a number of helpful suggestions.

I also wish to thank my friends Miss A. D. M. Hoare and Miss E. E. Phare for reading some of the translations in MS, and Miss E. E. H. Welsford and Mr C. E. Wright for reading through the proofs. Mr Wright in particular has spared neither time nor pains in his careful scrutiny. I should like also to thank Mr R. H. Rottmann, of Messrs Deighton, Bell and Co., Cambridge, for the trouble which he took to procure Rybnikov's collection for me, as well as more recent collections from Russia and Esthonia, which without his help I could not have obtained. I welcome this opportunity of acknowledging a series of similar obligations to him, lasting over twenty years. I am indebted to Herr Karl Baedeker for permission to use his maps of the Kremlin and environs, and of the Great Kremlin Palace, Moscow; and to the Hakluyt Society for permission to reproduce the portrait of Ivan IV. Finally I should like to thank the Syndics of the Cambridge University Press for undertaking the publication of the book, and the staffs of the University Press and the University Library for their unfailing and courteous help while the work was in progress.

N. KERSHAW CHADWICK

CAMBRIDGE
June, 1932

INTRODUCTION

SCIENTIFIC interest in Russian popular poetry is of comparatively recent date even in Russia itself. Before the beginning of last century such poetry was neglected and almost unknown. The collection and publication of popular poetry on a large scale in Russia during the latter half of last century was no doubt due indirectly to the influence of the Romantic Revival of Western Europe, reacting first on Russian men of letters, such as Pushkin and Lermontov, and ultimately on the more intellectual of the official classes. Percy's *Reliques* and Macpherson's *Ossian* probably acted as a stimulus to the interest in Russian popular poetry no less potent than that of Byron in literary circles. The scientific collection and investigation of oral poetry as a living form has therefore been carried on under exceptionally favourable circumstances in Russia. The lower classes, backward and illiterate, continued to derive their entertainment from the old traditional forms of poetry, while the officials and landed gentry of the more progressive type, especially those in the neighbourhood of Moscow and St Petersburg, had acquired the literary outlook of the Romantic Revival, simultaneously with the scientific and critical methods which followed it in Western Europe only at a later period.

The narrative and heroic poems of Russia are called *byliny* (sg. *bylina*), or *stariny* (sg. *starina*). The word *bylina* is said to be derived from the past participial form (*byl*) of the verb *byt'*, 'to be', and signifies 'that which has been', 'past occurrences'. By an extension of meaning the word is also applied to poems celebrating contemporary events. Such poems generally contain a narrative element. Sometimes, however, they consist wholly of speeches, as some of the following examples will show. In its application to the popular narrative poems relating to the ancient heroes the word *bylina* is said to be of literary origin. The native singers of Olonets and Siberia generally call both the heroic and the historical poems *stariny*,[1] 'stories of long ago'. I have used the term *byliny* throughout this book, as being more generally familiar. Although *byliny* sometimes relate to characters whose names are not mentioned, the great majority are concerned with well-known characters, sometimes, but not always, persons who figure in Russian history. Indeed the *bylina* is the most popular form of poetry relating to historical events in Russia at all periods, from the tenth to the nineteenth century.

The traditional mould in which this narrative poetry was carried on was certainly a living form down to the Revolution of 1917, and in remote districts will no doubt continue to be the popular form of entertainment for some time to come. But it is doomed to pass away here as everywhere else with the spread of education. Even in the province of Olonets on Lake Onega, the district in which the great majority of the *byliny* have been collected, the practice of singing *byliny* has for long been restricted to a limited area. Yet at Petrozavodsk in this same district, at the time when the early collections were made, the old men related how, fifty years earlier, it had been the custom in their little town for the *chinovniks* or officials, no less than the bourgeoisie and merchant classes, to meet together in the evenings to listen to the singing of *byliny*.[2] To-day if we would seek the oral remnants of ancient Kiev in their purest form we must go to the River Kolyma in North-Eastern Siberia, where it is said that one can still hear the ancient Russian songs and legends, the words and expressions of which are obsolete now in European Russia, and only to be found perhaps in the twelfth-century Russian work *Slovo o Polky Igorevê*.[3]

The *byliny* are purely oral in character, and their long

---

[1] Brodski, Mendelson and Sidorov, *Istoriko-Literaturnaya Khrestomatÿa*, vol. I (Moscow, 1922), p. 70, footnote.

[2] See Rambaud, *La Russie Épique* (Paris, 1876), p. 11.

[3] J. W. Shklovsky, *In Far North-East Siberia* (London, 1916), p. 12.

history is the history of oral tradition. They have never at any time formed a part of the written literature of the country, and it may be regarded as certain that they have never been seriously influenced from written sources. In modern times they have formed the répertoire of the peasant population all over Russia and Siberia. It is interesting to observe, however, that *byliny* relating to early times are cultivated by wide circles of singers only in remote districts. By the middle of the last century such *byliny* were believed to be almost extinct as a living form till Rybnikov discovered them still flourishing among the singers of the Government of Olonets on the shores of Lake Onega.[1] This discovery was so surprising and sensational to the educated world that it was treated with a scepticism similar to that which greeted Macpherson's *Ossian* in our own country.

Rybnikov has left us a picturesque account of his first experiences during his search for *byliny*. He was an officer in the Russian civil service, a *chinovnik*, stationed at Petrozavodsk on Lake Onega. He had reason to believe that *byliny* relating to the ancient heroes of Russia were not wholly dead among the villagers of the Olonets Government, and when in 1860 he was ordered to obtain statistics in that district on behalf of the Government, he was enabled to make persistent enquiries for singers familiar with *byliny*. He constantly heard of the great reputation of a travelling tailor known as 'the Bottle', who was a famous singer of *byliny*, and who roamed throughout the whole of the trans-Onega district; but his efforts to find either 'the Bottle' or other singers were unsuccessful for a long time. The peasants feared and distrusted a *chinovnik*, and even in that backward region it was not easy to come upon people who were actually familiar with poetry of the kind he was seeking.

[1] The original edition of Rybnikov's collection is very scarce. A new edition was published by Gruzinski in three volumes at Moscow in 1909, under the title *Pésni sobrannÿa P. N. Rybnikovym*, 'Songs collected by P. N. Rybnikov'. My references throughout the present volume are to Gruzinski's edition.

Success came unexpectedly one day when he and his companions were overtaken by a storm as they were crossing Lake Onega in a crazy boat, and took refuge on an island. Rybnikov has left us an account of this romantic incident.

On the island there was a smoky shelter, a shed, where in the summer and autumn time, in calm, in contrary and in stormy weather the people take shelter at night. Round the wharf were many boats from the north of the Onega, and the shelter was full of people to the point of overflowing. To speak the truth, it was excessively smelly and dirty, and although it was very cold, I felt no desire to go in and rest. I lay down on my bag beside the meagre wood fire, made some tea for myself over the embers, drank it, and ate some of my travelling supply, and then became warmed by the fire and gradually fell asleep. I was awakened by strange sounds. Up to now I had heard many songs and religious poems, but such a song as this I had not heard. Vivacious, fantastic, and gay, now it grew quicker, now it slowed down, and recalled by its tune something very long ago, forgotten by our generation. For a long time I was unwilling to awaken, and listened to every word of the song—so happy was I to remain totally overpowered by this new sensation.

In my sleep I fancied that three paces from me some peasants were sitting, and an old man sat singing, with a bushy white beard and bright eyes and kindly expression of face. Squatting on his heels beside the dying fire, he turned first to one neighbour, then to another, and sang his song, breaking off now and then with a smile. He ended one song, and began to sing another poem. Then I made out that he was singing the *bylina* of *Sadko the Merchant, the Rich Trader*. Needless to say I was on my feet in a moment, and prevailed upon the peasant to repeat his song, and wrote it down from his lips. I began to question him as to whether he did not know anything else. My new acquaintance, Leonti Bogdanovich from the village of Seredka, Kizhski district, promised to recite many *byliny* to me—of Dobrynya Nikitich, Ilya of Murom, Michael Potyk Ivanovich, of the noble Vasili Buslaevich, of Khotenushka Bludovich, of the Forty

Kalêki Men and Women, of the hero Svyatogor, but he knew
only incomplete versions, i.e. he could not complete the narratives. Consequently I wrote down in the end only such of his
byliny as served to supplement other versions by their details, or
such as offered wholly new matter. For the rest, on the first
occasion I wrote down somewhat reluctantly, and preferred to
listen. In the course of time I listened to many rare *byliny*;
I recollect ancient, superb melodies. The singers sang them with
exquisite voices and masterly declamation; but to be perfectly
honest, I never experienced again that fresh sensation which the
wretched versions of the *byliny* conveyed to me, sung by the
broken voice of old Leonti.[1]

The scepticism which greeted the publication of Rybnikov's collection was quickly silenced. In the year 1871
Gilferding set out to the same region in the hope of supple-
menting Rybnikov's work. He penetrated, as a matter of
fact, much farther to the north, and into more inaccessible
regions than Rybnikov had done, and was able to add
much valuable new material. At the same time he inter-
viewed many of the same singers whom Rybnikov had heard
and again recorded their *byliny*. A comparison of the
variant versions thus obtained affords valuable material for
the study of the composition and recitation of oral poetry
and the circumstances of oral transmission.[2]

While Rybnikov was making his researches in person
among the peasants in the neighbourhood of Lake Onega,
Kirêevski was publishing *byliny* collected from all over
Great Russia, from Archangel to Moscow, from Novgorod
to Siberia. Some of the *byliny* in his collection had already
been published from Kirsha Danilov's MS (cf. p. 8 below).
Others were obtained from albums and private MS collec-

[1] Rybnikov, *Pêsni*, vol. i, p. lxix f.
[2] Gilferding's collection was published at St Petersburg in 1875
under the title *Onezhskÿa byliny zapisannÿa A. F. Gilferdingom*,
'Byliny of Onega recorded by A. F. Gilferding'. A new edition
appeared, also at St Petersburg, and in three volumes, in 1894, under
the same title. My references throughout are to this later edition.

tions. While many of them relate to ancient times and are identical with, or variants of, those of Rybnikov and Gilferding, many again are quite modern. Kirêevski's collection is, in fact, the most representative collection of Russian *byliny* which has appeared. It was first published at Moscow, in four parts, during the years 1860–2.[1]

Each of these three great collections has a special interest of its own. Rybnikov, as a pioneer collector of narrative poetry relating to the Russian Heroic Age, holds the first place. His work is also extremely valuable for its collection of lyrics and ceremonial songs, and for the large amount of interesting information which he recorded relating to the singers themselves, both men and women, from whose recitation he noted down his texts. Gilferding's is the most comprehensive collection of *byliny* relating to heroic Russia which we possess, affording, as it does, an enormous number of narratives and variant versions. Kirêevski's collection is the most interesting from both a geographical and an historical point of view. Not only does it contain, as I have said, *byliny* from singers scattered over the whole Great Russian world and many parts of Siberia, but their subjects are drawn from all periods of Russian history. Rybnikov and Gilferding each obtained some examples of poems relating to modern times, but Kirêevski was the first to show the real wealth of popular poetry relating to historical events. In his volumes we have, as it were, a contemporary chronicle of Russian history from the viewpoint of the lower classes— a chronicle which in some cases, e.g. the pictures of Ivan the Terrible and the Period of Troubles, may well be used as a corrective to the views expressed by historians such as Karamzin. They supply the historical imagination required

---

[1] Kirêevski's collection was published by P. A. Bezsonov under the title *Pêsni sobrannÿa P. V. Kirêevskim ÿdannÿa obshchestvom lyubiteley rossiskoy slovesnosti* (Moscow, 1860, etc.). Bezsonov also included valuable supplementary and editorial matter. The edition was afterwards reprinted unchanged by Bezsonov at Moscow during the years 1868–74 under the same title.

to give colour and value to the scientific researches of serious historians into a period and conditions remote from those with which they are personally familiar.

Evidence is not wanting to prove that many MS collections of popular poetry had been made before the great collections of the last century. These, however, were made for the most part by private individuals for their own use. It is interesting to note that the earliest known collection of the popular poetry of Great Russia was made by an Englishman, Richard James, a graduate of Oxford, who in 1619, while serving as chaplain to the English merchants in Moscow, wrote down, or induced a friend to write down for him, six poems on contemporary events, of the kind known today as *byliny*. These poems are written on a few sheets put loosely into a note-book, which is preserved in the Bodleian Library at Oxford.[1] They are, as Bezsonov observes (*loc. cit.*), particularly interesting as affording rare examples of Russian popular poetry composed contemporaneously with the events celebrated and recorded during the earliest stages of its recitation in the place where it was composed, before it had suffered deterioration from oral transmission. Later in the same century (1688) a further small collection of *byliny* treating of contemporary events was made by Kalaidovich, but both this collection and that of James remained unpublished till long after the more recent collections had seen the light.

During the eighteenth century a collection of *byliny* was made by a certain Kirsha Danilov from the workers connected with the Demidov mines in the province of Perm, in the neighbourhood of the Urals. It is a matter for regret that nothing is known of Kirsha himself. He has been called the real originator of the modern interest in traditional oral narrative. It is possible that recent research in Russia may have succeeded in unearthing details relating to him which

[1] They have been published by the St Petersburg Academy and (in part) by Bezsonov in his edition of the collections made by Kirêevski and others (*Pêsni sobrannȳa P. V. Kirêevskim*, pt. VII, p. 56 ff.).

have not been accessible to me. In the absence of further information, however, I see no reason to regard his collection as differing in object and scope from those made occasionally for their own use by the few Olonets singers themselves who could write; and it would seem to be not improbable that his object in making the collection was similarly practical. A selection of twenty-five poems from Danilov's MS was published in 1804 under the title *Les anciennes Poésies russes*, and created considerable interest. In 1818 the famous Russian editor Kalaidovich published a more complete edition from the same collection, comprising sixty poems. In 1819 a further collection of *byliny* was published anonymously at Leipzig, apparently the work of a German resident in Russia, under the title *Fürst Wladimir und dessen Tafelrunde, alt-russische Heldenlieder*. The collection is of especial interest as containing, besides German translations of some of Kirsha Danilov's *byliny*, some additional pieces of which the Russian originals have not since been found.

The Western student is not wholly without guidance in beginning a study of the oral narrative poetry of Great Russia. Rambaud's French work on the subject, *La Russie Épique*, is an admirable and brilliantly written survey of the field, and although published as early as 1876, soon after the appearance of the first great collections, it still remains the standard work on the subject. Unfortunately it has long been out of print and is now rare. It contains an admirably selected series of translations (frequently abridged) within the text. Three years after the appearance of Rambaud's work, the German scholar Wollner published his *Untersuchungen über die Volksepik der Grossrussen* (Leipzig, 1879), which contains useful summaries of the *byliny*. Among the earliest translations in English are the small selection contained in Talvi's *Historical View of the Languages and Literature of the Slavonic Nations* (New York, 1850) and in Morfill's *Slavonic Literature* (London, 1883). Hapgood's *Epic Songs of Russia*, first published in 1886, and again in

1915 (London), consists of translations and adaptations of the oldest cycles of narrative poetry, and contains a brief introduction relating to their literary history. In 1915 also a charming little book, intended for children, was published at Cambridge by M. C. Harrison, with illustrations by Mrs Hugh Stewart, under the title *Byliny Book, Hero Tales of Russia,* which tells the stories of four of the older heroes. A small selection of translations of *byliny* is included also in the first volume of Wiener's *Anthology of Russian Literature* (London and New York, 1902–3). In 1921, L. A. Magnus published in London a critical account of this poetry, entitled *The Heroic Ballads of Russia.* Critical accounts of the narrative poetry as a whole, and also of individual poems, have appeared from time to time in periodicals, such as *Russkaya Mysl, Archiv für slavische Philologie, La Revue des Études Slaves, The Slavonic Review,* etc.

The *byliny* are all anonymous. There are no secular professional minstrels among the peasants of North Russia. The communities are too poor to support such a class. Specialisation is highly developed, however, and we have seen that certain singers enjoy a relatively high reputation. Sometimes the reciters are blind. We may instance Kuzma Romanov and Peter Kornilov, both from Olonets. Not unfrequently the art of singing *byliny* was handed on from father to son. Thus Ilya Elustafev bequeathed his art and his répertoire to his son Iev, and he in turn to his son Terenti Ievlev. Being himself something of a public entertainer among the peasants, Ilya had other pupils as well as his own descendants. Among them were Kuzma Romanov and Ryabinin, two of the best reciters in modern times. The *byliny* have all been handed down by oral tradition. Scarcely any of the singers can read or write, nor can they refer to any known author of the poems. They recite merely what they have heard from one another. Very rarely we hear that someone has formed a manuscript collection, but only as a mnemonic for himself. This was done by Kokatin, an inn-keeper in St Petersburg, who had taught Ryabinin some of his songs. We may suspect that the important MS collection of Kirsha Danilov from Perm (cf. p. 8 above) had a similar origin.

The *byliny* are sung[1] wherever the peasants are gathered together—in inns, round camp fires, in one another's huts. They are frequently sung in Olonets in the evenings in an *izba*, or peasant's wooden hut, crowded with eager listeners, who sit about on the bedstead, the wooden benches, the table, indeed anywhere where they can find room.

Lyatski, one of the more recent collectors and critics, has left us a vivid picture of a crowded Olonets *izba* on the evening when Nikifor Prokhorov (surnamed Utka), a contemporary of the younger Ryabinin, was reciting a *bylina*:

Utka coughed. Everybody became silent at once. He threw his head back and glanced round with a smile at those present, and seeing their impatient, eager, expectant expressions, he at once began to sing again. Little by little the face of the old singer changed; all its cunning disappeared, and it became childlike and naïve. Something inspired appeared in it; the dove-like eyes opened wide, and began to shine. Two little shining tears sparkled in them; a flush overspread the swarthiness of his cheeks; occasionally his nervous throat twitched.

He lived with his beloved *bogatyrs*; grieved in tears for the infirmity of Ilya of Murom, when he sat paralysed for thirty years, gloried with him in his triumph over Nightingale the Robber. Sometimes he broke off of his own accord, interpolating his own remarks. All the people present lived with the heroes of the *byliny* too. At times an exclamation of wonder involuntarily escaped from one of them; at times the laughter of another resounded through the room. From one fell tears which he involuntarily brushed away from his lashes. Everybody sat

---

[1] An account of the recitation of the *byliny* is contained in Ralston's *Songs of the Russian People*[2] (London, 1872), p. 36 ff.

without winking an eye while the singing was going on. Every sound of this monotonous but wonderfully gentle tune they loved.[1]

No instrument is in use in Olonets. The singers are called *Skaʒiteli*, i.e. lit. 'story-tellers', 'narrators'; but the tradition of musical accompaniment is clearly indicated in the current expression 'to sing a *bylina*'.[2] The tunes are said to be very monotonous, and few are known to any singer. The elder Ryabinin, one of the best singers of *byliny*, knew only two tunes; another of the best singers, Kuzma Romanov, knew only three;[3] 'the Bottle', another good singer, knew only one. Lyatski, writing as late as 1895, says that musical specialists who had listened to the younger Ryabinin, had not succeeded in obtaining any reliable versions of the tunes.[4] It may be doubted whether any subsequent attempts to note down these tunes have been really successful. The article of Delange and Malherbe in Lavignac's *Encyclopédie de la Musique*, vol. v, pt. i, p. 2486 ff., contains some interesting specimens of folk-tunes and notes on Russian peasant instruments in general, but makes no attempt at serious musical analysis, or comprehensive treatment. We may no doubt assume that the tunes retain some earlier system of scales than that in general modern use, as is not rare in folk-songs elsewhere.

The poems vary greatly in length. In general it may be said that those which relate to the early period are longer than those of more modern date, and that as we approach our own time the *byliny* grow briefer. Those of recent origin are generally comparatively short, the majority consisting of less than a hundred lines, though many of course are longer. On the other hand it is to be observed that great

---

[1] *Skaʒitel Ivan T. Ryabinin i ego Byliny*, 'The Reciter Ivan T. Ryabinin and his Byliny' (Moscow, 1895), p. 11.

[2] Rybnikov, vol. i, p. xciii; cf. Rambaud, *op. cit.* p. 12.

[3] Rybnikov, *loc. cit.*

[4] *Op. cit.* p. 25 f.

freedom is allowed in the recitation.[1] A poem as recited by one minstrel may consist of eleven hundred lines,[2] while another minstrel will recite what appears to be in nucleus the same poem in a hundred; or more frequently, will select only certain episodes from the many which relate to the hero in question, and recombine them into a single briefer *bylina*. Very often a single episode constitutes a complete *bylina*.[3]

It is not easy to draw a clear distinction between author and reciter.[4] Each recitation is, in some measure, a creative work. Gilferding observed that among the peasants of Lake Onega a singer never sang a *bylina* twice alike.[5] He tells us that in general the speeches of the heroes were remembered and transmitted verbally, and these vary little. On the other hand the narrative was not remembered by heart, but re-created afresh with each recitation from the singer's fund of epic material. In neither respect is usage consistent however. The artistic process in the mind of the singer and the large extempore element in his performance are no doubt greatly facilitated by the conventional character of the diction, form and subject-matter of the *byliny*. At the same time there can be no doubt that the personality of the reciters colours their versions to a considerable extent. A man of a passionate temperament is said to emphasise the warlike incidents and expressions, accompanying his recitation with great force and bravura of manner, while one of gentler temperament tends to tone down the narrative.[6] The

[1] See Rybnikov, vol. I, p. xciv f. An interesting instance of the free use of the poetical material made by the *Skazitel* I. T. Ryabinin will be found on p. 9 ff. of the paper by Lyatski to which reference has already been made.

[2] See e.g. the text of the *bylina* on Dobrynya Nikitich as recited by Kalinin, Gilferding, *Sbornik*, vol. I, p. 31 ff.

[3] See e.g. the text of the *bylina* relating the marriage of Dobrynya's wife during his absence, as recorded by Chukov ('the Bottle'), Rybnikov, vol. I, p. 162 ff.

[4] See Rybnikov, vol. I, p. cxiv ff.

[5] Gilferding, vol. I, p. 32.   [6] Rybnikov, vol. I, p. 413.

same writer adds that the *kalêka*, or wandering psalm-singer, Ivan Feponov, generally known as 'blind Ivan', when reciting *byliny*, always gave a religious colouring to his narratives, representing the heroes as constantly praying to God.[1]

The metres of the *byliny* have never been successfully analysed. They are generally described as 'a kind of rhythmical chant'. The lines vary in length within the poem, but on the whole poems tend to be composed in lines which correspond approximately in length throughout. The poem relating the *Healing of Ilya of Murom* in the *bylina* recorded by Kirêevski[2] is composed of long lines; the lines of the poem on Shchelkan Dudentevich[3] are much shorter. It is interesting to note that different localities favour different lengths of line. Poems obtained to the east of Lake Onega are generally composed in short lines of five or six syllables, whereas the same poem to the west of the lake is generally in long lines of eight or nine.

Although the character of the metre cannot be said to be established,[4] it is impossible to doubt that relics of metre still exist. The *byliny* are quite different from ordinary prose, and there can be no doubt that they are descended from medieval metres, such as the metre employed in parts of the twelfth-century work, the *Slovo o Polky Igorevê*; though the metre of the *Slovo* itself appears to be in a disintegrated condition. It has been noted above that the *byliny* are sung without accompaniment in the north, though this was not always so. The break-down of metre no doubt goes hand in hand with the deterioration in musical accomplishment. The monotony of the airs and the absence of variety are no doubt due to the same cause.

The importance of the musical accompaniment in regard

[1] Gilferding, vol. I, p. 32.
[2] Kirêevski, *Pêsni*, pt. I, p. 1.   [3] *Ibid.* pt. v, p. 186 ff.
[4] For some general observations on this point the reader may consult Magnus, *Heroic Ballads of Russia* (London, 1921), p. 14 ff.; Gilferding, vol. I, p. 39 ff.; Lyatski, *op. cit.* p. 25 f.

to metre is strikingly attested by Gilferding's experience among the Olonets reciters. Seeking out Abram Evtikhiev Chukov (nicknamed 'the Bottle'), who had formerly sung the *bylina* of *Mikhailo Potyk* to Rybnikov, he followed with Rybnikov's printed text while the *skazitel* sang him his *bylina*.

I was amazed by the difference, not in the subject-matter of the narrative, but in the versification. In the written text metrical structure is expressed only by the dactylic endings of the line; inside the line there is no sort of metre whatever. Yet when Abram Evtikhiev sang there was clearly discernible not only the musical cadence of the air, but also the fact that the line consisted of feet marked by tonic accents. I resolved to write down the *bylina* afresh; the *skazitel* offered to recite (*skazat'*) it to me word by word (*po slovesno*) without song.

Gilferding then wrote down the *bylina* of *Mikhailo Potyk*; the metre had disappeared, leaving nothing but broken prose like that of Rybnikov's version.

I tried to arrange this disjointed (*rublennaya*) prose into lines (*stikhi*), making the *skazitel* sing it repeatedly; but this proved impracticable because, as explained above, the reciters alter the *bylina* to some extent with every fresh recitation, transposing words and passages, now adding, now leaving out some lines, now employing different expressions. Having listened for some days...and made vain efforts to write the *bylina* down perfectly exact, with the metre preserved, as it is sung, I tried to get my rhapsodist friend to sing (and not to recite merely in words) the *bylina*; with such pauses between each line that it could be written down. This was easily explained to Abram Evtikhiev, and I once more attempted to write down his *bylina*. The air preserved the poetical metre...and the *bylina* got on to paper as it was actually sung.

Gilferding tried the same plan with the other singers and almost always with success.[1]

The *byliny*, that is to say, heroic narrative and speech

[1] Gilferding, vol. I, p. 39 ff.

poems, cover a period of nearly a thousand years. Several Cycles may be distinguished, which rarely overlap or encroach on one another. The Cycle which is generally regarded as the earliest deals with heroes who are so richly endowed with superhuman qualities as to be more supernatural than human. Chief of these are Volga, Mikula, and Svyatogor, with whom also is associated, and partly confused, Samson. Of the first three nothing appears to be certainly known from other sources. The fourth has undoubtedly borrowed his exploits, as well as his name, from the hero of the Old Testament. The association and confusion with Svyatogor is probably due to an identification of the latter with the biblical hero. The heroes themselves, and the feats which they perform, have their nearest affinities in the heroes of folk-tales. This is also true of the less common heroes, such as Kolyvan (who is perhaps to be identified with Samson), Shark Velikan, Sukhman Odikhmantevich, etc.

The heroes of this group are generally known as the 'Older Heroes'. They have been regarded as representing the débris of ancient Slavonic, sometimes even of 'primitive' Aryan, mythology. But there is no really valid evidence for assigning special antiquity to any of them. They have very little in common. Volga is a military prince who fights successfully with his *druzhina*, and repels invasions from without, even carrying his aggressions into the heart of Tsargrad. His personal attributes are the gift of shape-changing and supernatural wisdom, like those of Prince Roman of Galicia in a *bylina* translated by Rambaud,[1] and of Vseslav in the *Slovo o Polky Igorevê*. A close study of the diction of the *Slovo*, however, leads one to suspect that these supernatural features are due to an early local school of poetic diction of a highly figurative character, which at a later period has come to be interpreted literally. The process would be aided by the rarity of similes introduced by *kak* in the early period, instead of which metaphors, or the so-called negative comparative, were commonly used.

[1] Transl. Rambaud, *op. cit.* p. 236 ff.

Svyatogor and Mikula are even less protean and fantastic
than Volga. Both are more human than divine. Svyatogor
has much in common with heroes of folk-tale. His weapon
is a steel club. His prodigious strength is not too great to
allow of his riding a horse over the 'open plain' like any
other hero, though he does not appear at Kiev, and is not
allowed to enter Russia, by which is probably meant the
valley of the Dnêpr. Mikula is a strong ploughman, clearing
the virgin soil in some vast plain within the range of influence
of Volga and his *druzhina*. But the agrarian pioneer pushes
forward so fast that though Volga and his *druzhina* can hear
the echoes of his labours, they have difficulty in overtaking
him. When they succeed in doing so they learn that Mikula
has recently looted one of Volga's tributary cities. Mikula
consents to join his *druzhina*, but he makes his own terms.
The settler of the steppe is in a position to dictate to the
military princes of Old Russia.

The second, and by far the largest Cycle of *byliny*, is
located in and around Kiev. The earliest of the heroes to
whom a date can be assigned is Vladimir, the last of the
purely Scandinavian princes of Kiev, who was baptised in
988, and who is now generally regarded as the founder of the
Russian Empire. Round him by far the largest number of
stories are loosely grouped, much as the legends of the
knights of the Round Table are grouped round the person
of King Arthur. Like King Arthur himself, Vladimir is
never the principal figure of the stories, though he is the
Solnyshko ('Little Sun')[1] round whom the other planets
revolve. The minstrels who composed the *byliny*, however,
have identified him with Vladimir Monomakh who died in
1126, and have attributed to the early prince many of the

---

[1] The origin of the epithet is unknown, though many derivations
have been suggested, mostly of a romantic character. It is perhaps
worth remarking that the word 'Sun' is commonly applied to the heroes
in Tartar epic poems, as the word 'Moon' is to the heroines, and here
the words seem to be used in the sense of 'son' and 'daughter'. I suspect the Russian epithet is of Tartar origin.

features which properly belong to his namesake. Vladimir I was constantly engaged in hostilities against the Pechenegs, as Vladimir Monomakh was against the Polovtsy. In the *byliny* the enemies are the 'Tartars'.

The poems of the Kiev Cycle relate the adventures of the members of his *družhina* or body of personal followers, some of whom appear to be historical characters. Actual historical reminiscences are also preserved, no doubt, in the events narrated, though the history is viewed through a cloudy and distorted lens, and is often interspersed with *motifs* borrowed from folk-tales. Nevertheless the element of the marvellous and the superhuman is much less pronounced than in the Cycles of Volga, Mikula, Svyatogor, etc., and is quite subordinate to the heroic narrative of adventure. The heroes of this Cycle are too numerous, and their exploits too varied to be enumerated here. The favourite hero of all the reciters is Ilya of Murom, the 'Old Cossack' whose life is spent in warfare against the enemies of Russia. He is somewhat of a free-lance, and not permanently attached to Vladimir's *družhina*, though he is constantly associated in his exploits with the Kiev heroes. The most prominent member of the court is Dobrynya Nikitich, who is described as a nephew of Vladimir and his chief envoy. In addition to the other heroes whose exploits figure in the following *byliny* we may mention young Ivan Godinovich, the son of a serf, who presumed to raise his eyes to the daughter of Dimitri, the merchant of Chernigov, already betrothed to the Tartar Khan Koshchey the Deathless; to Ivan the Merchant's Son, who drank away all his patrimony, but who won a wager against Prince Vladimir that he would ride from Kiev to Chernigov—a distance of three hundred and thirty versts—and return between Mass and Matins; to Mikhailo Potyk Ivanovich the rover, who married the swan maiden and followed her alive into the tomb; to Khoten Bludovich, the wealthy noble, who married the widow of a rich merchant after a youth spent in heroic prowess; to Danilo Ignatevich, who retired to a

2

monastery after a life of warfare against the Tartars. All these and many others come and go, attracted by the splendour of Vladimir and his Queen Apraxya, from Tsargrad, from rich Galicia, from Novgorod the Great, and the trading centres of the Dnêpr.

A third Cycle relates to heroes of a different political milieu—the citizens of the wealthy trading city-state of Novgorod—'My Lord Novgorod the Great' as she was commonly styled by her citizens. This is a much smaller Cycle, chiefly occupied with the adventures of only two important heroes, Sadko the 'rich merchant', and Vasili Buslaevich. Of these the former must have been a very popular hero, since a large number of *byliny* are extant in which he is the leading figure. Other *byliny*—those of Terenti Danilovich and Akundin—appear to have been little sung by minstrels. The former is of interest as containing references in some versions to the trade of the Hanse towns, and the latter as preserving traditions of the old Novgorod traderoutes. The *bylina* of Terenti relates a humorous domestic contretemps of bourgeois life. Although heroic in metre and—to some extent—in style, it is quite Chaucerian in atmosphere and plot, and in its attitude to women. Like *Sadko* it presents a lively picture of the wealth and activity of Novgorod at the height of her prosperity.

The atmosphere and style of this Cycle as a whole differ considerably from those of the Kiev Cycle. They offer a relatively larger range of episode, increasing the number of incidents and narrating them in summary form. While retaining many of the characteristics of heroic narrative, the framework of the story is drawing closer to the style of the medieval metrical romances. Terence the merchant is frankly bourgeois in character. Like Sadko, Vasili Buslaevich belongs to the burgher class, and his exploits reflect the clashing interests of a rich trading community. In passing from the combats of the Kiev heroes to those of Vasili Buslaevich, we pass from the single combats on the plains of Troy to the encounters of the Montagues and Capulets in the streets of Verona. Moreover, a new element has entered into these poems—the element of burlesque. The reciter of the Novgorod *byliny* does not always regard his hero very seriously, and even the Church is not exempted from satire. The treatment of Vasili and his exploits is playful in tone, while his godfather the monk appears wearing the bell of the cathedral of St Sophia as a helmet, and using the clapper as a walking-stick.[1]

The *byliny* of the period intervening between the twelfth and the sixteenth centuries, relating to heroes of the older principalities, are not numerous. They are, moreover, slight in character for the most part, briefly narrating a single incident, or series of incidents, in summary form. Although attached to the names of medieval princes, many of them appear to have little relationship to actual history. These 'medieval' *byliny* belong to a different literary tradition from the preceding Cycles. The difference in style and diction will be apparent even in translations. Many of them share common characteristics of their own, both in regard to diction and poetic conventions, which suggest that they originated in a common poetical milieu—perhaps in a lost body of court poetry such as we have reason to suspect may have existed in Galicia.

Even the incidents relating to the Tartar domination seem to have produced few *byliny*. From the sixteenth century, however, begin the interesting series of *byliny* relating the exploits of the Cossacks of the Don and Volga, which are remarkable for their fidelity to history. The authentic exploits of such adventurers as Ermak, the conqueror of Siberia in the sixteenth, of the rebel Stenka Razin in the seventeenth, and of Mazeppa and Pugachev respectively in the eighteenth centuries left little to be desired in the way of incident, even by the most accomplished minstrel or the most exacting audience. But indeed it may be said of the *byliny* as a whole that each fresh Cycle becomes progressively nearer to historical fact as it approaches our own time, while

[1] *Slavonic Review*, vol. III, p. 56.

the atmosphere of the poems becomes farther and farther removed from that of the court.

The Princely Cycle of Moscow has had an uninterrupted life in the area in which it originated, as well as elsewhere, for over three hundred years. Its history has been continuous, and may be said to be still incomplete. This Cycle undoubtedly reached its highest development in the time of Ivan the Terrible, who, like Vladimir, has become the central figure of a wide circle of narrative *byliny*. In the Muscovite *byliny* the heroic spirit of the Kiev poems lives again, though the majority of the former are briefer. To the traditional heroic features of the earlier poems the events and achievements of the reign of the Terrible Tsar are peculiarly suited. The strangely interesting overlap of oriental barbarism and occidental humanism, with their resultant high lights and deep shadows, is well adapted to the crude and picturesque figurative style of Kiev court poetry. The novel offensive of Ivan's struggle against the Tartars, and the romance of the conquest of Siberia by a handful of heroic adventurers, are in themselves sufficiently akin to the bizarre adventures of Vladimir's own community on the Dnêpr to fit naturally into the old framework. Ivan's many matrimonial alliances and the consequent arrival of strangers at his court give ample scope for the introduction of the well-worn themes of the 'honourable feast', the rivalry between the native *dru-žhina* and the guests, with its resultant boasting, challenge, and single combat. The *bylina* of *The Tsar's Marriage with the Tartar Princess* might almost be taken for a poem of the Kiev Cycle with the proper names changed.

During the seventeenth century, alongside the *byliny* with which we are already familiar from Kiev and Novgorod, there grew up a briefer type of poem in which a single emotional situation is portrayed in detail, and which is largely occupied with speeches, not unfrequently a monologue. In these poems the old heroic metre is still kept, and also, in a large measure, the diction. In the attitude of the poet to his subject, however, a change is noticeable. The events and characters are not lifted on to the same exalted plane as in the earlier *byliny*. The heroic spirit has given place to a spirit of criticism, often of frank censure. The adjective *slavny*, 'glorious', 'exalted', applied to all heroes of the earlier *byliny* is often replaced by *zloy*, 'evil', 'accursed', 'wicked', which is even applied to crowned heads such as Boris Godunov. In this period it is a static description of the boyars.

It is doubtful if this brief type of *bylina*, consisting largely of speeches, was new. The second version of the *Lament of Xenya Borisovna* is so similar in form to the 'Lament of Yaroslavna' contained in the twelfth-century poem, the *Slovo o Polky Igorevê*, that we may believe the type to have had a continuous history. The latter is generally believed to be based ultimately[1] on popular models, and the most striking feature of these seventeenth-century *byliny* is their popular character. They represent the views of the Muscovite citizens on contemporary events. They are astonishingly outspoken. Many of them read like articles from an evening paper in a country where censorship of the Press is unknown. Nothing could illustrate better than these *byliny* the change which came over the political situation in the period following upon the death of Ivan the Terrible. The old autocracy has gone, the unity, stability, and oppressive rule of the old tsarist régime. The bourgeoisie has become a power and articulate; but it is not stabilised as yet. Had the tsarate been forced to depend for a longer period on the responsible citizenship and bourgeois funds of such men as Minin, the Russian Revolution of 1917 might never have taken place.

Interesting as are the *byliny* which represent the period between Ivan the Terrible and Peter the Great, they are not

---

[1] See Rambaud, *op. cit.* p. 217. V. Miller, however, considered the poem to be of literary provenance, and to have been borrowed by the author directly from Bulgarian sources. See the summary of Miller's views published by Hofmann, 'Beobachtungen zum Stil des Igorsliedes', in *Archiv für slavische Philologie* (1923), p. 89 ff.

numerous. In the reign of Peter the Great a revival of *byliny* seems to have taken place. A whole volume of Kirêevski is devoted to his reign alone. These *byliny* are completely reactionary in tone. The return to an autocratic monarchy has brought about a return to the old heroic type of *bylina*. The note of criticism and protest is silenced. It is a notable fact that many of the *byliny* of the reign of Peter are based on *byliny* originally composed for Ivan the Terrible. It has often been remarked how similar are many of the features of the two reigns, and the incidents of the private lives of the two tsars; and these similarities have facilitated the adaptation of the older *byliny* to the new incidents, or the composition of new *byliny* on the old models. Thus we again find in the reign of Peter a *bylina* commemorating the banishment of the tsaritsa to a monastery; but it is significant of Peter's suppression of popular expression that the name of the tsaritsa does not occur in the poem. The tsar had issued an order that her name must never be mentioned.

In the eighteenth and nineteenth centuries heroic narrative poems were still composed, but we rarely find the freedom and outspoken popular opinion of the Period of Troubles. Bezsonov regards the first of the variants which he records of the *byliny* on the death of the Empress Katharine II as inspired by party feeling directed against the Emperor Paul;[1] but the frank censure characteristic of the *byliny* of the preceding century has given place to innuendo. The attitude of heroic loyalty to the tsar, revived under Peter the Great, persisted down to the end. Even the Cossacks, so popular in the past, are not always exalted when they venture to rebel. The minstrels dare not extol the enemies of the reigning house; and in Central Russia Pugachev is roundly called a 'scoundrel dog, a cursed Cossack', and it is with evident satisfaction that his execution in the public square in Moscow is reported.[2] A number of *byliny* on the Seven Years' War show the vitality of the old heroic diction and manner of

[1] Kirêevski, pt. IX, p. 265.
[2] See Rambaud, *op. cit.* p. 338.

treatment. Those on the exploits and death of the loyalist Cossack General Krasnoshchokov are particularly interesting for the conservative nature of their treatment and the liberal use of heroic conventions in the conduct of the narrative.

It will be observed that the intellectual outlook of the Russian minstrels has hardly kept pace with the growing dignity of their subjects. This increasing disparity becomes most obvious when we come to the last large body of narrative heroic poetry which Great Russia has produced—that on the Napoleonic Wars. In the Tsar Alexander, as in his enemy Napoleon, the poets had subjects which might well have inspired a new school of heroic poetry. Tolstoy's *War and Peace* reflects the consciousness which was felt by all Russians, whether in the officers' quarters or the Moscow and Petrograd drawing-rooms, that they were living in an age of heroes. Yet when we read the *byliny* on the capture of Smolensk, and observe the part assigned to the Cossack General Platov and to the tsar himself, we are conscious of a paradox. The function of heroic poets is to glorify human action and exalt human beings; but in the pictures of Platov at the French court, of the Tsar Alexander cutting his beard, or receiving the intimation of Napoleon's approach, the poet has unconsciously reduced his heroes far below their actual human dignity. The epic manner and formulae are still preserved, but the exaltation has vanished, the epic figures have become puny. Above all, the presentation of the facts is distorted and unworthy of the great events and changes which were taking place. The breach between the minstrels and their old patrons, which shows itself in the poverty of the treatment of exalted subjects, has become final—a breach which was perhaps first foreshadowed when the travels of Peter the Great in search of enlightenment were described by an indulgent but uncomprehending minstrel as 'amusing himself abroad'.

The history of the *bylina* as a literary type is to be regarded, therefore, as the history of an art in its decline. The qualities which constitute its charm were acquired at a time when the minstrels moved in court circles and shared the intellectual outlook of their patrons. The greatest period in the heroic poetry of Russia is undoubtedly that of the heroes of Kiev. If we may judge by the traditions which have survived, this was the most productive period. The Kiev Cycle was the spontaneous outcome of an Heroic Age in Russia. The evidence of medieval records, such as monastic chronicles, and especially that of Nestor, makes this clear. While Moscow revived the form of the *byliny* in the sixteenth century and added to the ancient répertoire many new themes, it is impossible to suppose that she can be responsible in any sense for their origin, or have borrowed the stories of Kiev from written sources.[1] There can be no reasonable doubt that it was the court poets of Kiev and the narrative poems of the Kiev Cycle which set the standard in heroic narrative style which has persisted down to our own time.

The contribution of Moscow to the history of the *byliny* is a different one. The short popular song, consisting largely of speeches, which we know to be already widespread when the *Slovo* was composed, was developed in Moscow into a literary form admirably adapted to the celebration of contemporary events and to the expression of popular feeling. When this form is combined with narrative, it is still equally suited to the transmission of contemporary or recent news, as some of the following examples will show. It is curious that the form is hardly ever applied to the themes of the Kiev Cycle. It is reserved for contemporary history. The Muscovite singers never developed, as did the Norse poets, their ancient epic themes as subjects for the study of emotional situations.

One of the most interesting aspects of the *byliny* is the

[1] The suggestion has been made by Prince Mirsky that the *byliny* arose for the first time in the sixteenth century, deriving their style from Byzantine models and the subjects of the Kiev Cycle from books. See the *Slavonic Review*, vol. III (1924–5), pp. 78, footnote 1; 89. No evidence is adduced in support of this view however.

fidelity of their oral transmission. This is most clearly seen in the rigidity with which the different stories and Cycles are kept apart. Only very rarely does a hero stray from his own native environment into an alien milieu. But the conservatism is also strikingly apparent in the whole mise-en-scène, especially of the early Cycles. The political geography of the Kiev poems has preserved with great fidelity the memory of the city-state on the Dnêpr, and the local and restricted sphere of its influence. It knows nothing of Russia in its modern political connotation, or of any Russian cities except those in the valley of the Dnêpr and in the extreme south. It has not forgotten the tributary River Pochaina which flows into the Dnêpr at Kiev itself. The singers make constant reference to the characteristic features of the South Russian landscape which neither they nor their ancestors have ever seen—the 'open plain', the 'feather-grass of the steppe', the 'aurochs' which had long been extinct. Their verbal memory of obsolete titles shows the same fidelity. They know the heroes as *bogatyri*, a word borrowed from the Tartars at some period of the Tartar inroads. They remember the *polenitsy* or heroines who fight like men, though the term had long been forgotten in Russia, even by lexicographers. They recall in their constant references to Vladimir as *Solnyshko* (a diminutive of *Solntse*, 'Sun') the Tartar term generally applied to the eldest son or 'hero' of Tartar epic poetry. The peculiar and individual topography and political organisation of medieval Novgorod are not forgotten, or its turbulent citizens, its constant brawls, its *posadnik*, its *tysyatski*. They have not forgotten the names of the Tartar khans who destroyed their peace in the Middle Ages—Tugor K(h)an, Chol Khan, Mamai and others. Their familiarity with the topographical features and the architectural details of the Kremlin of Moscow is hardly less remarkable.

It is not surprising that in a literature so dependent on oral tradition, and carried on at so great a distance from the scenes where the action of the poems has taken place, the treatment as a whole should be highly conventional. This conventional treatment has been analysed in some detail in two interesting papers by V. Miller.[1] He pointed out that in addition to the prevalence of purely verbal conventions and epic formulae, the entire narrative is composed of a series of conventions, stock situations described in static terminology, which are introduced in various combinations. He further distinguished local peculiarities in the conventions employed in the *byliny*, pointing to local schools of composition. He quoted as an instance a conventional opening found in the *byliny* from Simbirsk which does not occur in a single *bylina* from Olonets in the collections of either Rybnikov or Gilferding.[2] This conventionality must have greatly facilitated the extempore elements which have been mentioned above as a distinctive feature of the recitation of the *byliny*.

The persistence and conservatism with which the *byliny*, collected from all over Great Russia and northern Asia, have retained the conventions associated originally with the *byliny* of the Kiev Cycle, are all the more remarkable in view of the fact that all trace of this Cycle has disappeared in precisely the district where it is believed to have grown up. In the valley of the Dnêpr round Kiev, where the court of Vladimir was held, and the heroes performed their exploits, scarcely a trace remains of their names or deeds. The disunion among the Russian princes of the Dnêpr, followed by the destruction of Kiev by the Tartars in 1240, and the consequent stream of migration northwards, are no doubt initially responsible in part for the wide distribution of themes and *motifs* derived from the poetry of this Cycle. In the meantime changing political conditions in and around Kiev inspired fresh schools of heroic poets to fresh efforts. The old themes were superseded in their native district by a totally new cycle of poems celebrating the exploits of the heroes of the rising community of the Zaporogian Cossacks and the

[1] 'Russkaya Bylina, eya Slagateli i Ispolniteli', in *Russkaya Mysl*, vols. IX, p. 143 ff., X, p. 1 ff.
[2] *Loc. cit.* vol. IX, p. 155.

Republic of Little Russia. This new school looked to the west for its literary traditions, and composed in rhyming strophic verse quite distinct from the *byliny*.

It is curious that nothing is really known as to the origin of the *byliny*, or of the class of people who were originally responsible for their composition and transmission. The word occurs first in the *Slovo o Polky Igorevê* (cf. p. 2 above), in the opening lines of which the singer announces that instead of following the elaborate and conservative poetical conventions of his predecessor Boyan he intends to compose in the new fashion—*po bylinam*. The exact meaning of the phrase is not clear. Does it mean 'in the style of a *bylina*', implying that the form now understood by that term was already in existence? Or does it mean 'according to actuality', i.e. in a literal narrative style as opposed to the figurative allusive style of Boyan? In either case we must suppose that something like our idea of a *bylina* was in the poet's mind.

V. Miller, who devoted special study to the subject, regards the *byliny* as the work of the *skomorokhi*, a class of jesters and minstrels who appear to be identical with the *veselÿe lyudi*, lit. 'joyous folk', also a class of popular entertainers.[1] These popular troupes went about the country from the later Middle Ages till the close of the seventeenth century singing and playing on the *gusli*. They were regarded with great disfavour by the Church, who looked with suspicion on their growing influence and insubordination. Already in the fifteenth century they had become a serious menace to ecclesiastical and civil authorities alike, and ecclesiastical letters and chronicles from the fifteenth to the end of the seventeenth century contain frequent denunciations of these troublesome people. Their prestige was so great that we learn from Kurbski, a contemporary writer, that Ivan the Terrible himself danced and feasted with *skomorokhi*.[2]

---

[1] Vsevolod Miller, *op. cit.* vols. IX, p. 143 ff., X, p. 1 ff.
[2] See Miller, *op. cit.* vol. X, p. 13.

The *byliny* themselves contain frequent references to the *skomorokhi* and *veselÿe lyudi*. The mischievous tendencies of the *skomorokhi* are referred to in the *bylina* of *Terenti Gost* from the Novgorod Cycle, where they are represented as wandering about the streets of Novgorod and taking an active part in Terenti's domestic affairs. In Kirsha Danilov's version of the *bylina* of *Stavr* the *veselÿe lyudi* are represented as entertaining the court. In the version of the *bylina* translated below which narrates the marriage of Dobrynya's wife Nastasya to Alyosha Popovich, Dobrynya himself appears at the feast disguised as a *skomorokh* and relates his adventures.[1] In the *bylina* of *Vasili Buslaevich* the hero joins a band of drunken *veselÿe lyudi*. Unfortunately in these and other instances which might be cited we are not told the actual words sung by the minstrels. It cannot be actually proved, therefore, that their songs were *byliny*. The words of the historian Tatishchev[2] are important here however:

I heard in the past from the *skomorokhi* ancient songs about Prince Vladimir in which they make mention of his wives by name, as well as those glorious men Ilya of Murom, Aleksêy Popovich, Nightingale the Robber, Dolk (? Dyuk) Stefanovich, and glorify their deeds; but of history, very little or nothing.[3]

The contemporary evidence of Olearius also suggests that the short contemporary *byliny* which rose to prominence in Moscow in the sixteenth and seventeenth centuries formed a part of the répertoire of the *skomorokhi*. He tells us that in Ladoga, on the outskirts of the earlier Novgorod dominions,

we listened to Russian music: when we were sitting at dinner there came two Russians with lutes and *gudkas* ('fiddles') who made their bows to the ambassadors, and began to play and sing

---

[1] See also Miller, *op. cit.* vol. x, p. 16.
[2] Tatishchev lived 1686–1750. He was the first Russian to write a history of Russia.
[3] See Miller, *op. cit.* vol. x, p. 19.

about the great mighty sovereign and tsar Michael Theodoro-vich.[1]

The reference is to the Tsar Michael Romanov I, who reigned 1613–45.

The question has often been asked: from what source has the narrative form of the *byliny* been derived? As early as 1868 Stasov published a volume, full of learning and valuable information, in which he attempted to prove that the *byliny* are oriental in Origin, form, and content; and there has been a growing tendency in modern times to regard the form of the *byliny*, and to some extent the subjects also, as of foreign, i.e. non-Slavonic, origin. Among recent writers who claim to have traced Russian heroic *byliny* to foreign sources we may mention Prince Mirsky, Abicht, V. Miller, Potanin, Veselovski, Rožniecki, and Schröder. Origins are looked for in Byzantine and Mongolian sources, in German, Galician, and Scandinavian—both the Scandinavia of the north, and the Scandinavian kingdoms on the Dnêpr, prior to the eleventh century.

The number and diversity of the views expressed make it exceedingly doubtful if any one of these countries can have been primarily responsible for the origin of the *byliny* as a literary type, though we may well believe that all have been laid under contribution at different periods for literary themes and *motifs*, orally transmitted, as we know to have been the case in regard to folk-tales. The geographical and historical relation of Byzantium to Russia make it exceedingly probable that its influence on its barbaric neighbour will be strong. We need not doubt that the oral literature of Galicia and the countries to the south have exercised a strong influence on the Russian *byliny*.

In regard to Scandinavia the position is somewhat different. I have myself noted similarities between the litera-

---

[1] Olearius, *The Voyages and Travels of the Ambassadors sent by Frederick, Duke of Holstein, to the great Duke of Muscovy and the King of Persia*, transl. by J. Davies (London, 1669), p. 7.

tures of the two peoples which cannot, I think, be accidental. There are, however, some important facts which should not be overlooked. The first, and the most important, is that the differences are infinitely greater than the similarities. Secondly, the Norse verse which comes in for consideration is invariably strophic, while the *byliny* and the greater part of the *Slovo* are non-strophic. Thirdly, many centuries have elapsed between the time when the Norse poems were written down and the first recorded notices of *byliny*. Much careful comparative work must be done on the literature of the two peoples, therefore, before any convincing conclusions as regards their literary relations are to be looked for.

There is yet another factor which comes in for consideration at this point. When the Norsemen first settled in Russia, we have reason to think that the native population with whom they would come principally into contact would be not Slavs but Finns and Mordvins. Novgorod is situated on Lake Ilmen, and while the former name is Slavonic the latter is Finnish. The evidence rather suggests a comparatively recent Slavonic settlement in Finnish territory. Norse colonies are believed to have settled on the Volga as early, if not earlier, than on the Dnêpr,[1] and the Volga ran throughout its course in non-Slavonic territory. The Cheremis, Chuvash, Mordvin, and other Tartar and Finnish and Mordvin tribes had—equally with the Slavs—opportunities of literary intercourse with the Norsemen. We know the Finns to have had a well-developed narrative poetry which had points of affinity with both Teutonic and Slavonic narrative poetry respectively. Unfortunately few of us who are interested in the two latter have any knowledge of Finnish, and we are therefore apt to overlook this factor in the literary problem. The problem is nevertheless a three-cornered one, and cannot be settled by facile generalisation based on observation of a few points of similarity between the two best known factors.

[1] Schröder, 'Skandinavien und der Orient im Mittelalter', in *Germanisch-romanische Monatsschrift*, vol. VIII (1920), p. 209.

There are reasons for thinking that the court of Vladimir of Kiev in the tenth century was in a stage of transition, and that the art of narrative may have shared the general change. It had been the custom in the past for the princes of the cities on the Dnêpr to bear Scandinavian names. Vladimir I, however, the son of Svyatoslav I by a Slavonic slave woman, called his sons by Slavonic names. It is also important to note that while the *byliny* of the Kiev Cycle look to Vladimir, a 'Scandinavian' prince, as their 'Sun', the centre of heroic life, none of the heroes of the *byliny* themselves, with the possible exception of Stavr, bear Scandinavian names. The most important of all the Kiev heroes is Ilya of Murom, the 'Old Cossack', a peasant hero of the Mordvin community of Murom. Other foreigners visited the court, such as Dyuk Stepanich from rich Galicia. The majority of the heroes bear Slavonic names. The story of Churilo Plenkovich, the native squire whose home Vladimir visited, and whom he took back with him to Kiev to act as his seneschal, no doubt faithfully represents Vladimir's relations with the landed gentry, especially such as seemed likely to cause him trouble. Nestor gives a story in which the Pechenegs are represented as challenging a member of Vladimir's *druzhina*, or comitatus, to single combat against one of their own champions. None of Vladimir's men was found who was willing to volunteer, and the king was in despair, when an old serving-man of his household came forward and volunteered that his youngest son should be brought. His strength was such, he said, that he would be able to overcome the Pecheneg. Vladimir consented joyfully, and the young peasant, probably a Slav, overcame the foe of royal Kiev, and was taken into Vladimir's *druzhina*.[1]

These indications, slight as they are, suggest that according to the traditions current at the time of the formation of the Kiev Cycle of *byliny*, Vladimir opened the ranks of his *druzhina* to the native population, and established a

---

[1] Nestor, *Chronicle* (ed. Léger, *Publications de l'École des Langues Orientales Vivantes*, 2ᵉ sér., vol. XIII, Paris, 1884), p. 102.

more native Slavonic, and therefore a more democratic spirit at his court. The fact that he called his sons by Slavonic names suggests that it was about his time that the language of the court changed from Scandinavian to Russian. This being so, it is not impossible that the native minstrels may have found their way to court at this period in the train of their Russian patrons, and gradually supplanted the Scandinavian raconteurs. This at any rate would account for the fame which has been accorded to the great Scandinavian king on the Dnêpr by a grateful body of Russian minstrels for nearly a thousand years.

But whatever the origin of the form of the Russian *byliny*, and whatever foreign influences may have made contribution to their subject-matter, there can be no doubt that the result is a literary genre which is, in its present form, purely and exclusively Russian. Stasov's monumental attempt to prove the Oriental origin of their form and content convinced no one. Miller and Abicht can at most point to a small contributory Greek element, by no means fundamental, in Russian native poetry. Had we known nothing of the Scandinavian colonies on the Dnêpr, and had Vladimir had a Slavonic name, probably no one would have recognised Scandinavian elements or affinities in the *byliny*. To overstress the points of contact between the *byliny* and the literatures of neighbouring peoples is as if one should call the Homeric poems, or certain books of the Homeric poems, Oriental in origin because a similar form and some few identical themes are to be found in certain Asiatic literatures. Russia has always been a through route geographically from both north to south and from east to west, and we may assume that intellectual transport has taken place to some extent. But the geographical and political unity of Russia has remained surprisingly constant, and, if we may judge from her written literature, the intellectual unit has also remained individual. After all, by far the nearest analogies of the *byliny* lie not with Oriental, Greek, or Norse poetry, but with the *narodne pjesme* of other Slavonic peoples, notably the Serbians and Montenegrins.

I

Volga Vseslavich or Svyatoslavich

VOLGA is one of the most interesting figures of Russian popular poetry. He is generally regarded as a magician, but he is more akin to the shamans of Asia. He stands in intimate sympathetic relationship with the world of nature. The state of the heavens and the elements are constantly noted as significant at his birth. He is said to have applied himself to learning wisdom; but it is occult wisdom, supernatural knowledge of nature, which is implied. Like a shaman he possesses the power of changing himself into all creatures of animate nature, and into whatever order of nature he enters he is himself supreme.

At the same time he is also a military chief, and has a *druzhina* like Vladimir in the Kiev Cycle. He is pre-eminent above all the heroes as a military leader. Vladimir I and the *bogatyrs* of Kiev are generally occupied in defensive warfare only, satisfied if they can defend the marches against the Tartar hordes. Volga alone habitually practises offensive warfare. The poet does not shrink from claiming victory for his hero over the Emperor of the Turks. Volga succeeds in making his way to the Great Tsargrad, whose ruler lives in permanent fear of his aggressive policy.

In spite of the absence of verisimilitude, the portrait of this hero, so clearly and so remarkably conceived, and so consistently portrayed through a number of variant *byliny*, can hardly be derived from folk-tale or Aryan mythology. Yet it is curious that there is no agreement among scholars as to Volga's identity. Rambaud and others have identified him with Prince Oleg, brother of Rurik, who figures in Nestor's Chronicle as leading his *druzhina* against Byzantium.[1] Nestor adds that the heathen Russians gave to Oleg

[1] Rambaud, *La Russie Épique*, p. 36.

the epithet of *Vêshchi*, the Sage or Sorcerer, on account of his wisdom. Rambaud also points out that one of Volga's patronymics is Vseslavich, and that in the *Slovo o Polky Igorevê*, l. 569 ff., shape-changing is attributed to Vseslav, prince of Kiev. Schröder accepts Rambaud's identification, but goes further, regarding both Volga and Oleg as identical with the Norse hero Helgi Hundingsbani.[1] Abicht has sought to trace the origin of the Russian *bylina* of Volkh- (i.e. Volga) Oleg in the story of Alexander as known to us from Pseudo-Kallisthenes.[2] The fantastic shape-changing and other magical practices attributed to Volga in the *byliny*, together with the similarity of the name, have led others, notably Chalanskij, to regard him as the son of Vseslav prince of the Polovtsy in the *Slovo o Polky Igorevê*.[3] Vsevolod Miller, one of the most learned and brilliant writers on Russian popular poetry, holds that the story of Volga draws upon several older stories, and regards attempts at the identification of the hero as a hopeless quest.[4] The similarity of Volga to Prince Roman of Galicia has already been remarked (p. 15 above).

In spite of the similarity of the names, there are serious philological difficulties in the way of an identification of the name Volgá with either Volkh or Oleg. Such philological equations could only be accepted if we regard the word as having been affected by analogy, possibly with some such word as the name of the river Vólga. And there is no satisfactory evidence for such an assumption.[5] Apart from the philological difficulty, however, Rambaud's identifica-

---

[1] *Germanisch-romanische Monatsschrift*, vol. VIII (1920), p. 287 f.
[2] R. Abicht, 'Ein Alexanderlied unter den russischen Bylinen', in *Die Festschrift für Alfred Hillebrandt* (Halle, 1913). The work of Abicht has not been accessible to me.
[3] *Velikorusskÿa Byliny*.
[4] Neither Chalanskij's nor Miller's discussions of Volga's identity have been accessible to me. For a summary of their views and those of Abicht I am indebted to Schröder, *loc. cit.*, and to Hofmann, *Archiv für slavische Philologie*, vols. XXXVIII, p. 89 ff., XXXIX, p. 228 ff.
[5] The analogy of the name of the hero Tikhi Dunai Ivanovich has been adduced.

tion with the historical Oleg, Rurik's brother, is tempting. Oleg, as he points out, was called *Vêshchi*, and was credited by the people with supernatural power. Oleg, no less than Volga, is referred to in terms of unusually poetical and figurative diction. Both are great military leaders credited with the exploit of carrying their aggressive warfare to the very gates of Tsargrad and making the Turkish Emperor tremble.

It may, of course, be objected that the figurative diction on which stress has been laid is not confined to either hero. Traces of it are widespread in association with other Russian heroes, historical and unhistorical, notably with Prince Roman of Galicia, himself a great conqueror also. It originates no doubt in the current poetic diction of the neighbourhood of Kiev during the period prior to its destruction by the Tartars, rather than in the supernatural achievements attributed by deliberate fiction to any single individual. On the other hand, it is noteworthy that Volga alone of all the heroes of the *byliny* is especially and consistently distinguished by these features. This at least makes it probable that whichever individual we select as Volga's prototype— whether Oleg, Roman or another—his origin and affinities are to be sought in Kiev and in the period to which these heroes belong.

In my opinion, however, it is Volga's military character even more than his supernatural attributes which lends support to Rambaud's identification with Prince Oleg. He is a hero of princely rank, who, at the age of fifteen, collects a *druzhina*, or group of military followers. Three cities are assigned to him by Prince Vladimir, where he rules land near Kiev in the manner of the Scandinavian princes of the Dnêpr in the ninth century. Here, surrounded by his *druzhina*, to whom he is superior in nothing but courage and skill, he subsists in time of peace on hunting and fishing, levying tribute, quelling rebellions, protecting with especial care the passages of the rivers, guarding his outposts against enemies from the south and east. In much of this he resembles closely

Prince Vladimir I himself. In venturing into the heart of the enemies' territory his great prototype is Oleg, who is said to have furnished his ships with wheels in order to cross the Steppe, and to have hung up his shield on the golden gates of Tsargrad.

Volga is variously called Svyatoslavich (or Svyatoslavgo-vich), Vseslavich, etc. Before accepting Rambaud's identi-fication without reserve it may be worth while to compare the character ascribed to Volga in the *byliny* with that of Vseslav as sketched for us in the great medieval Russian portrait gallery, the *Slovo o Polky Igorevê* (l. 569 ff.). Here we are told that Vseslav galloped about as a wild beast (*lyutim zverem*) at midnight, swathed in blue mist; as a wolf he galloped over the plains; he was a great conqueror, 'with his weapon he took hold of the golden throne of Kiev'; he 'opened wide the gates of Novgorod'. He was also a great administrator; 'he appointed cities to the princes'. But he himself raced as a wolf (*volkom*) from Kiev to Tmutorokan in the Crimea. His path would seem to have been the path of Volga; though he has allowed his son to outstrip him. But though Oleg is said to have reached Tsargrad, and un-doubtedly wrested an advantageous mercantile treaty from the Greeks, historians have doubted[1] if his achievement is not due to the unscrupulous eulogies of panegyrists. Tmutoro-kan, the great Tartar stronghold of the Crimea at this time, is a more likely objective than Tsargrad for the military adventurers of the Dnêpr, and it is not unlikely that the *Slovo* has preserved a more accurate historical record of this remarkable achievement than either Nestor or the *byliny*. Be this as it may, the intellectual and military affinities of both these heroes with Volga seem to justify us in ascribing the hero of the *byliny* to the same age and milieu as one or other of them, perhaps even in identifying him with Oleg himself. The evidence suggests that the popular hero Volga origi-nated not in folk-tale, or primitive Aryan myth, but in one

[1] See G. Laehr, *Die Anfänge des russischen Reiches* (Berlin, 1930), p. 95 ff.

of the phases of the ancient type of heroic community in the valley of the Dnêpr. He is not a timeless-nameless un-localised hero; he belonged in all probability to the tenth or the eleventh century, and ruled on the frontiers of Kiev.

VOLGA

Sung by Kuzma Romanov

Gilferding, *Sbornik*, vol. II, p. 172.

The red sun was sinking
Behind the dark woods, behind the broad sea,
Multitudes of stars studded the clear sky
When Lord Volga Buslavlevich was born
In holy Russia.   5
When Volga Buslavlevich was five years of age,
Lord Volga Buslavlevich went forth over the damp earth;
Damp mother earth was rent,
The wild beasts fled away into the forests,
The birds flew away up to the clouds;   10
And the fish scattered in the blue sea;
And Lord Volga Buslavlevich went
To learn all craft and wisdom,
All the various languages;
He collected a brave druzhina to him,   15
A brave druzhina and a bold,
Of thirty heroes save one;
He himself made up the thirty.
'Ho, you, my brave and bold druzhina,
Obey your mighty brother chief,   20
And perform the task I lay upon you.
Twist ropes of silk,
Spread the ropes along the damp earth,
And hunt martens, foxes,
Savage wild beasts, black sables,   25
And white hares that burrow,[1]

---

[1] *Sic.*

White hares, little ermines,
And hunt for three days and three nights.'
They hearkened to their mighty brother chief.
They performed the task laid upon them.   30
They twisted ropes of silk,
They spread the ropes across the dark forest, over the damp
    earth,
They hunted for three days and three nights,
But they could not catch a single creature.
Lord Volga Buslavlevich transformed himself,   35
He changed himself into a lion,
And leapt over the damp earth through the dark forest;
He rounded up martens, foxes,
And savage wild beasts, black sables,
And white, leaping hares,   40
And little ermines,
And is forthwith in the city of Kiev
With his brave druzhina.
And Lord Volga Buslavlevich speaks:
'My brave, my bold druzhina!   45
Obey your mighty brother chief,
And perform the task I lay upon you;
Twist snares of silk,
Spread the snares in the dark forest,
In the dark forest, right on the tree-tops.   50
Catch geese, swans, bright falcons,
And all kinds of little birds,
And snare them for three days and three nights'.
And they obeyed their mighty brother chief,
And performed the task laid upon them: 55
They twisted snares of silk,
They spread the snares in the dark forest, right on the tree-tops;
They snared for three days and three nights,
But they could not catch a single little bird.
Lord Volga Buslavlevich transformed himself into a bird;   60
He flew away to the sky.
He rounded up geese, swans, bright falcons,

And all kinds of little birds.
And forthwith they are in the city of Kiev,
He and his bold druzhina.   65
Lord Volga Buslavlevich speaks:
'My brave, my bold druzhina!
Obey your mighty brother chief,
Perform the task laid upon you:
Take axes for felling,   70
Build oaken ships,
Weave silken nets,
Depart over the blue sea,
Catch salmon and white salmon,
Pike, roach,   75
And precious sturgeon.
And catch them for three days and three nights'.
And they obeyed their mighty brother chief.
They performed the task laid upon them.
They fetched axes for felling,   80
They built oaken ships,
They wove silken nets,
They departed over the blue sea,
They fished for three days and three nights,
But they could not catch a single little fish.   85
Lord Volga Buslavlevich transformed himself into a pike,
And swam off through the blue sea.
He rounded up salmon and white salmon,
Pike and roach,
And precious sturgeon.   90
And forthwith they are in the city of Kiev,
He and his brave druzhina.
And Lord Volga Buslavlevich speaks:
'My brave, my bold druzhina!
Hearken to your mighty brother chief!   95
Whom should we send into the land of the Turks
To discover the tsar's intentions,
And what plans the tsar is planning,
And whether he intends to invade holy Russia?

If we send an old man, we shall have long to wait;   100
And if we send a middle-aged man, they will make him
    drunk with wine;
If we send a youth,
He will play too long with the maidens,
And make merry with the married women,
And chatter with the old crones,   105
And in that case also we shall have long to wait.
Manifestly it is Volga himself who must go'.
Lord Volga Buslavlevich transformed himself
Into a little bird, a tiny little bird;
He flew away through the sky,   110
And at once he is in the land of the Turks,
With the Turkish Santal,
At the white stone palace,
In front of the very windows;
And he hears a secret conversation.   115
The tsar is talking to the tsaritsa:
'Ah, Tsaritsa, Pantalovna,
Do you know this? Have you noticed?—
In Russia the grass sprouts not as of old,
The flowers bloom not as in the past,   120
And in Russia the grass grows not as in the past;
It is clear that Volga no longer lives;
And I shall go into holy Russia,
I shall take for myself nine towns,
I shall bestow them upon my nine sons,   125
And to you, Tsaritsa Pantalovna,
I shall present a costly mantle'.
The Tsaritsa Pantalovna made answer:
'Ah, Tsar Santal of the Turks!
I know this, I have noticed it:—   130
In Russia the grass grows exactly as of old,
The flowers are blooming just as in the past.
Last night I slept, and in my sleep I dreamed:
From the eastern quarter
A little bird came flying,   135

And from the western quarter
A black crow came flying;
They flew down into the open plain,
And tore at one another;
The little bird, the tiny little bird,   140
Stripped the black crow,
And plucked out all its feathers,
And scattered them all to the winds.
That was Lord Volga Buslavlevich,
But the black crow was the Turkish Santal'.   145
The Turkish Tsar Santal spoke:
'Ho Tsaritsa Pantalovna!
I intend to ride at once into holy Russia,
I shall take nine cities,
I shall bestow them upon my nine sons,   150
I shall bring for myself the costly mantle'.
Said the Tsaritsa Pantalovna:
'No, you will not take nine cities,
Nor bestow them upon your nine sons,
Nor bring for yourself a costly mantle'.   155
The Turkish Tsar Santal spoke:
'Ha, you old devil!
You only slept and dreamed an idle dream!'
And he struck her on her white cheek,
And then he turned, and struck her again on the other,   160
And he flung the tsaritsa on the brick floor,
And again he flung her a second time:
'I shall go into holy Russia,
I shall take nine cities,
I shall bestow them on my nine sons,   165
I shall bring for myself the costly mantle!'
Then Lord Volga Buslavlevich transformed himself;
He transformed himself into a grey wolf,
And trotted off to the stable-yard.
He went from one good steed to another   170
And tore the throat of every one.
And Lord Volga Buslavlevich transformed himself

Into a little ermine,
And ran off to the armoury.
He snapped the taut bows,   175
And tore the silken bow-strings,
And broke in bits the tempered arrows;
The sharp swords he made all jagged,
The steel clubs he bent double.
Then Lord Volga Buslavlevich,   180
Lord Volga Buslavlevich transformed himself
Into a little bird, a little tiny bird,
And forthwith he is in the city of Kiev;
And has transformed himself into a goodly youth,
And is with his brave druzhina.   185
'My brave, my bold druzhina!
Let us be off to the Turkish land.'
And they went into the Turkish land,
And took the Turkish host prisoners.
'My brave, my bold druzhina!   190
Let us now begin to divide the spoil.'
What was a dear bargain,
And what a cheap?
Good steeds went for seven roubles,
And a steel weapon for six roubles,   195
Sharp swords for five roubles,
Steel clubs for three roubles.
But the cheap bargain was the womenfolk.
Old women were priced at a quarter of a kopeck,
And married women at half a kopeck,   200
And fair maidens at a halfpenny.

II

Volga and Mikula

MIKULA SELYANINOVICH, 'the villager's son', is the great peasant hero of the *byliny*. He is a ploughman of the Steppe, and his horse, for all its noble equine lineage, has been harnessed to the plough. He is the glorification of the peasant ideal, and his characteristic features are his tremendous strength and his excellence in husbandry. The love and admiration of the popular singers for their ploughman hero can be seen in the wealth of technical details relating to ploughing and agriculture, and the emphasis which they lay on his skill and adroitness in driving his furrow and clearing the land. He is identified, to some extent, with St Nikolai, whom the peasants call Mikula, and who is the patron saint of agriculture.

The story of Volga's search for Mikula and the compact which they make together is sometimes followed by a sequel, according to which they proceed together to take possession of Volga's three cities. The cities were stoutly defended by the inhabitants, who did not welcome the new governor or his companion, and built a treacherous bridge against them. But Volga and Mikula leapt across the river on their good steeds and chastised the peasants into submission with their whips, so that from that time they were glad to pay tribute.

The stories associated with Mikula are not numerous, but it will be seen that they are very distinctive. Mikula excels in strength and speed, and in skill as a workman. He has none of the abnormal brain-power or the protean qualities of Volga. Supernatural elements are confined to what is hardly more than exaggeration of the normal. He is conceived on big lines. His little bags contain the weight of the whole world, but are not too heavy for him to carry with ease. He ploughs and clears the virgin soil of the Steppe just beyond the range of the military influence of Kiev, which has difficulty in overtaking the agrarian pioneer. The compact between the military prince, dependent, for his own part, on Kiev, with the agricultural settler of the Steppe can surely not be without political significance. Is not Volga's invitation to the turbulent agricultural countryman analogous to Vladimir's invitation to the country lad to come to Kiev to fight the Pecheneg champion, as related to us by Nestor? We would prefer to see in Mikula, not a divinity or Slavonic myth, or the Prince Kolaxais of Herodotus,[1] but a free agricultural yeoman, perhaps a settler, turning up the soil on the fringe of Russian military influence, showing his power and eking out his gains by robbing the 'robbers', and finally throwing in his lot with the princely caste. The wealth of technical agricultural detail points to a peasant milieu, and the story of Mikula may well have taken its present form in some comparatively recent democratic community—some pioneer agricultural community such as the Cossacks of the Ukraine, or the settlers in Orenburg or the north—where the audience would demand 'sound tendencies' in their minstrelsy—the heroic celebration of the free country yeoman and pioneer tiller of the soil.

VOLGA AND MIKULA

Sung by Trofim Grigorevich Ryabinin

Rybnikov, *Pêsni*, vol. i, p. 10.

When the red sun rose[2]
In the bright heavens
Then was young Volga born,
Young Volga Svyatoslavgovich.

[1] See Rambaud, *La Russie Épique*, p. 40.
[2] In the *byliny* Volga is generally said to be born as the sun was sinking.

Volga grew in strength and stature,   5
Eagerly Volga sought wisdom.
He could swim as a pike in the deep seas,
Fly as a falcon under the clouds,
Race as a grey wolf on the open plains.
All the fish sped away in the blue sea,   10
All the birds flew away beyond the clouds,
All the wild beasts fled away into the dark forest.
Volga grew in strength and stature.
He chose for himself a bold druzhina
Of thirty youths save one,   15
He, Volga, making the thirtieth.
His dear 'uncle' bestowed upon him,
Gracious Vladimir of royal Kiev,
Three cities with their peasants:
The first city was Gurchevets,   20
The second city was Orêkhovets,
The third city was Krestyanovets.
Young Volga Svyatoslavgovich,
With his bold druzhina,
He has gone to receive his cities.   25
He has ridden forth in the free, open plain,
He has heard a ploughman in the open plain:
A ploughman is ploughing in the plain, driving his plough
        before him,
The ploughman's ploughshare is grating against the stones,
The plough is scoring its track among the stones.[1]   30
Volga rode after the ploughman,
All day long from dawn till eventide,
With his bold druzhina;
But that ploughman he could not overtake.
Volga rode yet a second day,   35
A second day from dawn till eventide;
But he could not overtake the ploughman.

---

[1] Bezsonov points to the strong local colouring in the passage. In the districts of Zaonega and Pudoga in the north the land is so stony that the fields are literally strewn with stones.

The ploughman ploughs in the plain, driving his plough before
    him;
The ploughman's ploughshare is grating against the stones.
The plough is scoring its track among the stones.   40
Volga rode yet a third day,
A third day from dawn till noon,
And overtook the ploughman in the open plain.
The ploughman is ploughing in the plain, driving his plough
    before him,
From end to end he drives his furrows,   45
When he reaches one end he cannot see the other;
Roots and stones he tears up,
And all the mighty stones he rolls into the ditch.
The ploughman's mare is a light-bay,
The ploughman's ploughshare is of maple-wood,   50
The ploughman's ropes are of silk.
Volga spoke as follows:
'God speed you, ploughman!
Ploughing and tilling, and labouring on the land,
Driving your furrows from end to end,   55
Tearing up roots and stones'.
The ploughman spoke as follows:
'Need have I, Volga Svyatoslavgovich,
With your bold druzhina,
For God's speed to my labouring.   60
Are you riding far, Volga? By what road are you travelling
With your bold druzhina?'
'Ah, ploughman, good ploughman,
I am going to my cities to take possession—
To the first city Gurchevets,   65
To the second city Orêkhovets,
To the third city Krestyanovets.'
The ploughman spoke as follows:
'Ah, Volga Svyatoslavgovich!
I was in the city no longer ago than the day before yesterday,   70
On my light-bay mare;
I carried thence two whole bags of salt,

Two bags of salt of forty pud[1] each.
The folk there are no better than robbers.
They demand two kopecks toll; 75
But I had a leaded whip for toll.
I paid their two kopecks toll.—
Whoever was upright I left seated,
And whoever was seated I left prostrate.
And those who were prostrate would never stand again!' 80
Volga spoke as follows:
'Ah ploughman, good ploughman!
Let us go, you and I together,
To the glorious city of Gurchevets,
To receive the cities'. 85
At this the ploughman, that good ploughman,
Unbound the silken ropes,
Loosed his mare from the plough,
Drew the yoke from the mare;
They seated themselves on their good steeds and away they
rode. 90
The ploughman spoke as follows:
'Hearken, Volga Svyatoslavgovich!
I have left my plough in the furrow—
Not for the wayfarer, whether on foot or on horse,
But for the labouring peasant. 95
Let them take the steel plough,
For I shall do no more peasant's work with it.
Will you have the plough pulled out of the earth,
The clods shaken from the ploughshare,
And let the plough be thrown behind a willow bush?' 100
Young Volga Svyatoslavgovich
He sent of his bold druzhina
Five sturdy youths
To pull the plough out of the earth,
To shake the clods from the ploughshare, 105

---

[1] A *pud* is a weight of 40 Russian pounds or rather more than 36
English pounds.

To throw the plough behind a willow bush.
This bold druzhina,
Five sturdy youths,
Rode up to the plough of maple-wood,
They pulled the plough about by the handles,   110
But they could not pull it out of the earth,
Or shake the clods from the ploughshare,
Or throw the plough behind the willow bush.
Young Volga Svyatoslavgovich,
He sent a whole half-score   115
To pull the plough out of the earth,
To shake the clods from the ploughshare,
And to throw the plough behind the willow bush.
They pulled the plough about by the handles:
They could not raise the ploughshare out of the earth,   120
They could not shake the clods from the ploughshare,
Or throw the plough behind the willow bush.
He sent the whole of his bold druzhina:
They pulled the plough about by the handles,
But they could not pull the plough out of the earth,   125
Or shake the clods from the ploughshare,
Or throw the plough behind the willow bush.
The ploughman, the good ploughman spoke:
'Oh, Volga Svyatoslavgovich!
Your bold druzhina are a negligible band!'   130
The ploughman, the good ploughman rode up
On his light-bay mare
To that plough of maple-wood!
He seized the plough with one hand,
Pulled the plough from the earth,   135
Shook the clods from the ploughshare,
Threw the plough behind the willow bush.
They bestrode their noble steeds and rode away.
The ploughman's mare went at a trot,
But the horse of Volga set off at a gallop.   140
The ploughman's horse went with a will,
But Volga's horse lagged behind;

Then Volga began to cry out,
Volga began to wave his cap:
'Stop, stop, good ploughman!   145
If that mare were but a stallion
I would give five hundred roubles for it'.
The ploughman spoke as follows:
'Foolish Volga Svyatoslavgovich!
I took the mare as a foal from its mother's side,   150
And I paid five hundred roubles for her.
If this mare were but a stallion
That stallion would be beyond price'.
Volga Svyatoslavgovich spoke:
'Ah, ploughman, good ploughman!   155
By what name do they call you?
How do they address you in your own country?'
The ploughman spoke as follows:
'Ah, Volga Svyatoslavgovich!
I cultivate rye, and stack it in the rick,   160
I stack it in the rick, and lead it home,
I lead it home, and thresh it at home,
I rend it to shreds, and I brew drink,
I brew drink and supply it to the peasants.
The peasants generally hail me thus: 165
"Young Mikulushka, the villager's son"'.

III

Mikula and Svyatogor

THE figure of Svyatogor is more nebulous than that of Volga or Mikula. He resembles much more closely the giant of folk-tales, whose character seems to consist wholly in vast strength, and supernatural elements and *motifs* common to folk-tales are prominent in the *byliny* relative to him. He is, indeed, definitely styled a giant (*velikan*)—one of the few supernatural beings who are heroes of *byliny*. He is depicted not as living on Russian soil, but as being restricted to the high mountains and massive rocks. His name seems to mean 'Holy Mountain'. The *byliny* associated with him are wholly lacking in local associations or local colour. He is brought into association, however, not only with Mikula and Ilya of Murom, but also sporadically with other heroes both of Kiev and Novgorod, though the two latter associations are undoubtedly adventitious.

MIKULA AND SVYATOGOR

Dormidontov, *Kratki Kurs Istorii Russkoy Literaturÿ*, pt. 1 (Tallinn, 1923), p. 217 ff.

On the lofty mountains, on the holy mountains,
The giant hero Svyatogor dwelt;
But he was not allowed in holy Russia:
Damp mother earth could not carry him.
Once upon a time the hero felt a wish   5
To walk abroad in the free open plain.
He saddled his heroic steed,
And rode forth on his way.
His young heart was throbbing,
His strength vibrated in his sinews,   10
His energy was like to overflow,
And he was heavily burdened with his strength,

Heavily burdened, as if with a grievous load;
He could not control his heroic strength.
And he threw away his steel club   15
Which vanished out of sight above the clouds,
And caught it again in his white hand:
'If I should take to walking on the earth
I would fasten a ring to heaven,
I would bind an iron chain to the ring,   20
I would drag the sky down to mother earth,
I would turn the earth on its end,
And I would confound earth with heaven!'
Then he descried in the open plain
A good youth walking on foot;   25
Over the shoulders of the good youth
A little bag was slung.
He urges on his good steed to overtake him
With all his equine might—
The good youth walks on foot,   30
He cannot overtake him with his heroic steed.
When he is riding at an easy trot
The good youth ahead never hurries.
And Svyatogor hailed the good youth:
'Ho there, wayfarer, good youth!   35
Wait a moment, wait just a little moment;
When I put my good steed to the gallop
With all his equine might,
And you are walking in front on foot,
I cannot overtake you on my heroic steed;   40
While I am riding at an easy trot,
You are walking without hurrying yourself'.
The good youth, the wayfarer, waited for him,
Unslung from his sturdy shoulders
His little bags,[1] and laid them on the ground.   45

---

[1] I suppose these to be double bags or pouches to contain provisions
such as the *kaléki* are pictured as wearing slung over their shoulders in
the frontispiece to Bezsonov, *Kaléki Perekhoɀhie. Sbornik Stikhov i
Iɀslédovanie*, 2 vols. (Moscow, 1861, 1863).

Svyatogor addressed the good youth:
'Tell me, good youth,
What sort of load you have in your bag?'
The good youth made answer:
'Ah, you glorious, mighty hero!   50
Try to lift my load
On to your sturdy shoulders,
And set off with it into the free open plain'.
The glorious mighty hero dismounted
From his good steed and approached the little bag;   55
He seized hold of the little bag;
He seized hold first with one finger—
The little shoulder-bag did not stir from its place on the damp
      earth.
Then he seized it with one hand—
That little bag did not move wholly.   60
He laid hold of it with both hands—
It did not move completely from its place.
He seized hold of it with all his mighty strength,
But he fell down on his heroic white bosom,
On to that little shoulder-bag.   65
He clutched it with his whole mighty force,
He sank into the damp earth to his knees,
Not tears, but blood streams over his white face!
His young heart is spent.
Only a little breath could pass   70
Under that little shoulder-bag.
He spoke the following words:
'I never lifted such a load!
I am very strong, but I am not strong enough for that!
What burden have you in your bag?   75
Who are you yourself, bold, noble youth?
What is your own name and your father's name?'
The bold noble youth replied:
'In my little shoulder-bag
The weight of the whole world is contained,   80
And I myself am Mikula Selyaninovich'.

IV

Svyatogor

THE *byliny* relating to the friendship between Ilya of Murom and Svyatogor are not, as a rule, of a high artistic standard, and it is not easy to find a version which has consistently preserved the tradition intact throughout. In some versions Svyatogor is represented as having a wife whom he had miraculously freed from her covering of fir-tree bark, and transformed into a beautiful maiden. In these versions it is the wife who is responsible for secreting Ilya in her husband's pocket, till his horse protests that it is carrying three people, whereupon Svyatogor discovers Ilya's presence. In the version which follows it will be seen that in the early part of the *bylina* a certain amount of confusion has arisen with the preceding *bylina* of *Mikula and Svyatogor*, from which some of the lines had been transferred—very inappropriately—into the present text. The tradition of Svyatogor is better preserved on the whole in prose versions than in the poems.

SVYATOGOR

Sung by Menshikov

Gilferding, *Sbornik*, vol. III, p. 382 ff.

An old man rode in the open plain,
The old man rode up on to the holy mountains,
The old man came upon a hero;
And the hero was one who rode a horse, but he was asleep.
'What marvel is this?   5
Can it be mighty, powerful heroes
Fast asleep in white tents?'
And Ilya of Murom rode up,
And struck the hero hard, very hard,

The hero always rides on ahead.[1]   10
'Ah, so mighty a hero am I
That no hero has ever been able to keep his seat on his horse
    against me,
I must go up to him again.'
Then Ilya of Murom went up,
And struck him hard, very hard,   15
But the hero always rides ahead of him.
'What marvel is this?
It is clear that I have not hit hard enough.'
Then Ilya went up yet a third time,
And struck the hero hard, very hard,   20
And struck him over and over again.
Then the hero awoke from his sleep.
He seized Ilya with his right hand,
Thrust Ilya into his pouch,
And carried Ilya for two whole days.   25
But on the third day the horse began to stumble,
The horse's legs began to fail him.
Then Svyatogor struck his noble steed:
'Why, my steed, art thou stumbling?'
The horse spoke as follows: 30
'And how could I fail to stumble?
I have been carrying for three days
Two mighty, strong heroes,
And for a third I am carrying a heroic steed'.
Then Svyatogor took Ilya out of his pouch;   35
They pitched the tent of white linen,
And he and Ilya began to take repose.
And he and Ilya swore brotherhood together on their crosses,
They named themselves sworn brothers on the cross.[2]
They rode and wandered in the holy mountains,   40
Then together they descended the holy mountain,
They came into a broad open space,

    [1] This line, which seems strangely out of place here, is no doubt
borrowed from the *bylina* of *Mikula and Svyatogor*.
    [2] I.e. brothers by exchange of crosses.

Into a green meadow.
Then they discovered a great marvel,
A great marvel, a mighty wonder,   45
A stone structure, a tomb stood there before them.
Ilya spoke as follows:
'Hearken, my sworn brother,
For whom has this tomb been built?'
And they dismounted from their good steeds,   50
And Ilya laid himself down in that tomb.
But Svyatogor spoke as follows:
'Hearken, my sworn brother!
Not for you has that tomb been built.
Let me lie in that tomb'.   55
Then Svyatogor lay down to sleep in that tomb.
Svyatogor spoke as follows:
'Hearken, my sworn brother,
Shut the oak lid on me'.
Svyatogor spoke as follows: 60
'Hearken, my sworn brother,
It is pleasant living here in the tomb.
But come now, my sworn brother,
Open the oak lid'.
Then Ilya of Murom tried to raise the oak lid,   65
But he could not lift off any of the planks.
'Hearken, my sworn brother,
I cannot lift any of the planks.'
'Hearken, my sworn brother,
Hearken now, Ilya of Murom!   70
Strike it with my battle club.'
Then Ilya set to work to strike it with the club:
Where he struck, hoops of iron appeared.
Ilya spoke as follows:
'Hearken, now, my sworn brother!   75
Where I strike, hoops of iron appear'.
Svyatogor spoke as follows:
'Hearken, my sworn brother!
It must be that God has appointed my death here'.

Then Svyatogor began to feel the approach of death, 80
And he foamed at the mouth.
Svyatogor spoke as follows:
'Hearken, my sworn brother!
Place your lips to my foam,
Then will you ride on the holy mountain, 85
And you will not fear heroes,
No mighty bold hero of them all'.

V

The Healing of Ilya of Murom

ILYA of Murom is the hero of a large number of *byliny*. He is constantly called the 'peasant's son', and the 'Old Cossack'. Murom was in early times in Mordvin territory, and Ilya evidently possessed horse and weapons. It is possible, therefore, that 'peasant's son' means that he belonged to the agricultural squirearchy of the Mordvin population. Vladimir's reluctance to receive him into his court was probably connected with his origin and class. On the other hand his great exploit against Tsar Kalin, the Tartar Khan, is believed to have reference to the Battle of Kalka, which took place in 1228. In this battle the Polovtsy, a people of Tartar extraction settled in South-West Russia, supported by their allies, the Russians of Kiev and the Galicians, who were connected with them by marriage, attempted unsuccessfully to check a Tartar inroad. Ilya's part in this and other *byliny* would therefore be analogous to the part played by the Polovtsy, as defenders of the 'Russian' marches, i.e. of the territory watered by the Dnêpr. It is not improbable that the 'Old Cossack' was of Polovtsy extraction, and belonged to the Polovtsy population settled on Mordvin territory—an ally rather than a subject of Vladimir. If this is so we would suggest that the static epithet *stari*, 'old', applied to him in the *byliny*, is used in the sense in which we are familiar with it in the *Slovo o Polky Igorevê*, and refers not to his age, but to his race and the period in which they lived, to distinguish the earlier Tartar or Polovtsy element to which he belonged from those of later invasions.

The first of the following *byliny* embodies the theme with which we are familiar in early Teutonic literature, according to which a great hero is slow to develop, or is actually crippled in early life.

Ilya of Murom may possibly have had a historical existence however. In 1594 a German traveller, Erich Lassota of Steblau, states in his diary that he saw in the Cathedral of St Sophia at Kiev, the tomb, now destroyed, of Elia Morowlin, 'a famous hero or a *bogatyr* as they call them. Many stories are told about him'. Kolnoforsky, a Pole, stated in a book published in 1638 that Ilya lived about 1188. His portrait was also published among the saints of Kiev in the seventeenth century.[1] Even if we assume confusion with St Elias in all these cases, there can be no doubt that secular traditions of Ilya have been current from very early times. In his native village of Karachoro, in the province of Murom, peasants bearing the name of Ilyuchni claim descent from him in a direct line.[2] In the Norse *Thiðreks Saga af Bern*, which dates from the early part of the thirteenth century, we read that 'Ilias...a great chief and mighty warrior' was a half-brother of Valldimar (Vladimir), and possessed an earldom in Greece (i.e. South Russia).[3] There can be little doubt that the reference here is to Ilya of Murom. Other references are to be found elsewhere in the same saga, as well as in the *Fornaldar Sögur*.

The following *bylina* relates the healing of Ilya by Christ and two disciples disguised as *kalêki perekhozhie*. These *kalêki* were a fraternity of wandering singers whose répertoire consisted principally of religious poems, known as *stikhi*, similar in form and style to the *byliny*, but composed on Biblical and other sacred themes. These singers, who are often blind or cripples, wandered about the country in small groups, begging for alms, at fairs and along the high-roads. Many *kalêki* are familiar also with the *byliny* and other forms of popular secular poetry. Rybnikov obtained some fine specimens of such poetry from two *kalêki* whom he met in the Onega district and at the Shungsk Fair. A collection of their religious poetry has been published by

[1] Hapgood, *Epic Songs of Russia*, p. 263.
[2] Rambaud, *La Russie Épique*, p. 105.
[3] *Thiðreks Saga af Bern*, cap. 25 f.

Bezsonov,[1] together with an engraving of a group of *kalêki* from a famous picture in the Moscow art gallery.

THE HEALING OF ILYA OF MUROM

ll. 1–27, Kirêevski, *Pésni*, pt. 1, p. 1 ff. The whole is printed by Dormidontov, *Kratki Kurs Istorii Russkoy Literaturÿ*, pt. 1 (Tallinn, 1923), p. 182 f.

Who is there who could tell us about the old days,
About the old days, and what happened long ago,
About Ilya, Ilya of Murom?
Ilya of Murom, the son of Ivanov,
He sat among the stay-at-homes for thirty-three years;   5
There came to him poor brethren,
Jesus Christ Himself, and two apostles:
'Go, Ilya, and bring us a drink!'
'Poor brethren, I have no use in my arms or legs!'
'Stand up, Ilya, do not deceive us!'   10
Ilya stood up, exactly as if nothing were the matter;
He went off and fetched a bowl of huge measure,
And offered it-to the poor brethren.
The poor brethren motioned him to keep it.
The poor brethren addressed Ilya: 15
'Do you feel your strength great within you, Ilya?'
'If there were a pillar from earth to heaven,
And if there were a gold ring attached to the pillar,
I would take it by the ring and overturn holy Russia.'
'Go, Ilya, and fetch another bowl!'   20
Ilya went and brought it to them.
They signed to Ilya to keep it.
Ilya drained at one draught
The great bowl of huge measure.
They proceeded to question Ilya.   25
'Do you feel your strength great within you, Ilya?'

----

[1] *Kalêki Perekhoƶhie. Sbornik Stikhov i Iƶslêdovanie* ('Wandering Kalêki. A Collection of their songs and a Survey'), 2 vols. (Moscow, 1861, 1863).

'I feel the strength in me reduced by half.'
The wandering kalêki spoke:
'You will be, Ilya, a mighty hero,
And death in battle is not destined for you.   30
Fight and make war against all heroes,
And all bold polenitsy.[1]
But do not go to fight
With the hero Svyatogor:
The earth can hardly carry him.   35
Do not go to fight with the hero Samson:
He has seven angelic hairs on his head.
And do not fight with your relative Mikula:
Damp mother earth loves him.
Lastly, do not go against Volga Vseslavich: 40
He does not lay hold by force,
But by craft and wisdom.
Get for yourself, Ilya, a heroic steed.
Go forth in the free, open plain.
Purchase a first foal,   45
Put it in a stall for three months,
Every three nights lead the foal about the garden,
And roll the foal in three dews;
Lead him to a high fence.
When the foal takes to jumping the fence   50
From one side to the other,
Ride away on him where you will:
He will carry you'.
Then the kalêki disappeared.
Ilya went to his own father,   55
Where he was working at husbandry.
A space had to be cleared of oak-tree trunks.
He cut up all the oak trunks,
Cast them into the deep river,
And then went home.   60

---

[1] *Polenitsa* (pl. *polenitsy*), a heroine who fights like a man. Not uncommon in the *byliny*.

VI

Ilya of Murom and his Quarrel
with Vladimir

THE following *bylina* represents an early stage in the
relations between Ilya and Vladimir. It will be remembered that while Ilya is represented as frequently
present at Vladimir's court, he was never an actual member
of the *druzhina*, and is more often away on the frontiers
fighting against Vladimir's foes. Vladimir's omission to invite Ilya to the feast as related here is no doubt connected in
some way with Ilya's origin, whether referring to his rank
or race (cf. p. 57 above). The main body of the *druzhina* is
distinctly aristocratic, though there are many indications,
both in the *byliny* and in Nestor's Chronicle, that the ranks
of the Scandinavian courts on the Dnêpr were being thrown
open to the native Slavonic, and therefore the more democratic elements in the time of Vladimir I. He was the first
prince of Kiev to call all his sons by Slavonic names.

ILYA OF MUROM AND HIS QUARREL WITH VLADIMIR

Sung by Trofim Grigorevich Ryabinin

Gilferding, *Sbornik*, vol. II, p. 38 ff.

Glorious Vladimir of royal Kiev,
He prepared a glorious, honourable feast
For his host of princes and boyars,
And glorious, mighty, powerful heroes;
But there was one whom he did not summon to the feast—   5
The old Cossack, Ilya of Murom.
The old Cossack, Ilya of Murom,
Was much displeased,

But he did not know what he could do
Against this Prince Vladimir.   10
Then he took his taut, resilient bow,
And he took his tempered arrows,
He, Ilya, went into the city of Kiev,
And he began to wander through the city of Kiev,
And to stroll about the holy mother churches;   15
And he smashed up all the crosses on the churches.
He shot off all the gilded balls.[1]
And Ilya cried out with all his might,
With all his might he cried in a loud voice:
'Ho! you drunkards, you pot-house fellows,   20
Come out of your taverns and ale-houses,
And steal the gilded balls,
Take them into your taverns and ale-houses,
And drink your fill of wine'.
Then they reported it to Prince Vladimir: 25
'Ah, Vladimir, prince of royal Kiev!
You eat and drink at the noble feast,
While there is the old Cossack, Ilya of Murom,
Wandering through the city of Kiev,
And strolling about the holy mother churches.   30
He has smashed up the crosses on the holy churches,
And shot off all the gilded balls.
And Ilya, look you, is crying out with all his might,
With all his might he is crying in a loud voice:
"Ho! you drunkards, you pot-house fellows,   35
Come out of your taverns and ale-houses,
And steal the gilded balls,
Take them into your taverns and ale-houses,
And drink your fill of wine"'.
Then Vladimir, prince of royal Kiev,   40
He, Vladimir, began to consider within himself
How that he must be reconciled with Ilya.
And Vladimir, prince of royal Kiev,

[1] I.e. the round gilded ornaments on the pinnacles above the cupolas,
etc., often surmounted by a cross.

He prepared an honourable feast on yet a second day.
Then Vladimir, prince of royal Kiev,   45
He considered yet further within himself:
'Whom shall I send to summon to the feast
This old Cossack, Ilya of Murom?
I have no mind to go myself;
And to send Apraxya,[1] that would hardly be seemly'.   50
And then he went through his dining-hall,
He walked around the oaken table,
And he paused beside young Dobrynyushka:
He addressed Dobrynya as follows:
'Young Dobrynyushka, do you go forth   55
To the old Cossack, Ilya of Murom,
And enter the white stone palace,
And pass into the dining-hall,
Knock upon the door five times,
Then cross yourself in the prescribed manner,   60
Make your bow as it is enjoined,
Offer humble salutation, and beat with your forehead
Upon the floor of bricks,
Upon damp mother earth herself,
Before the old Cossack, Ilya of Murom,   65
And address Ilya as follows:
"Ah, you old Cossack, Ilya of Murom,
I have come to you from Prince Vladimir,
And from the Princess Apraxya,
And I have come to summon you to an honourable feast"'.   70
Young Dobrynyushka Mikitinets,
Very quickly he sprang to his nimble feet,
Flung his coat of marten-skins over one shoulder,
And his sable cap over one ear,
Went forth from the dining-hall,   75
Passed through the palace of white stone;
Dobrynya went to the city of Kiev.
When he had walked through the city of Kiev,
He came upon the old Cossack, Ilya of Murom,

                    [1] Apraxya was Vladimir's wife.

In his palace of white stone.
When he had reached the dining-hall,
He knocked upon the door five times;
He crossed himself in the prescribed manner,
He made his bow as it is enjoined,
He offered a humble salutation and beat with his forehead   85
Upon the floor of bricks,
Upon damp mother earth herself;
He addressed Ilya in the following words:
'Ah, my sworn brother,
Old Cossack, Ilya of Murom!   90
I have been sent to you from Prince Vladimir,
And from the Princess Apraxya,
To summon you to an honourable feast'.
Thereupon the old Cossack, Ilya of Murom,
Very quickly he sprang to his nimble feet,   95
Flung his cloak of marten-skins over one shoulder,
His sable cap over one ear;
They left the dining-hall,
And they passed through the palace of white stone,
They went forth into the city of royal Kiev,   100
They came to Prince Vladimir,
To the glorious, honourable feast.
There was Vladimir, prince of royal Kiev.
Behold him walking about his apartment,
And glancing through the lattice!   105
Said he to the Princess Apraxya:
'Can those be two Russian heroes coming towards me,
To my glorious, honourable feast?'
And they entered the palace of white stone,
And they went up into the dining-hall.   110
There Vladimir, prince of royal Kiev,
With the Princess Apraxya,
Went up to the old Cossack, Ilya of Murom;
They took him by the white hands,
They addressed him in the following terms: 115
'Ah, you old Cossack, Ilya of Murom!

Your seat was indeed the humblest of all,
But now is your seat highest of all at the table !
Seat yourself at the table of oak'.
Then they ate his sweet food,   120
And drank honeyed drink,
And then Vladimir and Ilya were reconciled.

VII

Ilya and Nightingale the Robber

THE following *bylina* is the most popular of all the *byliny* connected with Ilya among the Russian singers. No entirely satisfactory explanation of the picturesque story of Nightingale has ever been found. It seems on the whole not unlikely that he was a robber chief, perhaps also a merchant, who had his 'nest', or home, beside the high-road from Chernigov to Kiev, whence he swooped down on passing caravans. His name Nightingale (Solovey) is peculiarly difficult to explain. The comparison with Nightingale Budimirovich, also a wealthy merchant, is, of course, obvious.

ILYA AND NIGHTINGALE THE ROBBER

Sung by Ryabinin

Rybnikov, *Pésni*, vol. I, p. 15 ff. (cf. Gilferding, *Sbornik*, no. 74).

The old Cossack, Ilya of Murom,
Set out on his good steed
Past the city of Chernigov:
Under Chernigov the troops were quite black,
Quite black, like black crows.   5
He urged his heroic steed
Into the midst of that mighty host.
He trampled them with his horse and slew them with his spear,
He trampled down and slew the host in a short time,
And he rode up to the town of Chernigov.   10
The men of Chernigov came to meet him,
And opened to him the gates of the city of Chernigov,
And invited him to become the governor of Chernigov;

Ilya answered them as follows:
'Ho, you men of Chernigov!   15
I will not come to you to be governor in Chernigov,
But do you tell me the direct high-road,
The direct high-road to the city of royal Kiev'.
The men of Chernigov made answer:
'Ho, you bold, you mighty, noble youth,   20
You glorious hero of holy Russia!
It is five hundred versts[1] to Kiev by the direct high-road,
By the indirect road it is a whole thousand.
The direct high-road is blocked with fallen timber,
Blocked with fallen timber and grown over with grass: 25
The wild beast does not wander there,
The black raven does not fly there;
At this Black Morass,
At this leaning birch tree,
At the glorious cross of Levanidov,   30
At the glorious River Smorodina,[2]
Sits Nightingale the Robber, the son of Odikhmantov,
Sits Nightingale in a damp oak.
Nightingale whistles like a nightingale,
He shrieks, the wretch, like a wild beast: 35
The dark forests bow to the earth,
All the herbage and grass withers up,
The azure flowers wilt,
Every mortal creature falls dead'.
Ilya of Murom urged on his heroic steed.   40
He rode off along the direct high-road,
He took his silken whip in his hand,
He struck his steed on his sleek flank,
He made his steed gallop with all his mighty strength.
His good heroic steed sped on,   45
Leaping from mountain to mountain,

----

[1] A Russian *versta* is about ⅔ of a mile in length.
[2] Neither the River Smorodina nor the cross of Levanidov has
been identified, though both are frequently mentioned in the *byliny* of
the Kiev Cycle.

Springing from hill to hill,
Passing over rivers and lakes at a stride.
He galloped up to that Black Morass,
To the glorious leaning birch tree,   50
To the cross of Levanidov,
To the glorious River Smorodina.
Whereupon Nightingale the Robber, the son of Odikhmantov,
      began to whistle;
He whistled like a nightingale,
That rascal robber roared out like a wild beast: 55
The dark forests bowed to the earth,
Every mortal creature lay lifeless.
The good steed of Ilya of Murom began to stumble;
He struck the steed on its sleek flank,
He struck the steed and addressed it: 60
'Ho, you food for wolves, you grass-bag;
Will you not go on, or can you not carry me?
Never can you have heard the whistle of a nightingale,
Or heard the roar of a wild beast,
And never can you have witnessed the blows of heroes,   65
That you now stumble over roots, you dog!'
He brought his heroic steed to a stand,
He unhitched his taut, resilient bow,
From his right stirrup of steel;
He fixed a tempered arrow,   70
And drew his silken bow-string;
He shot at Nightingale the Robber,
Putting out his right eye from its socket.[1]
Nightingale fell to the damp earth;
The old Cossack, Ilya of Murom,   75

    [1] *Kositsa.* The word properly means the hair round the eyes, and
so, by an extension of meaning, that part of the head or skull where
this hair is; the temple, temple bone. In popular poetry it would seem
that the reciters (*skaziteli*) sometimes understood it in the sense of
kosa, 'a curved knife', and the word is invariably translated by Rambaud in this sense. It is obvious that it would be inappropriate here,
however. See the *Slovar Russkago Yazika*, published by the Imperial
Academy of Sciences, Petrograd, 1891–1917, p. 2334, *s.v.*

He bound him to his right stirrup,
To his right stirrup of steel.
He rode over the free, open plain,
To Nightingale's nest.
And from Nightingale's nest   80
His eldest daughter Neveyushka descried him;
Neveya spoke as follows:
'Our father is riding over the free, open plain,
He is seated on a good, heroic steed,
He is leading a boorish lout   85
At his stirrup of forged steel'.
His second daughter Nenilushka looked out;
Nenila spoke as follows:
'Our father is riding over the free, open plain,
He is seated on a good, heroic steed,   90
He is leading a boorish lout
At his stirrup of forged steel'.
His third daughter, Pelka, looked out;
Pelka spoke as follows:
'A boorish lout is riding   95
Over the free, open plain,
He is leading our noble father
At his stirrup of forged steel.
His right eye has been shot from its socket.
Ho, you, our dear husbands!   100
Seize your hunting-poles,
Make haste into the free, open plain,
Slay the boorish lout'.
Those sons-in-law of Nightingale,
They seized their hunting-poles,   105
They made haste into the free, open plain,
Intending to belabour the country lout.
Nightingale cried out to them with all his might:
'Oh, my dear sons-in-law!
Cast aside your hunting-poles!   110
Conduct this hero of holy Russia
Into my Nightingale nest,

Feed him with sugared food;
Give him honeyed drink to drink;
Bestow precious gifts upon him'....   115
He did not ride to Nightingale's nest,
He rode to the city of Kiev,
To gracious Prince Vladimir.
He entered the prince's spacious court-yard,
He stood his horse in the middle of the court-yard,   120
He went into the palace of white stone.
And Prince Vladimir had left the Church of God
Where he had been for the Easter Mass.
He seated himself at the table of oak,
At the round table,   125
Eating sugared foods,
And drinking honeyed drinks.
Ilya of Murom went into the palace of white stone;
He crossed himself in the prescribed manner,
He made his bow as it is enjoined,   130
On three, on four, on all sides he bowed,
To Prince Vladimir in particular,
And to all his royal retinue.
Prince Vladimir began to question him:
'Whence do you come, mighty, noble youth?   135
By what name do they call you?
How do they address you, bold youth, in your own home?'
Ilya answered him as follows:
'I come from the town of Murom,[1]   140
From the glorious village of Karachoro;
They call me Ilya by name,
Ilya of Murom, the son of Ivanov'.
Vladimir proceeded to question him:
'And how long is it since you left Murom,   145
And by what road did you come to the royal city of Kiev?'
Ilya answered him as follows:

   [1] It will be observed that the numbering of the lines is incorrect at
this point. I have followed the numbering of the Russian text for convenience of reference.

'I attended Matins in Murom
And arrived in time for Mass at the royal city of Kiev.
My business on the road delayed me: 150
I came by the direct high-road,
The high-road past the glorious city of Chernigov,
Past the glorious River Smorodina'.
Vladimir spoke as follows:
'You mock us to our faces, fellow!   155
You lie in our faces, fellow!
Under the city of Chernigov lies the infidel host,
By the River Smorodina sits Nightingale the Robber, the son of
    Odikhmantov—
Nightingale who whistles like a nightingale,
The rascal robber, who roars like a wild beast'.   160
Ilya spoke as follows:
'Vladimir, prince of royal Kiev!
Nightingale the Robber is in your court-yard,
Chained to my right stirrup of steel'.
Then Vladimir, prince of royal Kiev,   165
Instantly leapt to his nimble feet,
Flung his mantle of marten-skins over one shoulder,
His sable cap over one ear,
Very, very quickly he ran into the spacious court-yard,
And went up to Nightingale the Robber.   170
He addressed Nightingale as follows:
'Come, give us a whistle, Nightingale, like a nightingale;
Give a roar, now, rascal, like a wild beast!'
Nightingale answered Prince Vladimir:
'Vladimir, prince of royal Kiev!   175
I do not eat your food to-day,
And I will not obey you.
I eat with the old Cossack, Ilya of Murom;
And him I will obey'.
Vladimir said to Ilya of Murom: 180
'Oh, old Cossack, Ilya of Murom,
Tell him to whistle like a nightingale,
Tell him to roar like a wild beast'.

Ilya spoke to Nightingale the Robber:
'Give us a whistle now, Nightingale, like a nightingale,   185
Roar out now, Nightingale, like a wild beast'.
Nightingale answered Ilya of Murom:
'Ah, you old Cossack, Ilya of Murom!
My wounds are caked with blood,
And no sugared drinks have passed my lips.   190
I cannot whistle like a nightingale,
I cannot roar like a wild beast'.
Ilya spoke to Prince Vladimir:
'Vladimir, prince of royal Kiev!
Pour out a goblet of green wine there—   195
Not a little cup—a huge measure,
And mix it with mellow mead,
And offer it to Nightingale the Robber.
When the sugared drink has unsealed his lips
He will whistle up for us like a nightingale,   200
He will roar out for us like a wild beast'.
Vladimir, prince of royal Kiev,
Very, very quickly he went into the palace of white stone,
Poured out a goblet of green wine,
But not a little cup—a huge measure,   205
And mixed it with mellow mead,
And offered it to Nightingale the Robber.
Nightingale the Robber, the son of Odikhmantov,
He took that goblet in one hand,
He drained that goblet at one draught.   210
Ilya of Murom said to him:
'Come, now, whistle up, Nightingale!—but only half the whistle
    of a nightingale!
Give a roar now!—but only half the roar of a wild beast!'
Then Nightingale began to whistle like a nightingale;
He gave a roar, the wretch, like a wild beast.   215
At that nightingale whistle,
At that wild beast roar,
A tremendous pother arose.
The dark forests bowed to the earth,

And the pinnacles of the houses were bent awry,   220
The glass windows were shattered,
And every mortal creature lay lifeless;
But Vladimir, prince of royal Kiev,
Stood firm, for he covered himself up in his cloak of marten-skins.
This occurrence exasperated Ilya of Murom.   225
He mounted his good steed,
Rode out into the free, open plain,
He cut off Nightingale's turbulent head,
He cut off his head, and he cried:
'You have caused enough fathers and mothers to weep,   230
You have widowed enough young wives,
You have orphaned enough little children!'
Then they sang the dirge[1] for Nightingale.

---

[1] Lit. the 'glory' (*slava*), probably the *De Profundis*. See Rambaud, *La Russie Épique*, p. 138; here the expression is not intended to be taken literally. As commonly elsewhere in the *byliny*, it simply means 'that was the end of Nightingale'.

VIII

Alyosha Popovich

ALYOSHA POPOVICH is Dobrynya's sworn brother, but he proves himself unfaithful, and marries Dobrynya's wife during his absence. He is the son of a priest, though in the following *bylina* he is represented as illiterate himself, while his servant Ekim is the scholar. This is quite in keeping with Alyosha's character as a mighty *bogatyr*. We have referred (p. 57 above) to the *bylina* of Tsar Kalin, in which Alyosha, Dobrynya Nikitich, and others defend the people of Kiev against the Tartar host; and Alyosha and Dobrynya are constantly engaged in single combats against the Tartars and other enemies of Kiev. His greatest exploit is the slaying of the monster Tugarin, who is generally represented as a winged dragon. In spite of his heroism he is no favourite with the minstrels. He is portrayed as a rough and ill-bred mocker, constantly stirring up strife among the heroes of Vladimir's court, and his ultimate discomfiture and punishment are openly approved in the *bylina* of Dobrynya Nikitich. The heroic poets do not love the 'pope's' son, and the anti-clerical bias is the more marked since no disapproval seems to be meted out to any other heroes of the Kiev Cycle.

It is now regarded as certain that Alyosha Popovich was a historical person. An Alexander (i.e. Alyosha) Popovich of Rostov is mentioned in a *povêst*, or story, preserved in a MS from Tver, where he is described first as in the service of the grand prince Vsevolod Yurevich, and then as offering his own submission and that of his *druzhina* to the grand prince Mstislav Romanovich of Kiev. He is also said to have a servant Torop—a name which is no doubt preserved in Trofim, which in its turn appears instead of Ekim in certain variants of our *bylina*.

In the Chronicle of Nikon, Alexander Popovich and his

servant Torop are also mentioned as having been slain at
the Battle of Kalka. The entry may be not independent of
heroic poetry; but there can be little doubt that in the name
of Alyosha's enemy Tugarin is preserved the name of the
Polovtsy Khan *Tugor-kan*, who did much damage to the
Russians at the close of the eleventh century.[1]

ALYOSHA POPOVICH

Recorded by Kirsha Danilov

Kirêevski, *Pêsni*, pt. II, p. 70 ff.

From the fair city of glorious Rostov,[2]
Like two bright falcons flying,
Rode forth two mighty heroes,
By name—young Alyoshenka Popovich
And young Ekim Ivanovich.   5
The heroes are riding shoulder to shoulder,
Stirrup to heroic stirrup:
They are riding and wandering over the open plain.
They have met nothing in the open plain,
They have seen no birds flying overhead,   10
They have seen no wild beasts running.
The only thing they have come upon in the open plain
Is three broad roads:
At the juncture of these roads stands a fiery[3] stone,
And on the stone an inscription is written.   15
Young Alyosha Popovich speaks up:
'Ah you, my brother, Ekim Ivanovich!
You are a man instructed in letters—
Look at the inscription on the stone,

---

[1] See Brodski, Mendelson and Sidorov, *Istoriko-Literaturnaya
Khrestomatÿa*, vol. I (Moscow, 1922), p. 105; cf. also Magnus, *Heroic
Ballads of Russia*, p. 47; Rambaud, *La Russie Épique*, p. 105; Hapgood, *Epic Songs of Russia*, p. 270.
[2] Presumably Rostov on the Don.
[3] 'Fiery', or 'burning' (*goryuchi*), is a static epithet of a stone in the
byliny.

Which is written on the stone'.   20
And Ekim leapt from his good steed,
And looked at the inscription on the stone,
Which indicated the directions of the broad roads:
The first road leads to Murom,
The second road to the city of Chernigov,   25
The third to the city of Kiev,
To gracious Prince Vladimir.
Then said Ekim Ivanovich:
'O brother, young Alyosha Popovich!
By which road do you wish to ride?'   30
Young Alyosha Popovich replied:
'We had better ride to the city of Kiev,
To gracious Prince Vladimir'.
Forthwith they turned their good steeds
And rode away to the city of Kiev.   35
Hardly had they reached the River Safat,
Ere they paused in the green meadows.
Ekim¹ must pasture the good steeds.
There they pitched two white tents,
For Alyosha wished to seek repose.   40
And when they had rested for a short time
Young Ekim hobbled their good steeds
And sent them into the green meadow,
And himself lay down in his tent to seek repose.
The autumn night passed away,   45
Alyosha awoke from sleep,
Stood up early, very, very early,
Washed himself at break of day,
Dried himself with a white towel,
And turned to the east to pray to God.   50
Young Ekim Ivanovich,
Quickly he went after their good steeds,
And led them to drink in the River Safat;
And Alyosha commanded him
Quickly to saddle the good steeds.   55

    ¹ The text has 'Alyosha', which is obviously an error.

When Ekim had saddled the good steeds,
They made ready to ride to the city of Kiev.
Then there came to them a wandering kalêka,[1]
Wearing foot-gear of seven silks,
Shod with pure silver,   60
Their tops studded with red gold,
A mantle of sables, falling low,
A Saracen hat from Greek lands,
And a travelling whip[2] weighing thirty pud,[3]
And filled with fifty pud of lead from the East.   65
He spoke as follows:
'Hearken, bold, brave youths!
I have seen Tugarin the Dragon's son.
Tugarin is three sazhens[4] high,
Between his sloping shoulders is a span of one sazhen,   70
Between his eyes is the width of a tempered arrow,
The steed beneath him is like a ferocious wild beast,
From his jaws pour burning flames,
From his ears issues a column of smoke'.
Young Alyosha Popovich made a bargain with him: 75
'Oh, brother, wandering kalêka!
Give to me your kalêka dress—
Take my heroic garb—
Your foot-gear of seven silks,
Shod with pure silver,   80
Their tops studded with red gold,
Your sable mantle, falling low,
Your Saracen hat from Greek lands,
Your travelling whip weighing thirty pud,
And filled with fifty pud of lead from the East'.   85
He gave Alyosha Popovich his kalêka dress—
He did not refuse him—

[1] For the *kalêki*, see p. 58 above. The Greek hat is characteristic of the dress of the *kalêki*, pilgrims, etc.
[2] Properly a leather strap weighted with lead at the end; a hurl-ball.
[3] For *pud*, see p. 47, footnote 1, above.
[4] A Russian *sazhen* is rather more than seven English feet.

And dressed himself in heroic garb.
Swiftly Alyosha dressed himself up as a kalêka,
And took the travelling whip,   90
Which was fifty pud in weight,
And took a steel poniard to be ready for use,
And went to the River Safat.
There he caught sight of young Tugarin the Dragon's son,
Roaring in a loud voice.   95
The green oaks trembled,
And Alyosha Popovich almost died:
'Hearken, wandering kalêka!
Have you heard or seen traces anywhere
Of young Alyosha Popovich?   100
For I want to pierce him with my lance,
To pierce him with my lance, and burn him with fire'.
Then Alyosha spoke as a kalêka:[1]
'Hearken young Tugarin, Dragon's son!
Come a little nearer to me,   105
I cannot hear what you say'.
And young Tugarin the Dragon's son came up to him;
Young Alyosha Popovich went up
And stood in front of Tugarin the Dragon's son.
He gave a cut at his rebellious head with his whip,   110
And broke his rebellious head.
Tugarin fell upon the damp earth.
Alyosha leapt upon his black breast.
Then young Tugarin the Dragon's son besought him:
'Oh, you wandering kalêka!   115
Are you not young Alyosha Popovich?
If you are indeed young Alyosha Popovich,
Let us swear brotherhood together'.
Now Alyosha did not trust his enemy;
He cut off his head,   120
Stripped him of his patterned robe—
Worth a hundred roubles—and put it on himself,
Bestrode his good steed,
And rode off to his white tent.

---

[1] The *kalêki* were often cripples. Alyosha pretends to be deaf.

Now Ekim Ivanovich beheld him— 125
Ekim and the wandering kalêka;
They were afraid of him, and mounted their good steeds,
And rode away toward the town of Rostov.
And young Alyosha Popovich overtook them;
Ekim Ivanovich turned round; 130
He drew out his war club of thirty pud,
And flung it at him—
He thought it was young Tugarin the Dragon's son.
And it struck Alyosha Popovich on his white breast,
Knocking him from his Circassian saddle, 135
So that he fell upon the damp earth.
Then Ekim Ivanovich
Leapt from his good steed, and sat upon his breast,
Intending to pierce his white breast.
But he caught sight of the wondrous gold cross upon him; 140
He lamented, crying to the wandering kalêka:
'This must have befallen me, Ekim, for my sins,
That I should have slain my own brother'.
And they both took to shaking and rocking him,
And they made him drink a foreign dram; 145
And with this he revived.
Then they conversed together and exchanged garments:
The kalêka put on his kalêka dress,
And Alyosha his heroic attire,
And the patterned robe of Tugarin the Dragon's son 150
He placed in his saddle-bag.
They mounted their good steeds,
And all rode off to the city of Kiev,
To gracious Prince Vladimir.

(In Kirsha Danilov's version, from which this translation is
made, the *bylina* contains 215 additional lines, relating the subsequent arrival of Tugarin at Kiev, and his death in single combat
at the hands of Alyosha Popovich. Obviously two variant
versions of the death of Tugarin have been combined in one
bylina with no attempt at reconciling the contradiction. See
Bezsonov's note *ad loc.*)

IX

The Absence of Dobrynya

DOBRYNYA NIKITICH is the most prominent member of Vladimir's court at Kiev. He is referred to in the *byliny* as a nephew of Vladimir and a 'prince boyar', though in a variant he is represented as the son of Nikita, a rich merchant of Ryazan who had left him a great fortune.[1] Vladimir constantly employs him as ambassador on far journeys and during his absence tries to marry his faithful wife Nastasya to his sworn brother, Alyosha Popovich (see p. 74 ff. above). Dobrynya is always represented in the *byliny* as a very polished gentleman, as befits a royal envoy and ambassador.

He is the hero of many exploits. First he slew the serpent of the mountain which haunted the River Pochai (cf. p. 94 below). He pursued the *polenitsa* (cf. p. 60 n. above) Nastasya, daughter of Mikula, but was defeated, and Nastasya took him as her husband. He made war on the Baba Yaga, the witch of the mountain, and with the help of Ilya of Murom was able to overcome her. He is constantly referred to as waging war against the enemies of Vladimir, along with Ilya of Murom and Alyosha Popovich.

There can be little doubt that Dobrynya was a historical person. The chronicles mention two Dobrynyas. One was the uncle of Vladimir I—not his nephew, as in the *byliny*. Reference is made to a later Dobrynya in the Chronicle of Nikon (*s.a.* 1224), where we are told that Alexander Popovich with his servant Torop,[2] Dobrynya Golden Belt of Ryazan, and seventy great and brave *bogatyrs* were slain

---

[1] Kiréevski, *Pésni*, pt. ii, p. 69; cf. Magnus, *Heroic Ballads of Russia*, p. 47.

[2] I.e. the Trofim who figures in place of Ekim in some versions of the *bylina* of *Alyosha Popovich* (see p. 74 ff. above).

in the Battle of the Kalka,[1] by the Tartars, 'through the wrath of God at our sins'. This battle, as we have seen, is believed to be the one described in a *bylina* which relates the encounter of Ilya of Murom and Tsar Kalin.[2]

THE ABSENCE OF DOBRYNYA

Sung by Abram Evtikhiev Chukov, known as 'the Bottle'

Rybnikov, *Pésni*, vol. I, p. 162 ff.

Dobrynya Nikitich spoke
To his dear lady mother:
'Ah, my dear lady mother!
Why did you bear the unfortunate Dobrynya?
Why, when you had borne me, my dear lady mother,   5
Did you not tie me to a white, hot stone
In a little bag of fine linen,
And cast me into the blue sea?
I should have slept for ever in the sea.
I should not have wandered over the open plain,   10
I should not have slain innocent souls,
I should not have shed blood needlessly,
I should not have drawn tears from parents,
Nor widowed young wives,
Nor made young children orphans'.   15
His lady mother made answer:
'For your own sake I would gladly have borne you, my child,
With the fortunate destiny of Ilya of Murom,
With the strength of the hero Svyatogor,
With the boldness of bold Alyosha Popovich;   20
I would have gladly borne you with the beauty of Osip the Fair,
I would have borne you with the elegant bearing
Of Churilo Plenkovich.
But I bore you with the courtesy of Dobrynyushka Nikitich.

[1] See p. 57 above.
[2] Gilferding, *Sbornik*, vol. II, p. 178 ff. Cf. Hapgood, *Epic Songs of Russia*, p. 270.

This is your only gift; God has given you no others,   25
God has given you no others; He has not endowed you further'.
Quickly, very quickly, Dobrynya saddled his steed,
Dobrynya rode forth into the open plain.
His dear mother escorted him,
Bade him farewell, and turned back,   30
Returned home, and began to weep;
She walked about the palace,
She raised her voice on high,
Dolefully, with lamentation.
At his right stirrup   35
Dobrynya's dear wife escorted him,
Young Nastasya Nikulichna.—
She spoke as follows:
'When will Dobrynyushka come home,
When may we expect Dobrynya from the open plain?'   40
Dobrynya Nikitich made answer:
'Since you have asked me
I will tell you:
Await Dobrynya for three years.
If I do not come in three years, wait three more;   45
But when six years are fulfilled,
And I have not come home from the open plain,
Think of Dobrynyushka as one dead,
And do you, Nastasya, as you will;
Either live as a widow, or marry,   50
Marry a prince or a boyar,
Or a mighty Russian hero;
But do not marry my sworn brother
Bold Alyosha Popovich'.
She waited for him for three years,   55
Day after day, as the rain falls,
Week after week, as the grass grows,
Year after year, as the river flows.
And the end of the three years came;
But Dobrynya did not return from the open plain.   60
She waited for him for another three,

Again day after day, as the rain falls,
Week after week, as the grass grows,
And year after year, as the river flows.
And now the end of six years had come;   65
But Dobrynya did not return from the open plain.
At that hour, at that time,
Alyosha came from the open plain;
He brought sorrowful tidings
That Dobrynya Nikitich was dead.   70
Then his dear lady mother,
Piteously she mourned for him.
Her bright eyes shed tears,
Her white face grew sorrowful,
For her dear child,   75
For young Dobrynya Nikitich.
Then our Sun Vladimir went about
Seeking a match for Nastasya Nikulichna:
'How can you live as a young widow,
Spending your youth in this way?   80
Marry either prince or boyar,
Or a mighty Russian hero,
Or else bold Alyosha Popovich'.
Nastasya Nikulichna made answer:
'I have carried out my husband's behest,   85
I have waited for Dobrynya for six whole years,
But Dobrynya has not returned from the open plain.
Now I will carry out the behest of his wife:
I will wait for Dobrynya for another six years;
When twelve years' time has elapsed,   90
Then I shall be ready to marry'.
Again day after day, as the rain falls,
Week after week, as the grass grows,
Year after year, as the river flows!
The end of six years came.   95
Twelve whole years were completed,
But Dobrynyushka did not return from the open plain.
Then our Sun Vladimir went about

Seeking a match for Nastasya Nikulichna,
Seeking a match, and urging her: 100
'How can you live as a young widow,
Spending your youth in this way?
Marry either prince or boyar,
Or a mighty Russian hero,
Or else bold Alyosha Popovich'.   105
She did not marry prince or boyar
Or a mighty Russian hero,
But she married bold Alyosha Popovich.
They are holding a feast for three days;
To-day they go to holy Church,   110
To receive the crowns of gold.[1]
Now Dobrynya chanced to be at Tsargrad,
And Dobrynya's horse stumbled:
'Oh, you food for wolves, you bear's skin!
Why are you stumbling to-day?'   115
The good steed addressed him,
Addressed him in human voice:
'Ah, my beloved master!
You see not the misfortune which has befallen you:
Your young wife Nastasya Nikulichna   120
Has married bold Alyosha Popovich;
They are holding a feast for three days;
To-day they go to holy Church,
To receive the crowns of gold'.
Dobrynya Nikitich flew into a rage;   125
He took his silken whip,
He beat his steed about the legs,
About the legs, the back legs,
So that his steed set off at a gallop,
From mountain to mountain, from hill to hill,   130
Leaping rivers and lakes,
Extending his legs to their full stride.
It is not a bright falcon in full flight,

---

[1] In the Russian marriage service crowns are placed on the heads of the bride and bridegroom.

It is a noble youth racing in his course.
He did not pass through the gates, but over the town wall,   135
Past the bastion towers,
To the widow's dwelling.
He rode into the court-yard unannounced,
He entered the palace without introduction.
He did not ask leave of the porters at the gates;   140
He did not ask leave of the door-keepers at the doors;
He thrust everybody aside by the scruff of the neck.
Boldly he entered the widow's palace,
Held the cross in the manner prescribed,
Made his bow as it is enjoined,   145
And to the venerable widow in particular:
'Hail to you, venerable widow, Mamelfa Timofeevna!'
All the door-keepers and porters followed him in;
They spoke as follows:
'Honourable widow, Mamelfa Timofeevna!   150
When this bold, good youth
Rode up from the open plain in his swift career,
He did not ask leave of us, the porters at the gates,
At the doors he did not ask leave of the door-keepers.
He thrust us all aside by the scruff of the neck'.   155
The honourable widow addressed him:
'Ah, you bold, noble youth!
Why do you trespass in the orphan's dwelling?
Why do you enter the palace unannounced?
If only my beloved child were alive,   160
Young Dobrynya Nikitich,
He would cut off your rebellious head
For your boorish conduct'.
Dobrynya Nikitich spoke:
'Are you not in grievous error?   165
Yesterday I parted from Dobrynya;
Dobrynya set off for Tsargrad,
And I set off for Kiev.
He swore blood-brotherhood with me.
He asked after his beloved wife,   170

After young Nastasya Nikulichna:
Where is Nastasya Nikulichna?'
'Dobrynya's dear wife is married.
They are holding a feast for three days;
To-day they go to holy Church.   175
It has chanced but now in the sixth year
That Alyosha has come from the open plain,
Bringing sorrowful tidings,
That Dobrynya Nikitich is dead.
He lies slain in the open plain;   180
His rebellious head crushed,
His sturdy shoulders pierced,
He lies with his head in a willow bush;
I have lamented him sorely.'
Dobrynya Nikitich spoke: 185
'He swore brotherhood with me:
If you are going to the feast at Kiev,
Do you bring my skomorokh attire,[1]
And bring my gusli of maple-wood,
And lay them all in another room on the table'.   190
They brought him his skomorokh attire,
They brought him his gusli of maple-wood,
The youth dressed himself as a skomorokh,
And went to the splendid, honourable feast.
He went to the royal dwelling unannounced,   195
He went into the palace without introduction;
He did not ask leave of the porters at the gates,
He did not ask leave of the door-keepers at the doors,
He thrust everybody aside by the scruff of the neck.
Boldly he entered the royal palace,   200
Held the cross in the manner prescribed,
Made his bow as it is enjoined,
And to our Sun Vladimir in particular.
He spoke as follows:
'Hail, our Sun, Vladimir of royal Kiev,   205

[1] Being Dobrynya's sworn brother, and therefore his representative,
he had the right to make use of his property.

And to your Queen Apraxya!'
They all followed him in clamouring:
'Vladimir, our Sun of royal Kiev!
When this bold, good youth
Rode up from the plain in his swift career,   210
And even now comes as a skomorokh,
He did not ask leave of the porters at the gates,
He did not ask leave of the door-keepers at the doors,
He thrust us all aside by the scruff of the neck,
And immediately entered the royal palace'.   215
'Ha, you, bold skomorokh!
Why do you come to the royal dwelling,
To the royal dwelling unannounced?
Why do you come into the palace without introduction,
Without asking leave of the porters at the gates,   220
And without asking leave of the door-keepers at the doors,
But coming directly into the royal palace?'
The skomorokh gave no heed to these words,
The skomorokh did not hearken to these words:
'Tell me, which is the skomorokh's place for me?'   225
Vladimir of royal Kiev replied in anger:
'That is the skomorokh's place for you,
On that glazed oven there,
On the glazed oven, behind the stove'.
Hastily he jumped on to the place indicated,   230
On to the glazed oven;
He tightened his silken strings,
His golden cords,
And began to wander over the strings;
He began to sing snatches of song,   235
He played a tune from Tsargrad,
And in his song he recounted all that had taken place in Kiev,
Both of old and young.
Then everyone at the feast grew silent,
They spoke as follows: 240
'Who can this bold skomorokh be?
He cannot be a Russian,

This bold noble youth!'
Vladimir of royal Kiev spoke:
'Ah, thou bold skomorokh!   245
Descend from your seat behind the oven,
Sit with us at the table of oak and eat bread,
And let us carve white swans.
For your joyous minstrelsy
We will give you your choice of three places: 250
The first place is the seat next to me,
The second is the place opposite me,
The third is where you will,
Where you will; for you are welcome'.
The skomorokh did not sit beside the prince,   255
The skomorokh did not sit opposite the prince,
The skomorokh seated himself on a bench
Opposite the betrothed princess.
The bold skomorokh spoke:
'Vladimir, our Sun of royal Kiev!   260
Grant that I may pour out a goblet of green wine,
And that I may offer this goblet to one whom I know of,
To one whom I know of, since I am welcome'.
When he had poured out a goblet of green wine,
He dropped his gold ring into the goblet,   265
Handed it to the betrothed princess,
And spoke as follows:
'Young Nastasya Nikulichna!
Take this goblet in one hand,
And drain the goblet at one draught: 270
If you drink to the dregs, you shall see good;
If you drink not to the dregs, you shall not see good'.
She took the goblet in one hand,
She drained the goblet in one draught,
And in the goblet she espied her gold ring   275
With which she had been betrothed to Dobrynya.
She spoke as follows:
'Our Sun, Vladimir of royal Kiev!
This is not my husband who sits beside me,

But that is my husband who sits opposite to me,   280
That is my husband sitting on the bench,
Who has given me a goblet of green wine'.
She sprang up from her place at the table of oak
And fell at Dobrynya's nimble feet:
'Pardon! Pardon! Dobrynya Nikitich,   285
Pardon me the wrong I have done you,—for my folly,
In that I have not fulfilled your behest;
I have married bold Alyosha Popovich'.
Dobrynya Nikitich spoke:
'I do not marvel at your woman's wit,   290
For a woman's hair is long and her wit is short:—
Where you take them, thither they go,
Where you carry them, thither they ride;
But I marvel at our Sun Vladimir,
And the young Princess Apraxya,—   295
Our Sun Vladimir here acting as *svakh*[1]
And the Princess Apraxya as *svakha*,
And marrying away the wife of a living husband!'
Then our Sun Vladimir was ashamed,
And Alyoshenka Grigorevich spoke: 300
'Pardon! Pardon, my sworn brother,
In that I have taken my seat beside your beloved wife,
Beside young Nastasya Nikulichna'.
'May God pardon you your fault, brother,
In that you have taken your seat beside my beloved wife,   305
Beside young Nastasya Nikulichna;
But for this second fault, brother, I will not pardon you:
When you returned from the open plain at the end of the first
        six years,
You brought sorrowful tidings
That Dobrynya Nikitich was dead,   310
That he lay slain in the open plain,
His rebellious head crushed,
His sturdy shoulders pierced,

---

[1] The matchmakers, male (*svakh*) and female (*svakha*), take a leading part in Russian weddings.

His head lying in a willow bush,
So that then my dear lady mother—   315
Piteously she bewailed me;
Her bright eyes shed tears,
Her white face grew sad:
For this wrong I will not forgive you.'
He seized Alyoshka by his yellow curls,   320
He dragged Alyoshka over the table of oak,
He flung Alyoshka about the brick-built floor,
He seized his riding whip,
And set about belabouring him with the butt-end.
You could not distinguish between the blows and the groans.

Everybody, my brothers, marries in his day,   326
But may God not grant that that Alyoshka marry:
Alyoshenka was only just married,
Only just married when he was parted from his wife.
Then Dobrynya took his beloved wife,   330
Young Nastasya Nikulichna,
And went to his dear lady mother,
And there they greeted one another.
They tell the story of Dobrynya for all time
On the calm blue sea,   335
For you all to hear, good people.

X

The Youth of Churilo Plenkovich

CHURILO and his father, the tall and massive old Plenko, are interesting figures, living on their own estate on the River Pochai[1] just beyond Vladimir's territory, and on the fringe of his range of influence. Nothing is known of them from historical sources, but the picture afforded by the *byliny* of their relations with Vladimir is interesting and instructive, and undoubtedly reflects historical conditions. Occupied in hunting and fishing, they trespass ever farther into his territory, till the ruler of Kiev turns his attention to his troublesome neighbours and pays them a visit. Churilo offers ample payment for his trespasses in the shape of presents, but Vladimir follows his consistent policy and 'invites' young Churilo to his court at Kiev—an invitation which we may interpret as a command. Vladimir knew well how to take a pledge of good behaviour from the troublesome native aristocracy, and at the same time enlarge the ranks of his own bodyguard. In young Churilo, however, he had found a troublesome recruit. Like Alyosha Popovich, he stirs up strife in the court of Kiev by his gibes and insults, as we shall see in the *bylina* of *Dyuk Stepanovich*. Moreover his golden curls and finery proved too attractive to the ladies of Kiev, and Vladimir was glad to cut short the term of Churilo's service and send him back to old Plenko, his father. Churilo's love adventures were ultimately his undoing, and he was killed in an encounter with an outraged husband named Bermyag.

[1] It has been suggested that this name is a reminiscence of the historical name of the River Pochaina in Kiev. See Brodski, etc., *op. cit.* p. 93, note 1.

THE YOUTH OF CHURILO PLENKOVICH

Sung by Ivan Pavlovich Sivtsev

Rybnikov, *Pêsni*, vol. II, p. 524 ff.

In the glorious city of Kiev,
By gracious Prince Vladimir,
A splendid, honourable feast was given
For the company of princes and boyars,
For powerful, mighty heroes,   5
For all the bold fighting-women.
The white day drew to evening,
And the prince was making exceeding merry.
He mounted the grand staircase,
And looked out, gazing into the open plain.   10
From far, far off in the open plain,
A crowd of people made their appearance;
All the people of Kiev are coming,
Beating the ground with their foreheads and making complaint:
'Our dear Sun, Prince Vladimir!   15
Award us, Sire, a just judgment
Against Churilo Plenkovich.—
To-day as we were on the River Soroga,
Strangers made their appearance;
They cast silken fishing-nets,—   20
The strands were of seven silks,
The nets had floats of silver,
And gilded sinkers.
They caught dace,
But for us, dear lord, there is no catch,   25
And for thee, Sire, there is not a fresh morsel.
And we have no guerdon from thee;
They all call themselves, give themselves out to be
Churilo's druzhina'.
That crowd went into the court-yard,   30
And a fresh one made their appearance from the plain;
All the people of Kiev came,

Beating the ground with their foreheads and making complaint:
'Our Sun, our Prince Vladimir!
Award us, Sire, a just judgment   35
Against Churilo Plenkovich.—
To-day in the quiet creeks,
Strangers made their appearance,
Shooting geese and swans,
And little grey-feathered duck.   40
For us, dear lord, there is no catch,
And for thee, Sire, there is not a fresh morsel,
And we have no guerdon from thee'.
That crowd went into the court-yard,
And a fresh one made their appearance from the plain;   45
All the people of Kiev came,
Beating the ground with their foreheads and making complaint:
'Our dear Sun, our Prince Vladimir!
Award us, Sire, a just judgment
Against Churilo Plenkovich.—   50
To-day we were in the dark forests,
When strangers made their appearance,
Laying silken snares,
Catching martens and foxes,
And black Siberian sables: 55
For us, dear lord, there is no catch,
And for thee, dear lord, there is no booty,
And we have no guerdon from thee'.
That crowd went into the court-yard,
And a fresh one made their appearance from the plain.   60
Five hundred youths came riding:
The mounted youths were all alike,
Their mounts were all of the same bay colour.
Their bridles and reins were of Saracen make,
Their saddles were of gold,   65
The shoes on their feet were of green morocco,
The leather worn by the youths was of elk-skin,
The coats they wore were of blue and scarlet,
Girt with girdles of many coloured strands,
Their caps were crowned with gold;   70

The youths on their steeds gleamed like candles,
The steeds beneath them flew like falcons.
They rode until they came to the city of Kiev,
And began to lay waste Kiev;
They pulled up the onions and garlic,   75
They broke off the cauliflowers,
The old men and women they put out of existence,
The young men and women they insulted,
The fair maidens they dishonoured.
All Kiev beat their brows before the prince.   80
Princes and princesses besought him,
Boyars and their wives besought him,
And all the men of the city:
'Award us, Sire, a just judgment
Against Churilo Plenkovich.—   85
To-day even here in the city of Kiev,
Churilo's druzhina rode in among us'.
Then our Sun, Prince Vladimir, spoke:
'Foolish are you, you princes and boyars,
And stupid, you trading merchants!   90
I do not know Churilo's estate,
I do not know Churilo, or where his home is'.
The princes and boyars made answer:
'Our dear lord, Prince Vladimir!
Churilo's home, mark you, is not in Kiev,   95
Churilo's home is not near Kiev,
Churilo's home is on the River Pochai,
Churilo's home covers seven versts.[1]
All around his home is fenced with steel
And all the doors are pivoted,   100
All the entrance doors are fitted with glass,
The thresholds are of precious fishes' teeth;
In Churilo's home
There are seventy terems[2]'.

[1] Or, is seven versts distant?
[2] The upper apartments in great houses and palaces, where people
of high rank lived.

Then the prince set off for the River Pochai;   105
He rode off with his princes and boyars,
With the merchants, the trading strangers.
When he came to the River Pochai,
At the wondrous cross of Levanidov,
At the holy mosque of Boris,   110
He shook his head and began to speak:
'Upon my word, they have not exaggerated!'
Churilo's home is on the River Pochai,
At the wondrous cross of Levanidov,
At the holy mosque of Boris;   115
Churilo's home covers seven versts,
All around his home is fenced with steel,
The entrances are fitted with glass doors,
The thresholds are of precious fishes' teeth.
In Churilo's home,   120
On two, on three sides,
There are as many as seventy terems,
And in these terems lives Churilo himself.
Churilo has three apartments with casement shutters,
And three apartments with lattice windows,   125
And in another three the windows are glazed.
From those high terems
On to the brick pavement
There came a tall old man.
The old man was dressed in a coat of sable,   130
And above it he wore costly green samite.
His buttons were of chased work,
Of chased work and cast of pure gold.
He bowed, bowed low to them,
And spoke words of greeting: 135
'Welcome, Vladimir, to my lofty hall,
To my lofty hall to eat my bread'.
Vladimir replied as follows:
'Tell me, tall old man!
By what name are you called?   140
For I would know whose bread I eat'.

'I', said he, 'am Plenko the merchant of the Soroga;[1]
Moreover I am Churilo's father.'
Vladimir entered the lofty hall,
He entered the hall and marvelled.   145
Beautifully were the halls adorned.
The floor was of pure silver,
The stoves were all of glazed tiles,
The supports were covered with silver,
Churilo's ceiling was covered with black sable,   150
On his walls were printed curtains,
In the curtains were sash windows,
The hall was a copy of the sky.—
The full moon of heaven rode aloft.[2]
All its other delights cannot be told.   155
The prince seated himself at the table of oak,
He peeped through a little window,
And gazed far out over the open plain.
A crowd appeared from the open plain,
Five hundred youths came riding.   160
The mounted youths were all alike,
Their mounts were all of the same bay colour,
They were all stallions of Latin breed.[3]

[1] *Gost Sorozhanin.* The meaning is uncertain. For alternative suggestions, see Magnus, *Heroic Ballads of Russia,* p. 183 f.

[2] In the apartment of the daughters of the Tsar Alexis in the royal terem of the Kremlin the wall was decorated with frescoes of landscapes, and the part surrounding the windows was painted to represent a blue sky with white clouds. See Rambaud, 'Les Tsarines de Moscou', *Revue des Deux Mondes,* vol. CVII, 1873, p. 516.

[3] The version sung by an 'Old Man' of Kolodozero adds the following picturesque details:
'The youths wore kaftans of scarlet cloth,
Girt with girdles of many coloured strands.
The boots on their feet were of green morocco,
The points were like the points of awls, and the heels high,
Round the tips of the toes an egg could be rolled;
Beneath the heel a sparrow could fly,
A sparrow could fly, could flit to and fro'.
(Rybnikov, *Pêsni,* vol. II, p. 460.)

Vladimir spoke as follows:
'Tell me, Plenko, merchant of the Soroga!   165
Is not this Churilo Plenkovich coming?'
'That is not Churilo Plenkovich:
Those are Churilo's cooks coming,
Who brew Churilo's green wine.'
That crowd went into the court-yard,   170
And a fresh one made their appearance from the plain;
Five hundred youths came riding:
The mounted youths were all alike,
Their mounts were all of the same bay colour,
They were all stallions of Latin breed,   175
Their bridles and reins were of Saracen make.
And Vladimir spoke as follows:
'Tell me, Plenko, silk merchant of the Soroga!
Is not this Churilo Plenkovich coming?'
'No, Sire, that is not Churilo Plenkovich: 180
Those are Churilo's seneschals coming,
Who stand by Churilo's table of oak.'
That crowd went into the court-yard,
And a fresh one made their appearance from the plain.
A thousand youths arrived—and more;   185
In the midst of the troops rode the handsome youth,
The youth was wearing a coat of sables,
And over it precious green samite.
His buttons were all of chased work,
Of chased work and cast of pure gold,   190
Like costly apples of Siberia.
Vladimir sat at the table of oak,
He began to fidget about uneasily:
'Alas! What will become of me?
Either here comes a tsar from the Horde,   195
Or else here comes the king of Lithuania,
Or here come wooers
For my beloved niece,
My darling Zabava Putyatichna'.
Plenko the merchant of the Soroga addressed him: 200

'Fear not, Vladimir, be not alarmed:
Here at last is my son really coming,
My very young son, Churilo Plenkovich'.
Churilo came on, amusing himself,
Leaping from steed to steed,   205
Springing from saddle to saddle,
Over three and on to a fourth;
Casting his spear on high,
Throwing and catching it from hand to hand.
Churilo came to the River Pochai,   210
His troop dispersed to their quarters.
They told Churilo of the stranger guests,
And Churilo took his golden keys,
And went to the store-house,
And took forty times forty black sables,   215
Many pairs of foxes and martens,
And made presents to Prince Vladimir,
And presented all the boyars with foxes,
And presented all the merchants with martens,
And presented all the common folk with gold treasure.   220
And so Vladimir spoke as follows:
'Although there have been a number of plaintiffs against Churilo,
And a vast number of petitioners,
I will not on this occasion give judgment against Churilo'.
And Vladimir spoke as follows: 225
'Young Churilo Plenkovich!
Will you come to be my seneschal,
To be my seneschal, my cup-bearer?'
Some buy themselves off from a misfortune in this way,
But Churilo gleaned misfortune for himself.   230
He went to Vladimir as seneschal,
As seneschal, as cup-bearer.
And they rode away to the city of Kiev,
And came to the city of Kiev.
The dear lord, Prince Vladimir,   235
Having a fine new seneschal,
He gave an honourable feast.

The youthful Churilo Plenkovich
Went and stood at the table of oak,
Tossing his yellow curls.   240
His yellow curls flowed freely down,
Like scattered pearls rolling hither and thither.
The youthful Princess Apraxya
Was carving the flesh of the swan.
And she cut her fair right hand,   245
And spoke as follows:
'Marvel not at me, my gentlewomen,
In that I have cut my fair right hand;
I was gazing on the beauty of Churilo,
On his golden curls,   250
On his gold rings,
And my bright eyes were dazzled'.
And then she added:
'Our dear lord, Prince Vladimir,
The youthful Churilo Plenkovich,   255
He must not be set to this service;
He must be our chamberlain,
And lay soft rugs for us to lie on'.
The dear lord, Prince Vladimir,
Took Churilo from that service,   260
And placed him in a different office—
That of courteous marshal,
To go through the city of Kiev,
And invite guests to his honourable feast.
The youthful Churilo Plenkovich   265
Went through the streets and alleys,
Tossing his yellow curls:
His yellow curls flowed freely down,
Like scattered pearls rolling hither and thither.
As they gazed on Churilo's beauty   270
The nuns in their cells tore off their habits;
As they gazed on Churilo's beauty
The young girls uncovered themselves....
As they gazed on Churilo's beauty

The pretty lasses tore off their head-dresses.   275
The young Princess Apraxya
Spoke to Prince Vladimir:
'Our dear lord, Prince Vladimir!
The youthful Churilo Plenkovich
Must not be set to this service.   280
He must be our chamberlain'.
Vladimir saw that a catastrophe had befallen him,
And he spoke to Churilo as follows:
'Young Churilo Plenkovich!
Either you must enter a cloister or go home,   285
I do not require you any longer in my household'.
Young Churilo Plenkovich,
He made his bow and he left the hall,
And out went Churilo into the city of Kiev,
And away rode Churilo to the River Pochai,   290
And continued to live on and take his pleasure.

XI

Dyuk Stepanovich

LIKE the *bylina* of Churilo Plenkovich, the following story reflects certain historical elements at the court of Vladimir, though no historical information is available relating to the person of Dyuk himself. In contrast to Churilo, who belongs to the wealthy local squires, perhaps of princely, perhaps only of mercantile rank, Dyuk belongs to the proud line which occupied the Galician throne—the throne later to be filled by the mighty Prince Roman and his son Daniel, who was crowned by the Pope in 1254. Coming from wealthy Galicia he expresses his unbounded contempt for the simpler conditions of Vladimir's court. These conditions are reflected elsewhere in a story told in Nestor's Chronicle, according to which Vladimir's *druzhina* are represented as complaining that they have to eat from wooden spoons. In contrast to this, however, it must be remembered that in 1075 Burhard of Worms, the ambassador of the Emperor Henry IV at the court of Svyatoslav, 'was amazed at the quantity and magnificence of the treasures he saw there' (Hapgood, p. 276). The visit of the haughty Dyuk of princely rank to Vladimir's court is in itself a tribute to the brilliance of Kiev at this period. We have already seen (p. 61 above) that Vladimir's policy was democratic and calculated to attach the native independent princes to his standard. Visits from foreign princes such as Dyuk Stepanovich and from foreign merchants, such as Solovey Budimirovich, and Stavr Godinovich, show that he was equally alive to the advantages of a wealthy cosmopolitan element in their midst. All these elements were necessary if Kiev was to enjoy comfort and immunity from the incursions of the nomads, whether Pechenegs, Polovtsy or Tartars.

The *bylina* is interesting from a literary point of view also.

The closing lines may be compared with a passage in the *Epistle from Tzar Ivan the Indian to Tzar Manuel the Greek*, which reads as follows:

If thou desirest to know all my power, and all the wonders of my Indian realm, sell thy kingdom of Greece and purchase paper, and come to my Indian realm with thy learned men, and I will permit thee to write down the marvels of the Indian land; and thou shalt not be able to make a writing of the wonders of my kingdom before the departure of thy spirit.[1]

The *Epistle* is included in the same MS as the *Slovo o Polky Igorevê* to which reference was made above. This MS has been assigned to dates varying from the fourteenth to the sixteenth centuries respectively. The latter date is probably correct.[2] The corresponding passage in the *bylina* is interesting, therefore, both as suggesting that the two compositions belong in origin to the same literary milieu, and also as testifying to the remarkable verbal fidelity of the oral tradition preserved in the *byliny*.

Equally interesting from the literary point of view are the speeches in which Dyuk contrasts the conditions in his own home with those of Galicia. These are composed in artificial antithetical style, each set of categorical items which form the contrasted pictures being of approximately equal length and similar form. This set of what appear to be practically strophic speeches is introduced by a peculiar phrase:

Stal zagadochki Vladimiru otgadyvat

which seems to mean literally 'Dyuk proposed riddles to Vladimir'.[3] This, however, can hardly be the true significance of the phrase. The word *zagadka* seems to signify popular learning, such as riddles, gnomic poetry and poetry of peasant wisdom. I think, therefore, that the *bylina* of

[1] Hapgood, *Epic Songs of Russia*, p. 276. For the 'Indian realm', see p. 103 n. below.
[2] See Magnus, *The Tale of the Armament of Igor* (Oxford, 1915), p. i f.
[3] The most recent editor explains the phrase thus: *zadavat zagadki*, 'to propose riddles'. See Rybnikov, *ed. cit.* vol. I, p. 100, footnote I.

Dyuk has embodied a popular song of gnomic character
in which the rich and the poor man's dwellings are contrasted
in a series of alternative descriptive phrases, just as the
Slovo o Polky Igorevê has incorporated a popular song
form in the Lament of Yaroslavna.

DYUK STEPANOVICH

Sung by Trofim Grigorevich Ryabinin

Rybnikov, *Pésni*, vol. i, p. 98 ff.

Dyuk Stepanovich, the prince's son, made ready to travel
From the glorious, rich city of Volhynia,
From wealthy India;[1]
Dyuk prepared to set off to the glorious city of Kiev,
Desiring to gaze upon Prince Vladimir,   5
And the mighty Russian heroes.
His dear mother said to him,
The honourable widow, Nastasya Vasilevna:
'Young Dyuk Stepanovich, prince's son!
If you make ready to go to the city of royal Kiev,   10
Desiring to gaze upon Prince Vladimir,
And the mighty Russian heroes,
Remember when you are drunk with the green wine
Not to boast of your possessions
Against the mighty Russian heroes'.   15
Dyuk bestrode his good steed,
And he rode over the free, open plain,
To the glorious city of Kiev.
And he came to Prince Vladimir in the spacious court-yard,
He entered the palace of white stone,   20
He made the sign of the cross in the prescribed manner,
He made his bow as it is enjoined;
On three, on four, on all sides he bowed,
And asked for Prince Vladimir.

[1] India in the *byliny* signifies, not the India of to-day, but the
wealthy countries of Galicia and Volhynia.

Vladimir was not at home: 25
Prince Vladimir had gone to the church of God,
To pray to the Lord God,
To kiss the divine cross.
Dyuk Stepanovich, the prince's son,
He walked through the glorious city of Kiev, 30
And entered the cathedral church,
He held the cross in the manner prescribed,
He made his bow as it is enjoined;
On three, on four, on all sides he bowed,
To Prince Vladimir in particular, 35
And to all his royal retinue.
On Vladimir's right hand
Was young Dobrynya Nikitinets,[1]
On Vladimir's left hand
Was Churilo Plenkovich. 40
Prince Vladimir began to question the youth:
'Tell me now, young man, and inform me,
From what horde,[2] and from what land are you?
By what name do they call you, bold youth,
How do they address you in your own country?' 45
Dyuk Stepanovich, the prince's son, made answer:
'I come from accursed[3] Galicia,
From wealthy India,
From the glorious, rich city of Volhynia,
I am young Dyuk Stepanovich, the prince's son'. 50
Churilo spoke as follows:
'Ho, Vladimir of royal Kiev,
The fellow mocks us to our faces,
He lies to us to our faces:
His is not Dyuk's bearing, 55

---

[1] The more usual form is Nikitich.
[2] A term borrowed from the Tartars.
[3] The adjective is static and must not be supposed to be intended literally by Dyuk. It is the customary Russian description in the *byliny* of Galicia, Lithuania, Poland, etc., because, belonging to the Roman Church, they were regarded as heretics.

His is not Dyuk's speech,
He must be some nobleman's serf'.
This speech was displeasing to Dyuk.
The speech was displeasing, it was not to his liking.
When they had prayed to the Lord God,   60
And had kissed the holy cross,
They left the cathedral church,
They walked through the city of Kiev.
Young Dyuk Stepanovich, the prince's son,
Put a riddle to Prince Vladimir.   65
Dyuk spoke as follows:
'Vladimir, prince of royal Kiev,
You do not have in Kiev such things as we have;
Your floors are paved with brick,
And your balustrade is of white hazel-wood,   70
And you walk on brick floors.[1]
Copper nails are used in clamping.
You flaunt about in gaudy clothes.
Whereas with us in glorious wealthy India,
In the glorious rich city of Volhynia,   75
In the house of my dear mother,
The honourable widow, Nastasya Vasilevna,
The floors are of white hazel-wood,
The balustrades are composed of silver;
Crimson carpets are spread,   80
While you walk on floors of white hazel-wood:
These crimson carpets
Are not held in place by copper nails,
And people do not flaunt about in gaudy clothes at my home'.
Prince Vladimir thought fit to ignore this speech.   85
When they entered the white stone palace
Of gracious Prince Vladimir,
And came into the dining-hall,
And seated themselves at the table of oak,
On their round stools,   90
They ate sugared food,

[1] This line is obviously out of place.

Rolls of millet flour were handed round.[1]
Dyuk Stepanovich, the prince's son,
Took his millet roll in his hand,
Took a bite of the outer crust,   95
And threw the middle to the dogs.
He spoke as follows:
'Vladimir, prince of royal Kiev,
You do not have in Kiev such things as we have;
The casks are made of oak,   100
And bound with hoops of fir-wood,
And in these cool spring water is stored,
And with this they knead your rolls;
Your stoves are faced with brick,
Heated with fir-wood for fuel,   105
Your oven-brooms are composed of fir-twigs,
And with these they bake your rolls.
Now with us in wealthy India,
In the glorious, rich city of Volhynia,
Belonging to my dear mother,   110
The honourable widow, Nastasya Vasilevna,
The casks are made of silver,
And bound with hoops of gold,
And in these mellow mead is stored,
And with this they knead our rolls.   115
Our ovens are built of brick,
Heated with fuel of oak,
Our oven-brooms are made of silk,
And thus do they bake the rolls in my home'.
Prince Vladimir thought fit to ignore this speech.   120
They offered him heady liquors to drink,
They poured out a goblet of green wine,
And handed it to Dyuk Stepanovich;
Dyuk Stepanovich, the prince's son,
He took the goblet in his white hand,   125
And lifted it to his delicate lips;
That liquor did not please him,

[1] *Kalachi*, fine wheaten rolls of peculiar shape.

He cast it all forth across the golden table,
Over the glorious hall,
And spoke as follows: 130
'Vladimir, prince of royal Kiev:
You do not have such things in Kiev as we have;
With you the casks are made of oak,
And bound with hoops of fir-wood,
And in these your heady wine is stored.   135
And in these deep cellars
The heady wine is like to choke one.
Whereas in our wealthy India,
In the glorious, wealthy city of Volhynia,
Belonging to my dear mother,   140
The honourable widow, Nastasya Vasilevna,
The casks are made of silver,
And bound with hoops of gold;
And in these our heady wine is stored,
And hung on chains of copper.   145
They are hung in a strong draught;
When a strong draught blows,
The air passes through the cellar,
By this means the heady wine never chokes us.
When one has emptied a goblet   150
One's soul burns for another'.
Prince Vladimir thought fit to ignore this speech.
Churilo Plenkovich came up
To that table of oak,
In a fine smock without girdle,   155
In a pair of fine stockings without shoes.
Churilo spoke to him as follows:
'Why all this boasting, you nobleman's serf,
Of your possessions and your wealth?
Let us lay a great wager together,   160
That during three years at all times
We will ride about the city of Kiev
On our good heroic steeds,
Wearing a change of dress,

A change of dress every day,   165
Every day wearing one new one after another,
One new one after another, each better than the last'.
Dyuk replied as follows:
'You propose, Churilo Plenkovich,
To lay a great wager with me   170
While you are living in royal Kiev,
And have store-houses full of new clothes;
Whereas I, on the contrary, am on a visit.
My clothes, therefore, have to be carried here'.
And Dyuk Stepanovich laid a great wager with him   175
That during three years at all times
They should ride about the city of Kiev,
On their good heroic steeds,
Wearing a change of dress,
A change of dress every day,   180
Every day wearing one new dress after another,
One new one after another, all costly garments;
Then Dyuk Stepanovich, the prince's son,
Very, very quickly he sat down at the writing-table,
Quickly he wrote letters in cursive hand,   185
He wrote these letters and sealed them up,
Put them in his travelling bags,[1]
And went into the spacious court-yard,
To his heroic steed,
Laid these travelling bags   190
Under his splendid Circassian saddle,
And despatched his good steed into the open plain.
His good steed set off over the open plain
To glorious, wealthy India.
The good steed came running into the spacious court-yard,   195
Into the spacious royal court-yard.
Dyuk's beloved grooms perceived him,
And that the good steed had come from Dyuk Stepanovich,
And they told his dear mother,

---

[1] A double bag which can be thrown over the shoulders or the
saddle. Cf. p. 51 n. above.

The honourable widow, Nastasya Vasilevna: 200
'Of a truth, Dyuk Stepanovich is dead'.
Then very, very quickly she ran into the spacious court-yard,
Went up to the good steed,
And began to lament bitterly,
And spoke these words: 205
'My beloved son Dyuk Stepanovich
Has lost his rebellious head
In holy[1] mother Russia!'
And the beloved grooms went up to him,
And proceeded to unsaddle the good steed;   210
And under the Circassian saddle,
On the saddle-cloth of seven silks,
They found the letter-bags,
And handed them to the honourable widow, Nastasya Vasilevna.
Very quickly she took them in her white hand,   215
Very, very quickly she tore open the bags,
Yet more quickly she read the handwriting of the letter,
And greatly did she rejoice over the news
That her beloved son was alive,
Dyuk Stepanovich, the prince's son.   220
She ordered her dear grooms
To scatter white millet before the steed,
And she ordered them to bring fresh spring water;
Very quickly she went into the palace of white stone,
Seized her golden keys,   225
And went into the deep cellar;
She took valuers with her,
She took valuers and assessors,
And they folded and packed costly garments,
And meted them out for three years' time,   230
Every day to wear one new dress after another,
One new one after another, all costly garments.
She ordered her beloved grooms
To saddle the heroic steed.

[1] A static adjective applied by Orthodox Russians to their own country, as opposed to Catholic Galicia.

Under the Circassian saddle   235
They placed a silken saddle-cloth,
A silken saddle-cloth, brand-new,
And under this saddle-cloth they laid a written letter,
And to this Circassian saddle
They bound the costly garments,   240
And sent the steed to the city of royal Kiev.
The good steed departed over the open plain—he did not tarry,
Very, very quickly he came running to the city of royal Kiev,
To the spacious court-yard of Prince Vladimir.
Dyuk Stepanovich came into the spacious court-yard.   245
From that Circassian saddle
He unloaded the precious apparel;
From under the silken saddle-cloth
He took the written letter,
From his dear mother,   250
From the honourable widow, Nastasya Vasilevna.
He entered the palace of white stone,
And donned costly garments,
And rode through the city of Kiev,
With young Churilo Plenkovich.   255
On their good heroic steeds
They went on riding, day after day,
Day after day, and so year after year,
They continued to ride during three years' time.
And on the last day they rode to Easter Matins;   260
Young Churilushka Plenkovich
Put on a costly garment;—
The threads of one set of stitching were of pure silver,
The other threads were of red gold;
The buttons were shaped as bold youths,   265
The loops were shaped as fair maidens:
When they were buttoned they were locked in close embrace,
When they were unbuttoned, they just kissed.
Vladimir surveyed on his right hand
The young Churilo Plenkovich,   270
And Vladimir spoke as follows:

'Young Dyuk Stepanovich, the prince's son,
Has pledged and lost all his rich possessions'.
But young Dyuk Stepanovich, the prince's son,
He donned a costly garment;   275
The threads of the stitching of the dress were of pure silver,
And the other threads were of red gold.
The buttons were shaped as bold youths,
The loops were shaped as fair maidens.
When they were buttoned, they were locked in close embrace,
When they were unbuttoned, they just kissed;   281
On Dyuk's head he wore a hat;
In front of it was the semblance of the red sun,
And behind, the semblance of the bright moon,
And the crown of the hat glittered like fire.   285
Quiet Dunai Ivanovich[1] spoke to him:
'Vladimir, prince of royal Kiev!
Look now on your left hand:
Young Churilo Plenkovich
Has pledged and lost his rebellious head'.   290
They mounted their good steeds and rode off
Through the glorious city of Kiev,
To gracious Prince Vladimir.
They came into the spacious court-yard,
And seated themselves at tables of oak   295
On their round stools;
They ate sugared foods,
They drank honeyed drinks.
Churilo Plenkovich came up,
He came up to the table of oak,   300
In a fine smock without girdle,
In a pair of fine stockings without shoes,
And Churilo spoke as follows:
'Why all this boasting, you nobleman's serf,
Of your great possessions and wealth?   305
Let us lay a great wager together,

    [1] One of Vladimir's retinue, himself the hero of a number of
byliny.

That on our good heroic steeds
We will ride away beyond the free, open plain,
And leap across the glorious mother Dnêpr'.
Young Dyuk Stepanovich, the prince's son,   310
He answered him, now, as follows:
'Ah, Churilo Plenkovich!
It is simple enough for you to lay a great wager with me;
While that heroic steed of yours
Is attended by his dear grooms,   315
Eating white millet,
Drinking fresh, spring water.
Mine, on the contrary, is a travelling nag,
A travelling nag, a jaded steed'.
Then his heart sank;   320
Very quickly he ran into the spacious court-yard,
Leant against his horse's flank,
He leant there and made complaint:
'Ah, my good, heroic steed!
I dare not lay a great wager, and pledge myself,   325
That I and Churilo Plenkovich
Would leap across the river, mother Dnêpr,
On our good heroic steeds'.
His good steed spoke to him in human speech:
'Have no fear, Dyuk Stepanovich,   330
Lay the great wager with him:
I will carry you across the river, mother Dnêpr,
On my invisible equine wings;
I will not fall short of my elder brother,
And still less of my younger brother.   335
My elder brother belongs to Ilya of Murom;
My second brother to Dobrynya Mikitits;[1]
I am the third brother and belong to Dyuk Stepanovich;
It is the fourth brother that Churilo Oplenkovich has'.
Then he went into the palace of white stone,   340
And they laid the great wager,
And proceeded to saddle their good steeds.
Young Dyuk Stepanovich, the prince's son,

        [1] Cf. note to line 38 above.

Went into the spacious court-yard,
And with his own hands he saddled his good steed;   345
He saddled it and made it ready.
Then Dyuk bestrode his good steed,
And rode with young Churilo Plenkovich
Over the glorious, free, open plain;
And they rode away beyond the free, open plain,   350
With their whole equine strength,
And leapt across the river, mother Dnêpr,
On their good heroic steeds:
Young Dyuk Stepanovich, the prince's son,
He leapt across the river, mother Dnêpr,   355
On his good, heroic steed,
And with a single equine bound
He leapt quite a whole verst[1] beyond;
And he looked over his right shoulder,
When his comrade did not follow him,   360
Young Churilushka Oplenkovich.
Churilo Plenkovich had gone splash into the middle of the Dnêpr,
With his good heroic steed.
Young Dyuk Stepanovich very quickly turned back,
Made a leap across the river, mother Dnêpr,   365
And pulled Churilo Plenkovich out by his golden curls,
Out of the river, mother Dnêpr,
And placed Churilo on the steep bank,
And addressed Churilo as follows:
'Ha, Churilushka Plenkovich!   370
You are not one who should boast,
Nor are you one who should lay a great wager.
Your part should be simply to parade Kiev,
To parade Kiev at the heels of the womenfolk'.
And they went to the royal city of Kiev.   375
Then Vladimir, prince of royal Kiev,
He proceeded to send valuers
Into wealthy India
To make an inventory and value Dyuk's possessions.

[1] I.e. $\frac{2}{3}$ of a mile.

Thither were sent quiet Dunai Ivanovich,   380
And secondly Vasili Kazimirovich,[1]
And thirdly the bold hero Alyoshenka Popovich.
They mounted their good steeds and rode off
And came to wealthy India,
To the spacious court-yard of Dyuk Stepanovich.   385
They did not send their horses to the messenger's yard,
They stationed their horses in the middle of the court-yard,
They went to the palace of white stone,
They burst open five doors.
They entered the palace of white stone,   390
They prayed to the Lord God,
They held the cross in the manner prescribed,
They made their bow as it is enjoined;
On three, on four, on all sides they bowed,
To the honourable widow, Nastasya Vasilevna in particular. 395
'Greetings, honourable widow, Nastasya Vasilevna,
Mother of Dyuk Stepanovich!'
She spoke as follows:
'I am not the mother of Dyuk Stepanovich,
I am Dyuk's water-carrier'.   400
They entered the second apartment,
Again they bowed low:
'Greetings, honourable widow, Nastasya Vasilevna,
Mother of Dyuk Stepanovich!'
She spoke as follows: 405
'I am not Dyuk's mother,
I am Dyuk's laundress'.
They went into a third apartment,
Again they bowed low:
'Greetings, honourable widow, Nastasya Vasilevna,   410
Mother of Dyuk Stepanovich'.
She spoke as follows:
'I am not Dyuk's mother,
I am Dyuk's table-maid'.
Fair maidens conducted them to Dyuk's mother.   415

[1] Another member of Vladimir's court, and a hero of *byliny*.

They bowed and they marvelled:
'Greetings, honourable widow, Nastasya Vasilevna,
Dyuk Stepanovich's mother!'
Dyuk's mother made answer:
'Ye bold, stout, good youths!   420
I know neither your names nor your rank.
What is the purpose of your visit?
Tell me, are you come to make an inventory of the orphan's estate?'
They answered her as follows:
'Dyuk Stepanovich himself has sent us   425
To make an inventory of his wealth and possessions'.
She plied them with sugared foods,
She gave them honeyed drinks to drink:
When they had emptied a goblet, their lips stuck together,
When they had emptied a second, their souls burned for a third,
And the fourth goblet did not make them drunk.   431
She took them into a deep cellar,
She set them to enumerate and value the horse trappings.
They enumerated and valued
Those horse trappings for three whole years,   435
They valued them for three years and for three days,
But they could not value those horse trappings.
She took them into a deep cellar
To enumerate and value his wealth and possessions.
There hung casks of pure silver,   440
And others hung full of pure gold,
And a third group was full of round pearls.
Those valuers
Could not give their total,
Or make an inventory of the wealth and possessions.   445
Then they wrote to the city of royal Kiev,
To glorious Prince Vladimir:
'Glorious Vladimir of royal Kiev!
Sell your city of royal Kiev
In exchange for embossed writing paper,   450
And sell, moreover, the city of Chernigov for pens and ink,
Then may you make a list of Dyuk's possessions'.

XII

Nightingale Budimirovich

THE hero has not been identified with any historical character. The most popular view is that he was a Norse viking. The most serious exposition of this theory is that of Stanislas Rozniecki, *Varægiske Minder i den Russiske Heltedigtning* (Copenhagen, 1914); but his arguments do not seem to me to be convincing. The name Budimir is Gothic in form—as is also Vladimir. Possibly Budimir belonged to the Gothic colony on the Black Sea, to which reference is made in the *Slovo o Polky Igorevê*. Clearly Nightingale is represented as a merchant prince, but heroes of many different regions are represented in the *byliny* as meeting at Vladimir's court, as was no doubt the case in actual fact (cf. pp. 50, 61 above). The island of Kadolski, Nightingale's home, has never been identified, though it occurs very frequently in the *byliny*.

NIGHTINGALE BUDIMIROVICH

Sung by Potap Antonov, Lake Onega
Gilferding, Sbornik, vol. 1, p. 517 ff.

From the island of Kadolski,
From the River Danube,
Came fifty ships in full sail.
On one of these ships
Were thirty youths save one;   5
Nightingale himself made up the thirty,
And his dear mother made thirty and one.
Bravely were the ships adorned,
Bravely were the ships bedeckt.

Stem and stern were shaped like an aurochs,   10
The broad sides were in the fashion of an elk.
The sails were of rich damask,
The ships' anchors were of steel,
The anchors had silver rings,
The ropes were of the seven silks;   15
Where the rudder was it was hung
With precious sables from foreign parts;
(Where the eyebrows should be it was decked
With precious foreign fox-skins;
In the place of the eyes it was inset   20
With sapphire stones from foreign lands.[1])
And on this ship
Was young Nightingale Budimirovich.[2]
He spoke as follows:
'All you, my bold druzhina!   25
Perform the task I lay upon you,
Obey your mighty chief,
Bring telescopes,
Look out over the glorious blue sea,
Towards the city of Kiev,   30
Towards gracious Prince Vladimir,
And sight the ships' anchorage'.
And they climbed the tall mast,
They performed the task laid upon them,
They obeyed the mighty chief,   35
They looked out over the glorious blue sea,
Towards the city of Kiev,
Towards gracious Prince Vladimir,
And sighted the ships' anchorage.
Soon were they under Kiev with their ships,   40
And ran into the ships' anchorage,

---

[1] The last four lines are supplied from the corresponding version of this *bylina* recorded by Rybnikov, vol. II, p. 420, l. 24 ff. Gilferding's text contains only one line in the parallel passage, and the text is obscure.
[2] In Gilferding's text the name appears as Gudimirovich; but Rybnikov's corresponding text has preserved the more usual form.

Lowered the sails of rich damask,
Cast the steel anchors;
Young Nightingale Budimirovich spoke:
'Lower a gangway of silver, 45
Lower a second one overlaid with gold,
Lower a third of whalebone.
Take acceptable gifts,
Marten-skins and fox-furs from foreign parts'.
They took the gifts in their white hands; 50
His mother took figured damask,
And he himself took his gusli[1] of maple-wood,
And he crossed the gilded gangway,
His mother crossed the silver one,
And all his druzhina the gangway of whalebone. 55
And they went to Vladimir's court-yard.
He entered the palace of white stone,
Held the cross in the manner prescribed,
Made his bow as it is enjoined,
On three, on four, on all sides, 60
And to Prince Vladimir in particular.
They presented him with the precious offerings,
And his mother gave the figured damask
To the young Princess Apraxya.
The princess took it in her white hand, 65
She took it and she marvelled:—
Not so much at the foreign damask itself, precious though it was,
As at the foreign patterns woven in the damask !
Vladimir proceeded to question him,
Vladimir proceeded to examine him: 70
'Tell me, good youth, from what land you come,
And by what name you are called?'
Nightingale went up quite close to the prince,
And bowed very low before him:
'I come from the Danube, 75
I come from the island of Kadolski;

---

[1] A stringed instrument, like a recumbent harp, frequently mentioned in the *byliny* of the Kiev Cycle.

I am a bold, brave hero,
I am young Nightingale Budimirovich'.
'Why have you journeyed hither to me?
To carry on trade, or to visit me,   80
To visit me, or to settle here?'
Nightingale made answer,
Young Nightingale Budimirovich:
'Neither to carry on trade, nor to visit you,
I have come to you to settle here.   85
Bestow upon me a little plot
Close beside you.
You have a young niece,
Young Zabava Putyatichna,
In whose green garden   90
Oaks and elms have grown up.
Permit me to hew them down,
To cast them forth out of the garden,
And to erect there three terems,
All brightly decorated'.   95
Vladimir replied as follows:
'For your gentle words,
For your prudent speech,
Go now into the green garden,
Do as you have suggested'.   100
Thereupon Nightingale went,
Young Nightingale Budimirovich,
To his bold druzhina
Of thirty youths save one:
'Perform the task I lay upon you,   105
Obey your mighty chief,
Take now in your white hands
Your hatchets of steel,
Make for yourselves pickaxes and shovels,
Go at once into the green garden,   110
Hew down all the oaks and elms
And cast them forth out of the garden,
And dig up the roots.

Erect there three terems, neither more nor less,
All brightly decorated,   115
To be ready by daybreak for me to go and live in'.
They performed the task laid upon them,
They obeyed their mighty chief,
And seized their hatchets of steel,
Made for themselves picks and shovels,   120
Hewed down the oaks and elms,
And when they had cast them forth out of the garden,
They erected there three terems,
All brightly decorated;
At the peep of dawn they went to live there.   125
When it was still very early dawn
Zabavushka had already arisen,
Young Zabava Utyatichna;
She washed herself with water till she was quite clean,
She dried herself with a little towel till she was quite dry, 130
She said her prayers to the Lord God,
And then she looked out of her little window;
Then she was astonished,
Then she marvelled:
'What miracle is this which has occurred?   135
Has the wine or ale gone to my head?
Behold, in my gardens
The thicket of oaks and elms is all felled,
They are cast forth out of the garden'.
Zabava flung her mantle over one shoulder,   140
Thrust her shoes on to her bare feet—
And went out into the green garden.
When she came to the first terem,
In the first terem someone was speaking in an undertone:
It was the mother praying to God,   145
She was entreating God on behalf of her dear son,
The young son of Budimir.
When she came to the second terem,
In the second terem there is a rattling and jingling,
A rattling and jingling as of golden treasure;   150
Nightingale is counting over his golden treasure,

His golden treasure which is beyond counting.
When she reached the third terem,
There they are playing on the gusli of maple-wood;
They are playing dances from Novgorod,   155
Others they play from Jerusalem,
And accompany them with sweet refrains.
Zabava Utyatichna drew near
And entered the white tent.[1]
She held the cross in the manner prescribed,   160
She made her bow as it is enjoined,
On three, on four, on all sides,
To the druzhina in particular.
She seated herself on the newly hewn bench,
She sat there the whole day from early morn,   165
All day from early morn till eventide,
And from eventide till midnight,
And from midnight until broad daylight.
Now at dawn, very, very early,
The gentle, bold youth came,   170
Young Nightingale Budimirovich,
And he spoke as follows:
'What sort of a maiden is this who does her own wooing,
What unknown maiden is this?'
Zabava sprang to her nimble feet,   175
Zabava bowed to the very ground:
'Greetings to you, bold, noble youth,
Young Nightingale Budimirovich!
You are a youth as yet unmarried,
And I am a marriageable maid'.   180
The gentle, bold, noble youth made answer,
Young Nightingale Budimirovich:
'For all things, maiden, for all things I love you,
But for one thing, maiden, I love you not at all,
That you, a maiden, have wooed for yourself. . . .   185

---

[1] A static formula. Actually Zabava enters the upper apartment
(*terem*) in which Nightingale is stationed. In most versions of the
bylina it is Nightingale himself who sits and plays on the *gusli*, while
it is the *druzhina* who count his treasure.

Betake yourself now, maiden, to your own dwelling,
Beat the ground with your forehead[1] and bow low
To Prince Vladimir,
And beg him to hold an honourable feast'.
So the maiden went to her own house,   190
The maiden beat the ground with her brow
Before Prince Vladimir:
'Hearken now, my uncle,
Vladimir, prince of royal Kiev!
In your faceted palace,[2]   195
For me, your dear niece,
Hold an honourable feast,
So that I may have guests and boasting'.
And so her uncle held for her,
He held an honourable feast.   200
At this feast they made merry,
They drank, and ate, and took their pleasure.
Then came the bold youth,
Young Nightingale Budimirovich;
He took the maiden by her white hands,   205
And he went with the maiden to the Church of God,
And with gold rings they were betrothed,
And with gold crowns they were crowned.
Nightingale went up to Vladimir
And tendered his warmest thanks,   210
He expressed his high esteem for him,
His high esteem and gratitude.
Then Nightingale went to his own house there.
Nightingale proceeded to live his life,
And they spent their time together.[3]   215

[1] A static formula for a respectful obeisance. The expression is believed to have originated in the humiliating observances imposed on the Russians by the Tartars.

[2] A Muscovite expression; derived from the great reception chamber in the Kremlin, on one side of which there was a balustrade of stones cut into facets on their outer surface.

[3] The text contains eight additional lines, but they have been omitted in the translation as having little bearing on the story.

XIII

Staver

STAVER—or, more correctly, Stavr—Godinovich, the hero of the following *bylina*, is in all probability to be identified with a certain Stavr mentioned in the Chronicle of Novgorod, *s.a.* 1118, who is associated with Vladimir II. The name is not Slavonic in form. It looks like a Norse form, though it is unknown to me elsewhere as a proper name in either Norse or Slavonic sources. Stavr is spoken of as a *sotski*, a ruler of one of the 'hundreds' into which Novgorod with its suburbs was divided. The presence of Stavr in sulky mood in Kiev at Vladimir's feast may be a reflection of the historical event when Vladimir II summoned all the nobles of Novgorod to Kiev to take the oath of allegiance to him. It is said that on this occasion Stavr was sent into exile.[1] It is to be remarked, however, that Stavr Godinovich is most frequently associated in the *byliny*, not with Novgorod, but with Chernigov.

Stavr's wife Vasilissa, or Vasilista in our version, belongs to the class of women in the *byliny* known as *polenitsy*, women who go about and fight and undertake heroic exploits like men. Analogies are to be found in the Norse Sagas (e.g. the heroine Hervör in the *Saga of Hervör and Heithrek*).[2]

[1] Hapgood, *Epic Songs of Russia*, p. 269.
[2] Transl. Kershaw, *Stories and Ballads of the Far Past* (Cambridge, 1921).

STAVER

Sung by Abram Evtikhiev Chukov ['the Bottle']

Rybnikov, *Pêsni*, vol. I, p. 202 ff.

In the glorious city of Kiev,
It happened that gracious Prince Vladimir
Made a banquet, an honourable feast,
For his company of princes and boyars,
For all the merchants invited and received,   5
Invited and received, and come from afar.
All had eaten their fill at the honourable feast,
All had drunk their fill at the honourable feast,
All at the feast began to boast of this and that.
One boasts his good steed,   10
One boasts his silken breeches,
One boasts his villages with their hamlets,
One boasts his towns with their suburbs,
One boasts of his dear mother,
But the foolish one boasts of his young wife.   15
From the land of Lyakhovits[1]
Came young Staver Godinovich.
He sat at the table, but no boast he made.
Vladimir of royal Kiev questioned him:
'Now, Staver Godinovich!   20
Why do you sit and make no boast?
Have you no village with its hamlets?
Have you no towns with their suburbs?
Have you no good steeds?
Or no dear mother whom you honour,   25
Or no fine young wife?'
Staver Godinovich spoke:
'Even though I have a village with its hamlets,

---

[1] This name, like the 'Politovski land' mentioned in l. 311, is used
of Poland, or, more exactly, the land of the western Slavs. See Zeuss,
Die Deutschen und die Nachbarstämme (Göttingen, 1904), pp. 98 ff.,
603 f. Cf. also *Streitberg Festgabe* (Leipzig, 1924), Karte II.

Even though I have a town with its suburbs,
I am not a youth to boast of them.   30
Even though I have good steeds—
I have so many steeds I cannot ride them all—
I am not a youth to boast of them.
Even though I have a mother whom I honour,
I am not a youth to boast of her.   35
Even though I have a young wife:
Even then I am not a youth to boast of her:
She would outwit all you princes and boyars,
And hoodwink you, our Sun Vladimir'.
A hush fell upon the feast,   40
And they spoke as follows:
'Our Sun, Vladimir of royal Kiev!
Let us shut up Staver in a deep cellar:
Then let Staver's young wife
Outwit all us princes and boyars,   45
And hoodwink you, our Sun Vladimir.
And let her deliver Staver from his cellar!'
Now Staver had his servant there,
Who mounted Staver's good steed,
And rode to the land of Lyakhovits,   50
To Vasilista[1] Mikulichna.[2]
'Hearken, Vasilista, daughter of Mikula!
There you sit, drinking and taking your ease.
You know not the misfortunes which have befallen you:
How your Staver Godinovich   55
Has been shut up in a deep cellar.
He boasted of you, his young wife,
That you could outwit all the princes and boyars,
And hoodwink their Sun Vladimir'.
Vasilista Mikulichna made answer: 60
'I cannot ransom Staver with money;
I cannot rescue Staver by force;

[1] The singer has corrupted the name which should be Vasilissa.
[2] The daughter of the hero Mikula and sister of Dobrynya's wife
Nastasya.

If I am to rescue Staver at all
It must be by my woman's wit'.
Very, very quickly she ran to the barber,   65
Cut off her hair like a young man,
Transformed herself into Vasili Mikulich,[1]
Collected a bold druzhina
Of forty bold archers,
Forty bold wrestlers,   70
And rode to the city of Kiev.
Before she reached the city of Kiev,
She unfolded a fair white tent,
Stationed her druzhina at the white tent,
And set off alone to the Sun Vladimir.   75
She beat the ground with her forehead and made her bow:
'Greetings to you, our Sun Vladimir of royal Kiev,
And to the young Princess Apraxya!'
Said Vladimir, prince of royal Kiev:
'Whence do you come, bold, good youth,   80
From what horde, from what land?
By what name do they call you,
How do they address you in your own country?'
The bold, noble youth made answer:
'I come from the land of Lyakhovits,   85
I am the son of the king of Lyakhovits,
I am young Vasili Mikulich.
I have come to you on a friendly mission,
To woo your beloved daughter'.
Vladimir of royal Kiev replied: 90
'I will go and discuss it with my daughter'.
He went to his darling daughter:
'Hearken, my darling daughter!
An envoy has come from the land of Lyakhovits,
The son of the king of Lyakhovits;   95
Young Vasili Mikulich is he;
He has come on a friendly mission,
To woo you, my beloved daughter;

[1] The masculine form of her own name.

How shall I receive the envoy?'
His darling daughter replied: 100
'My sire and my dear father!
What are you now thinking of?
Will you bestow a maiden in marriage on a woman?
Her words, her speech are entirely those of a woman;
Her delicate fingers are exactly those of a woman; 105
You can see the traces where she has worn rings;
She presses her thighs together and keeps them held close'.
Vladimir of royal Kiev made answer:
'I will go and make a test of the envoy'.
He went to the envoy from the land of Lyakhovits, 110
Young Vasili Mikulich:
'Now, young Vasili Mikulich!
Would you like after your travels on the road
To go into a steam bath?'
And Vasili Mikulich made answer: 115
'That would be not unpleasant after the journey!'
They heated a steam bath for him.
While Vladimir was making himself ready,
The envoy had steamed himself in the bath,
Left the bath and saluted him: 120
'Many thanks for the steam bath!'
Said Vladimir of royal Kiev:
'Why did you not tarry for me in the bath?
I would have come into the bath to increase the steam for you,[1]
To increase the steam and pour water over you'. 125
Vasili Mikulich gave answer:
'You are in your own home,
Your own princely abode,
Whereas I am on an embassy,
And I cannot spare much time for adorning my person, 130
I cannot spend long steaming myself in the bath;
I have come on a friendly mission,
To woo your beloved daughter'.

[1] For an account of the Russian steam bath, see Hapgood, *Russian Rambles* (London, 1895), p. 267. Cf. also p. 175 ff., below.

Said Vladimir of royal Kiev:
'I will go and discuss it with my daughter'.   135
He went to his darling daughter:
'Hearken, my darling daughter!
An envoy has come from the land of Lyakhovits,
He has come on a friendly mission,
To woo you, my beloved daughter;   140
How shall I receive the envoy?'
Then his darling daughter answered him:
'My sire and my dear father!
What are you now thinking of?
Will you bestow a maiden in marriage on a woman?   145
Her words, her speech are entirely those of a woman;
Her delicate fingers are exactly those of a woman;
You can see the traces where she has worn rings'.
Vladimir of royal Kiev made answer:
'I will go and make a test of the envoy'.   150
He went to Vasili Mikulich,
And spoke as follows:
'Young Vasili Mikulich!
Would you like after your steam bath
To take a rest in a warm bed?'   155
'That would not be unpleasant after the bath.'
When he entered the warm bed,
And lay down on the wooden bedstead,
He laid his head where his feet should be
And he laid his feet on the pillow.   160
When Vladimir of royal Kiev arrived
And looked into the warm bed—
There are the broad heroic shoulders.[1]

---

[1] The singer has not brought out the point of this manœuvre quite
clearly. In the version recorded by Gilferding, *Sbornik*, vol. II, p. 410,
Vladimir promises his daughter to make the test in the following
words:
'We will ensconce him in the royal feather bed.
If he is a man, there will be a little hollow where his shoulders have
    pressed,
But if a woman, it will be under her hips'.

The envoy from the land of Lyakhovits,
Young Vasili Mikulich spoke: 165
'I have come on a friendly mission,
To woo your beloved daughter;
When will you come to terms with me?'
Vladimir of royal Kiev replied:
'I will go and discuss it with my daughter'.   170
He went to his beloved daughter:
'Ah, my darling daughter!
An envoy has come from the land of Lyakhovits—
Young Vasili Mikulich is he:
He has come on a friendly mission,   175
To woo you, my beloved daughter.
How shall I receive the envoy?'
His darling daughter answered him:
'My sire and my dear father!
What are you now thinking of?   180
Will you bestow a maiden in marriage on a woman?'
Said Vladimir of royal Kiev:
'I will go and make a test of the envoy'.—
'Hearken, young Vasili Mikulich!
Would it please you to go and amuse yourself with my courtiers,
To go with them into the spacious court-yard,   186
And shoot at a gold ring—
Into its sharp edge—
And split it in two pieces with your arrow,
So that they shall be of equal size and both alike?'   190
The prince's archer began to shoot first.
The first time he shot, his arrow fell short;
The second time he shot, he overshot the mark;
The third time he shot, his arrow did not come down.
When Vasili Mikulich began to shoot,   195
He quickly stretched his taut bow,
Pressed his tempered arrow upon it,
Shot it into the golden ring,
Into its sharp edge,
And split it in two pieces with his arrow.   200

They were of equal size and both alike.
He spoke as follows:
'Our Sun Vladimir of royal Kiev!
I have come on a friendly mission,
To woo your beloved daughter;   205
When will you come to terms with me?'
Vladimir of royal Kiev replied:
'I will go and discuss it with my daughter'.
He went to his darling daughter:
'Hearken, my darling daughter!   210
An envoy has come from the land of Lyakhovits—
Young Vasili Mikulich is he:
He has come on a friendly mission,
To woo you, my beloved daughter.
How shall I receive the envoy?'   215
His darling daughter answered him:
'What are you now thinking of?
Will you bestow a maiden in marriage on a woman?
Her words, her speech are entirely those of a woman;
Her delicate fingers are exactly those of a woman;   220
You can see the traces where she has worn rings'.
'I will go and make a test of the envoy.'
He went to Vasili Mikulich,
And spoke as follows:
'Young Vasili Mikulich,   225
Would it please you to go and amuse yourself with my
       boyars,
To wrestle together in the spacious court-yard?'
When they entered the spacious court-yard
Then young Vasili Mikulich
Seized one in one hand, another in the other,[1]
And a third he crushed between them.   230
Three at a time he laid them low,
And whoever he laid low did not rise again.
Vladimir of royal Kiev spoke:

[1] It will be noticed that the numbering of the lines is incorrect. I have followed that of the Russian text for convenience of reference.

'Young Vasili Mikulich!
Restrain your heroic heart,   235
Leave us some people to carry on the race!'
Vasili Mikulich gave answer:
'I have come on a friendly mission,
To woo your beloved daughter.   239
If she is not given honourably, I will take her ignominiously,
I will take her ignominiously—I will crush your sides in'.
He no longer went to ask his daughter,
He betrothed her forthwith.
They made a feast lasting three days,
On the third day they went to the Church of God.   245
Vasili grew sad and full of sorrow.
Said Vladimir of royal Kiev:
'Why, Vasili, are you unhappy?'
Said Vasili Mikulich:
'For this reason my heart is sad.   250
Either my father is dead,
Or else my mother has died;
Have you no player on the gusli,
Who could play on the gusli of maple-wood?'
Then they brought out their gusli players,   255
And they all played, but not gaily enough.
'Have you no young warders?'
They brought out the young warders,
They all played, but not gaily enough.
Said Vasili Mikulich: 260
'I heard from my dear father
That our Staver Godinovich had been shut up
In a deep cellar of yours:
He was an expert player on the gusli of maple-wood'.
Said Vladimir of royal Kiev: 265
'If I set Staver at liberty
I shall never see Staver again;
But if I do not set Staver at liberty
I shall anger the envoy!'
And he dared not anger the envoy—   270

He released Staver from his cellar.
He began to play on the gusli of maple-wood,
And Vasili Mikulich cheered up,
And spoke as follows:
'Do you recollect, Staver, do you recall,   275
How we played in the street as children,
You and I played at svaechka.[1]—
The silver nail was yours,
And the golden ring mine.
Sometimes I would strike,   280
And then it would be your turn'.
Staver Godinovich replied:
'Surely I never played at svaechka with you!'
But Vasili Mikulich continued:
'Do you recollect, Staver, do you recall,   285
How we even learned to write together?
I was the silver ink-stand,
And you the gilt pen.
Now I would make a flourish,
And then it would be your turn'.   290
Staver Godinovich made answer:
'Surely I never learnt writing with you!'
Vasili Mikulich spoke:
'Our Sun Vladimir of royal Kiev!
Will you let Staver go out to my white tent,   295
To look at my bold druzhina?'
Vladimir of royal Kiev observed:
'If I let Staver go, I shall never see him again,
But if I do not let Staver go, I shall anger the envoy!'
And he dared not anger the envoy.   300
He let Staver go out to the white tent,
To look at the bold druzhina.
They rode up to the white tent,
Vasili entered the fine white tent,
Put off her male attire,   305
And dressed herself in woman's clothes,

                    [1] A kind of game.

And spoke as follows:
'Do you know me now, Staver?'
Staver Godinovich gave answer:
'Young Vasilista Mikulichna!   310
Let us depart to the Politovski land!'
Vasilista Mikulichna replied:
'It does not beseem a fine youth like you
To steal away from Kiev like a thief:
Let us go and play out the wedding to the end!'   315
They went to the Sun Vladimir,
They seated themselves at the table of oak.
Vasili Mikulich spoke:
'Our Sun Vladimir of royal Kiev!
Why was Staver Godinovich shut up   320
In your deep cellar?'
Vladimir of royal Kiev replied:
'He boasted of his young wife,
That she would outwit all my princes and boyars,
And hoodwink me, their Sun Vladimir'.   325
'Ah, Vladimir of royal Kiev!
Now what are you thinking of?
Will you bestow a maiden in marriage on a woman—
On me, Vasilista Mikulichna?'
Then our Sun Vladimir was ashamed;   330
He hung his rebellious head,
And spoke as follows:
'Young Staver Godinovich!
For your mighty boast,
Trade in our city of Kiev,   335
In the city of Kiev, free of tax for ever!'
They set off to the land of Lyakhovits,
To the king of Lyakhovits.
There they sing the song of Staver for all time,
On the peaceful blue sea,   340
For all you good people to hear.

XIV

Sadko, the Rich Merchant of Novgorod

THE history of Sadko, the rich merchant of Novgorod, consists of three, or perhaps four, main periods. In one *bylina* published by Kirêevski[1] he appears to have lived originally on the Volga, and to have removed to Novgorod at the end of twelve years. In some versions[2] he appears to have begun life as a minstrel—a player on the *gusli* (cf. pp. 86, 131 above). When, however, the people began to grow tired of his music, a nymph of Lake Ilmen, or, in other versions, the Tsar of the Sea, granted him wealth. With this he bought ships, and set up as a merchant, and the second period of his life is spent in foreign voyages. In the third, he is cast overboard by his crew in the hope of allaying a storm, and spends thirty years in the palace of the Tsar of the Sea. At the end of that period, by the intervention of St Nikolai, he is restored to his crew on the quay at Novgorod, and it all seems to have happened in a single night.

In this story the supernatural plays a large part, larger than in the *byliny* of the Kiev Cycle, generally speaking. Some of the *motifs* are found widespread in other literatures. We may refer to the story of the Tsar of the Sea who dances to Sadko's music and whose dancing causes storms at sea. A story very similar to this was current in Japan in the eighth century.[3] The story of the nymph of Lake Ilmen is probably connected with the Rusalkas or water nymphs of Russian folk-lore, immortalised by Pushkin in his Opera *Rusalka*. Analogies can indeed be found in the literatures of other peoples for most of the *motifs* in the *byliny* of Sadko.

[1] Kirêevski, pt. v, p. 47 ff.
[2] E.g. the version transl. by Kate Blakey, *Slavonic Review*, vol. III, p. 57 ff.
[3] See my paper, 'Notes on Polynesian Mythology', in the *Journal of the Royal Anthropological Institute*, vol. LX (1930), p. 425 ff.

In spite of these elements from folk-lore, Sadko is generally believed to have had an historical existence. According to the chronicles of Novgorod and Pskov respectively, in 1167 one Sadko raised a stone church in Novgorod to the Saints Boris and Gleb—a fact which is noted in certain of the *byliny*.[1] At this period Novgorod was at the height of its prosperity, in the full stream of European commercial life. The story of Sadko, his great wealth, his trading enterprise, and his long voyages no doubt reflect some elements of the wealthy merchant princes of the rich northern city, in spite of the fantastic nature of his adventures. It has, indeed, been suggested that Sadko's name indicates that he was a Jew, of whom there were already many in Novgorod. He is a merchant in the true commercial sense of the term. He does not concern himself in the stormy politics of Novgorod when he is at home, or in piracy or warlike enterprises when abroad.

The Heroic Age of Novgorod was, indeed, a thing of the remote and forgotten past. The heroic form of poetry had lingered on as a tradition or been introduced from a more backward artistic milieu elsewhere, embodying new themes and a large element of the marvellous. Even the form was not unaffected by medieval Europe. The single incident worked up and elaborated, which is characteristic of the *byliny* of Kiev as a whole, is not unaffected in the story or Cycle of Sadko by the form of the medieval Chronicle poem of Western Europe, according to which a number of incidents are related in succession in more summary form. In the *bylina* of Vasili Buslaevich this tendency has gone much farther, resulting in what is practically a chronicle of the life of the hero.

[1] Brodski, etc., *op. cit.* p. 117[1]; Khrushchov, *O Drevne-Russkikh Istoricheskikh Povêstyakh i Skazaniyakh* ('Ancient Russian Historical Povêsty and Skazany', Kiev, 1878), p. 7; Rambaud, *La Russie Épique*, p. 153.

SADKO, THE RICH MERCHANT OF NOVGOROD

Recorded by Kirsha Danilov

Kirêevski, *Pêsni,* pt. v, p. 41 ff.

As over the sea, the blue sea,
There sailed, there sped thirty ships,
Thirty ships, one falcon ship
Belonged to Sadko, the rich merchant.
And while all those ships were flying like falcons,   5
One falcon ship was becalmed on the sea;
Sadko the trader, the rich merchant, spoke:
'Ho you clerks, you hired men,
You hired men, subordinates!
Assemble all of you in your places   10
And carve lots in heavy wood blocks,
And all of you write your names on them,
And throw them into the blue sea'.
Sadko threw a light one made of hops,
And on it he had inscribed his signature,   15
And Sadko himself pronounced judgment:
'Ho you clerks, you hired men,
Hearken to my just words:
Let us fling them into the blue sea.
Those of us which float upon the surface—   20
Theirs must be righteous souls,
But whichever of them sink into the sea—
We will drown them into the blue sea'.
But all the lots floated on the surface,
As if they had been ducks bobbing on the water.   25
One lot only sank into the sea,
Into the sea sank the lot made of hops,
The lot of Sadko, the rich merchant.
Sadko the trader, the rich merchant, spoke:
'Ho you clerks, you hired men,   30
Hired men, subordinates,
Cut lots made of willow,

And write all your names upon them;
And I pronounce this judgment upon them:
Whichever lots sink into the sea— 35
Theirs must be righteous souls!'
But Sadko threw in a steel lot,
Even of blue steel from beyond the sea,
A whole twenty pood in weight.
And all the lots sank in the sea.— 40
One lot only floated on the surface,
The lot of Sadko, the rich merchant.
Then spoke Sadko the trader, the rich merchant:
'Ho you clerks, you hired men,
You hired men, subordinates, 45
I myself, Sadko—I know, I see—
I have traversed the sea for twelve years.
To the Tsar beyond the Sea
I have never paid tribute, or duty,
And in the blue Khvalinsk Sea[1] 50
I never threw bread and salt.—
Upon me, Sadko, has death fallen;
And do you, ye traders, rich merchants,
You, my dear sworn companions,
All of you good vendors, 55
Bring me my cloak of sables'.
And hastily Sadko arrayed himself,
He took his resounding gusli,
With splendid strings of gold,
And he took his precious chessboard 60
With its golden pieces,
Its precious carved pieces,
And they lowered the gangway of silver,
Of silver covered with red gold.
Sadko the trader, the rich merchant, walked along it, 65
And let himself down into the blue sea;

[1] This name occurs very commonly in the *byliny*, and appears to be used of different seas. Here the geography of the poem makes it clear that the reference is to the Baltic.

He seated himself on his golden chessboard;
And the clerks, the hired people,
The hired people, the subordinates,
Drew back the gangway of silver,   70
Of silver covered with red gold,
Drew it on to the falcon ship,
And Sadko was left in the blue sea.
And the falcon ship departed over the sea.
And all the ships flew like falcons;   75
But one ship sped over the sea
Like a white hawk,—
The ship of Sadko, the rich merchant.
Loud were the prayers of the father and mother
Of Sadko, the rich merchant.   80
Calm weather set in
Bearing along Sadko, the rich merchant.
Sadko the trader, the rich merchant,...
Saw neither mountains nor shore...
Sadko was carried to the shore,   85
And there he, Sadko, marvelled.
Sadko emerged on the steep strand,
Sadko walked beside the fiery[1] sea,
He...came upon a grand izba,[2]
A grand izba, built entirely of wood;   90
He found the doorway and he entered the izba;
And there lay the Tsar of the Sea on a bench:
'All hail to you, trader, rich merchant,
God has granted me my heart's desire'.
And Sadko remained there for twelve years.   95
And then the Tsar of the Sea bethought him of Sadko.
'Play, Sadko, on the resounding gusli.'
And Sadko began to entertain the Tsar,
He began to play on the resounding gusli,
And the Tsar of the Sea began to caper and dance.   100
He plied this Sadko, the rich merchant,

[1] I.e. with the rays of the setting sun (Ed.).
[2] The *izba* is the wooden hut of the Russian peasants.

With drinks of every kind;
Sadko drank his fill of all kinds of drinks,
And Sadko fell down, for he was quite drunk.
And Sadko the trader, the rich merchant, fell asleep,   105
And in his sleep Saint Nikolai appeared to him,
And addressed him in the following words:
'Hearken, Sadko, trader, rich merchant!
Rend asunder your golden strings,
And cast away your resounding gusli.   110
Your playing has plunged the Tsar of the Sea into a fit of dancing,
And the blue sea has grown rough,
And the swift streams have overflowed.
Many falcon ships are sinking,
Many sinful souls are sinking,—   115
Souls of our orthodox people'.
At this Sadko, the trader, the rich merchant,
He rent asunder his golden strings,
And cast away his resounding gusli;
The Tsar of the Sea ceased capering and dancing,   120
The blue sea grew calm,
The swift streams became tranquil,
And in the morning the Tsar of the Sea began,
He began to exhort Sadko:—
For the Tsar of the Sea wished to marry Sadko,   125
And he brought before him thirty maidens.
Nikolai enjoined him in his sleep:
'Hearken, you trader, you rich merchant,
The Tsar of the Sea is about to marry you,
He is bringing thirty maidens.—   130
Do not take a fair, white, rosy one,
Take a kitchen wench,
The foulest kitchen wench of all'.
And then Sadko, the trader, the rich merchant,
He made his choice and did not hesitate,   135
And he took a kitchen wench,
The foulest kitchen wench of all;
Sadko awoke from his sleep.

He found himself close to the city of Novgorod,
And his left foot was in the River Volkhov;[1]   140
And Sadko leapt up; he was startled;
Sadko cast his eyes on Novgorod.
He recognised the church, his own parish,
That of Nikolai Mozhaiski.
He crossed himself with his cross,   145
And Sadko gazed on the River Volkh.—
From the blue Khvalinsk Sea,
Over the glorious mother, the River Volkh,
There sped, there flew towards him thirty ships.
One was the ship of Sadko himself, the rich merchant;   150
And Sadko the trader, the rich merchant, welcomed them,
His dear sworn companions.
All the ships came to shore.
They cast their gangways on the steep strand.
The sworn companions stepped forth on to the steep strand,
And there Sadko gave them greeting;   156
'All hail to you, my dear sworn companions,
And worthy clerks!'
And then Sadko the trader, the rich merchant,
Made valuation from all the ships in the customs office 160
Of his twenty thousand treasures—
The estimate was not completed in three days.

[1] The Volkhov is the river on which Novgorod stands.

XV

Vasili Buslaev

LIKE Sadko, the hero of the following *bylina* belongs to
the burgher class. He was well educated. He is
spoken of in the Chronicle of Novgorod as a *posadnik*
or governor, but in the opening lines of the following version I believe that we have an obscure reference to his
father's rank as *tysyatski*, the title of the second official of
Novgorod, next in rank to the *posadnik*. These ranks were
of technical significance and peculiar to the Republic of
Novgorod, and are sometimes forgotten or corrupted by
the reciters as something unfamiliar to them. The story of
Vasili and his exploits gives a vivid reflection of the clashing
interests and stormy politics which were such a prominent
feature of the city life of the rich trading Republic. His exploits are of a less romantic nature than those of Sadko. Those
of early life take place chiefly in the streets of Novgorod, and
partake of the nature of street brawls between himself and
his *druzhina*, and groups of truculent citizens. In later life he
ventures farther afield. Like a true son of My Lord Novgorod
the Great, he takes ship and visits foreign parts. His chief expedition is down the Volga to Tsargrad and on pilgrimage to
Jerusalem. He dies on the return journey from the Holy City.

The atmosphere of the *byliny* of Vasili is a strong contrast to that of Sadko. The supernatural element is very
slight and confined to the closing scenes. The style is simpler
and more literal, though the traditional heroic diction still
lingers on as a conscious literary artifice, used for the most
part humorously. In many versions the treatment of the
hero partakes of the nature of burlesque. This humorous
element varies according to the taste and personality of the
reciters. It will be seen that Kirsha Danilov regards his hero
with some seriousness. He would even persuade us that
Vasili was a champion of Christianity and a great benefactor

of the Church. He makes liberal contributions to the tradesmen's guild on the vigil of St Nikolai, and did he not himself
make a pilgrimage to Jerusalem? He did not wish to quarrel
with the citizens; indeed he tried to part the combatants; but
they boxed his ears.

It is probable that Kirsha's rationalised and church-loving
hero has preserved a truer form of the tradition than the
mock-heroic burlesque which is emphasised by the northern
school of reciters. It is possible that Vasili, like Sadko,
was a historical person, a good citizen and a supporter of the
Church. In the year 1171 the Chronicle of Novgorod records a notice of the death at Novgorod of 'Vaska Buslaevich', who is there styled the *posadnik*,[1] i.e. governor of the
city. Vasili, therefore, may be a contemporary of Sadko.
An early MS from Pskov also refers to one 'Fome Buslaevich' as Posadnik.[2]

The *byliny* of Vasili are interesting from a literary point
of view. The form shows a tendency to chronicle in rapid
succession events covering a long period of time, rather than
to concentrate on a single incident. They begin with a brief
account of his father, the worthy and politic old Buslaev,
and follow his son through his childhood and education, his
turbulent youth, his enterprising travels to his death. In this
respect they approximate more closely to the medieval
romances than to the narratives of Kiev. They may be free
of Western influence, however. The same form of chronicle
exists among the Kara-Kirghiz in the poem *Joloi* side by side
with the *Manas* poems, which select and elaborate only individual incidents from the career of the hero for treatment as
an artistic unit.[3]

Elements borrowed from folk-tale are common in the
byliny which relate Vasili's journey to Jerusalem. He en-

[1] Rambaud, *La Russie Épique*, pp. 144, 153; cf. Hapgood, *Epic
Songs of Russia*, p. 281 f. The version of the Chronicle of Novgorod
published by N. Forbes, Beasley, etc., does not mention either Vasili
or Sadko.

[2] Brodski, etc., *op. cit.* p. 110.

[3] See Radlov, *Proben der Volkslitteratur der Türkischen Stämme
Süd-Sibiriens* (St Petersburg, 1868), vol. v, *passim*.

counters a number of portents which lay a number of pro-
hibitions or *tabus* upon him. All of these he violates, and in
violating the last *tabu* he meets his end. The most interesting
is the incident of the skull. As he crossed a mountain he
chanced to kick a skull lying by the path. The skull speaks
to him in protest, claiming that it had once been a hero and
was deserving of his greater respect. But Vasili spat upon it
and passed on. The incident of the skull, and probably the
other *tabus* also, belong to the common body of ancient
Russian oral folk-lore. A similar incident is related in Nestor's Chronicle of Prince Oleg Svyatoslavich. It is curious
how commonly we find in the literature of all countries that
the violation of *tabu* involves a certain aggressive and
truculent attitude on the part of the hero. Lack of respect
for things held sacred by others brings its own punishment.
These *tabus* are the only resource which the more refined
and intellectual elements in the community can utilise effectively against strength and brutality. When they are enforced
effectively it is a sure sign that the Heroic Age is over. The
individualism and the strong local colour of the *byliny* of
Vasili are also post-heroic. These *byliny* are the work of
poets living in an advanced political milieu, applying with
humour and vivacity the traditional heroic narrative form to
contemporary political conditions for satirical purposes. The
result is a delightful mock-heroic poem unique in Russian
popular literature.

VASILI BUSLAEV

Sung by Fedotov

Rybnikov, *Pésni*, vol. 1, p. 368 ff.

Buslav lived in Novgorod,
Buslav lived for ninety years,
Buslav ruled as *tysyatski*,[1]

[1] The word in the text is *tysyachu* (n. *tysyacha*, 'thousand'), but the
singer no doubt referred to the office of *tysyatski*, the ancient title
of the second official of Novgorod next in rank to the *posadnik* or
governor.

But as long as he lived he was never too old to rule,
He was never too old to rule, he was never displaced.   5
Buslav never wrangled with the citizens of Novgorod,
He never disputed with stone-built Moscow.
He left behind him a beloved son,
Young Vasili Buslavevich.
And Vasili began to walk abroad in the city,   10
He began to play pranks on the children;
Whoever he pulled by the arm, the arm came off,
Whoever he pulled by the leg, that leg was no more.
Their mothers began to pursue Vasili,
They began to pursue him and make complaint: 15
'Hearken, honourable widow Amelfa Timofeevna!
Take away your dear son:
If you do not take away Vasili Buslaev,
We will duck him in the River Volkhov'.
In bitter sorrow   20
Vasili distilled green wine,
Vasili brewed sweet mead,
Vasili prepared an honourable feast
For the company of princes and boyars,
And for the citizens of Novgorod.   25
And Vasili spoke as follows:
'Whoever will empty a cup of green wine,
A cup containing a huge measure,
A cup weighing a heavy weight,
And whoever can endure my club of red elm-wood,   30
Let such come to my feast!'
Young Potanyushka came to the feast,
Young Potanyushka the valiant,
He came with limping gait and looks askance,
He took the cup in one hand,   35
He drained the cup at one draught.
Vasili Buslavevich beat him
About his rebellious head,
But Potanyushka endured it, he did not quail.   40
His golden curls were not ruffled,

He made his bow and went to the feast.
Kostya Novotorzhanin also came to the feast.
Then Vasili Buslavevich,
He set out the table of oak, 45
He spread it with sugared foods,
He spread it with honeyed drinks,
With mead which was quite mellow;
He rolled out casks into the fortified court-yard.
'Eat your fill of my food 50
And drink yourselves drunk on my drink,
Only do not take to quarrelling among yourselves'.
Then the citizens of Novgorod,
They ate their fill,
And they drank themselves drunk. 55
The red sun sank towards evening,
The honourable feast waxed merry,
And they all became merrily drunk,
And took to quarrelling among themselves.
And Vasili seized his club of red elm-wood, 60
And began to lay about him right and left,
And took to belabouring the guests.
And the guests left the honourable feast all maimed.
'Devil take you and your feast, Vasili!
There has been too much eating and drinking at the
feast, 65
And we have been crippled for life'.
Then the citizens of Novgorod,
They prepared their own honourable feast
For the company of princes and boyars,
And the mighty Russian heroes. 70
Vasili set off to the honourable feast;
But he did not go alone, he took his druzhina.
And his dear mother said to him:
'Hearken, my dear son,
Young Vasili Buslavevich! 75
You are going to an honourable feast
Where all the guests have been invited,

While you are going as an uninvited guest'.
'Hearken, dear mother,
Honourable widow Amelfa Timofeevna!   80
Even if I go as an uninvited guest,
Where there are seats, there I sit,
And what I can reach with my hand, I eat and drink'.
And Vasili went to the honourable feast;
But he did not go alone, he took his druzhina.   85
He held the cross in the manner prescribed,
He made his bow as it is enjoined:
'Greetings, Mikula Selyaninovich!¹
Greetings, Kozma Rodionovich!'
'Come along, Vasili Buslavevich,   90
Take a seat, Vasili, at the table of oak'.
Vasili took his seat in the place of honour;
Not alone did he seat himself, but his druzhina with him.
Then the guests who had been invited protested,
'Ho, Vasili Buslavevich,   95
You seat yourself in the place of honour
Though you are an uninvited guest,
And we other guests were invited'.
'Even if I am an uninvited guest,
Where there are seats, there I sit,   100
And what I can reach with my hand, I eat and drink'.
The red sun sank towards evening,
The honourable feast waxed merry,
And they all became merrily drunk,
And began to boast of this and that.   105
Then Vasili Buslavevich
In his drunken folly,
He laid a great wager,
To go at daybreak to the Volkhov,
To go with his druzhina,   110
And to fight against all the men of Novgorod.
Then Vasili left the honourable feast,

¹ The editor suggests that this is an error for Mikula or Vikula
Zinovevich. Cf. also Magnus, *Heroic Ballads of Russia*, p. 143.

His head drooped over his right shoulder,
His eyes were downcast towards the damp earth.
He went to the princely palace,   115
His dear mother greeted him:
'Alas, my beloved son,
Young Vasili Buslavevich.
Why are you distressed and afflicted?
Was the place assigned to you not according to your
    rank,   120
Or did they pass you by when handing round the cup,
Or have the citizens mocked you in their drunkenness?'
Vasili could not give his mother
Either response or greeting.
But his bold druzhina spoke: 125
'The place assigned to Vasili was according to his rank,
And they did not pass him by when handing round the cup,
Nor did the citizens mock him in their drunkenness;
But Vasili has laid a great wager
With the citizens of Novgorod,   130
To go at daybreak to the Volkhov,
To go with his druzhina,
And to fight against all the men of Novgorod'.
Then his dear mother,
The honourable widow Amelfa Timofeevna,   135
Thrust her shoes on to her bare feet,
Flung her sable cloak over one shoulder,
Took her golden keys,
And went into her deep cellars,
Filled a bowl with red gold,   140
And another bowl with pure silver,
And a third bowl with round pearls,
And came to the citizens at the honourable feast.
She held the cross in the manner prescribed,
She made her bow as it is enjoined: 145
'Greetings, Mikula Selyaninovich,
Greetings, Kozma Rodionovich!'
And she placed her gifts on the table of oak.

'Accept these gifts from Vasili
And pardon Vasili his fault'.   150
The citizens of Novgorod made answer:
'We will not receive gifts from Vasili,
And we will not pardon Vasili his fault.
Rather may God help us to overcome Vasili,
And to ride his good steeds,   155
And to wear his patterned robes,
And to take his golden treasure by force'.
Then the honourable widow Amelfa Timofeevna
Turned away from the honourable feast,
And kicked with her right foot   160
That cudgel of maple-wood—
And the cudgel flew away behind the fence,
Behind the fence, scattering everything in its course.[1]
Vasili slept till dawn and took his ease,
Unconscious of the misfortunes which had befallen him.   165
But a serving-maid approached him,
Coming for water to the spring,
And she addressed him thus:
'Alas, Vasili Buslavevich!
While you sleep and take your ease,   170
You are unconscious of the misfortunes which have befallen you:
Your bold druzhina are fighting
On the bridge over the Volkhov,
Their rebellious heads broken,
Their eyes all bandaged with kerchiefs'.   175
Then Vasili Buslavevich,
Very quickly he awoke from his heavy sleep,
Thrust his shoes on to his bare legs,
Flung his sable cloak over one shoulder,
And seized his club of red elm-wood,   180
And sped to the bank of the Volkhov.

[1] The singer has not remembered the story well at this point.
Vasili's mother hid his club, etc. in order to prevent his keeping his
compact to fight the citizens. She then administered a sleeping potion
and locked him up.

And an old monk from the Andronova[1] monastery encountered
    Vasili,
On the bridge over the Volkhov,
Wearing on his head the great bell of St Sophia.
And Vasili Buslavevich addressed him: 185
'Ho, you old monk of Andronova,
My godfather!
You did not receive an egg on Easter Sunday,
So I will give you an egg on St Peter's day'.
And he belaboured him with his club of red elm-wood   190
About the great bell of St Sophia,
And killed the old monk of Andronova, his godfather.
And he ran to the bank of the Volkhov,
And began to lay about him with his club:
Where he struck, a street was formed through the fallen,   195
Where he brandished his club a lane was made,
And he slew all the citizens of Novgorod.
And the citizens went to Vasili's mother.
'We pray you, dear mother of Vasili,
Honourable widow Amelfa Timofeevna!   200
Take away your dear son,
Leave enough of the citizens to carry on the race'.
Then his dear mother,
The honourable widow Amelfa Timofeevna,
She thrust her shoes on to her bare feet,   205
Flung her sable cloak over one shoulder,
And sped to the bank of the Volkhov,
Enveloped Vasili in her sable cloak,
And bore him off to her palace of white stone,
And cared for and tended the bold noble youth.   210

[1] Again the singer has omitted several details of the story. When
Vasili had been fighting for some time, and dealing great slaughter
among the men of Novgorod, they went to intercede with his mother,
who advised them to persuade his godfather, an old monk, to come and
appease him.

XVI

Vasili Buslaev

A VARIANT VERSION

Recorded by Kirsha Danilov, from the miners in Perm

Kirêevski, *Pésni*, pt. v, p. 14 ff.

(The following translation is from the abridged text published by
Dormidontov, *Kratki Kurs Istorii Russkoy Literaturÿ* (Tallinn, 1923),
p. 207 ff.)

In glorious Novgorod the Great,
Buslay dwelt for ninety years;
He dwelt with the people of Novgorod and never gainsaid
  them;
To the citizens of Novgorod
He never ventured a word of opposition.   5
Buslay lived to a good old age,
A good old age, and at last he died.
After his long life
He left his property
And all his noble estate;   10
He left a venerable widow,
The venerable Amelfa Timofeevna,
And he left a little child,
His young son, Vasili Buslaevich.
When Vasili was seven years old,   15
His dear mother sent him—
The venerable widow Amelfa Timofeevna—
To learn the art of reading.
And he mastered the art of reading.
She set him to writing with his pen,   20
And he mastered the art of writing.
She sent him to learn church singing,
And he mastered the art of singing.
And never had we had singing

In glorious Novgorod   25
To compare with that of Vasili Buslaev.
But Vasili Buslaevich began to consort
With drunkards and fools,
And the joyous, bold, fine youths.[1]
Then he took to drinking himself drunk,   30
And roamed about the city maiming people;
Whoever he caught by the arm—
He wrenched off that arm at the shoulder,
And whoever he seized by the spine,
That person shrieked, roared, and crept about on all fours. 35
There arose a great outcry,
And the citizens of Novgorod,
The burgesses and the merchants,
They lodged a great complaint
With the venerable widow Amelfa Timofeevna,   40
Against this same Vasili Buslaev;
And his mother proceeded to chide and rebuke him,
To chide and rebuke him, and to teach him sense;
But scolding was not to Vasili's liking.
He took himself off to an upper room,   45
He seated himself on a leather chair,
And he wrote proclamations in handwriting,
And the matter was set down skilfully:
'Whoever wishes to drink and eat at pleasure,
Let them throng to Vasili's broad court-yard,   50
And there drink and eat at will,
And receive patterned garments of all kinds'.
He dispersed the proclamations by the hand of his servant,
In the broad streets,
And in the narrow alleys,   55

---

[1] I think that this is a reference to the *veselÿe lyudi* (lit. 'joyous people'), a powerful guild or body of popular entertainers, who, together with the *skomorokhi* (see p. 27 above), played a prominent part in Russian social life from the late Middle Ages down to the close of the seventeenth century. Numerous ecclesiastical proscriptions were published against them, and they were finally suppressed.

And then Vasili stationed a vat in the midst of the court,
And filled the vat with green wine,
And dipped in it a goblet of huge measure.
Now in glorious Novgorod
The people were educated;   60
They read the writing of the proclamations,
And went to Vasili's spacious court,
To the vat of green wine;
First of all came Kostya Novotorzhenin.
Kostya entered the spacious court   65
And Vasili made trial of him,
He began to beat him with a club of red elm,
With a core in the centre
Of weighty lead from the east.
This elm club weighed twelve pud [1]   70
And he beat Kostya over his rebellious head;
But Kostya proved his worth, he did not flinch,
And on his rebel head the curls did not stir;
Vasili Buslaevich spoke:
'Hearken, Kostya Novotorzhenin!   75
Be my sworn brother,
More to me than a brother born'.
And when they had lingered together for a short time
There came two brothers of boyar class,
Luke and Moses, a boyar's sons.   80
They came into Vasili's spacious court.
Young Vasili Buslaevich,
At once he welcomed and made merry with these youths.
Then came citizens from Zaleshen,
But Vasili did not dare show himself to them.   85
Moreover there came the seven brothers Sbrodovichi;
There collected and assembled
Thirty youths save one,
And Vasili himself made the thirtieth;
Whoever came their way, him they felled,   90
They felled him and flung him forth.

> [1] Cf. p. 47, footnote 1, above.

Vasenka Buslaevich heard
That among the men of Novgorod
The vigil-ale was brewed, the barley brew.
So Vasili set off with his druzhina,   95
He went to the guild of St Nikolai:
'We will not pay you a paltry fee;
We will pay five roubles for every brother'.
And for himself Vasili gave fifty roubles.
And the churchwarden   100
Received them into the guild of St Nikolai.
Then they began by drinking the vigil-ale,
This same barley brew.
Then young Vasili Buslaevich,
He made off to the royal inn[1]   105
With his bold druzhina;
Here they drank their fill of green wine
And returned to the guild of St Nikolai.
The day drew towards evening,
From young and old   110
The boys then began wrestling,
And boxing in the ring.
From this wrestling of the boys,
From this fighting with fisticuffs,
A mighty brawl arose;   115
Young Vasili tried to part the combatants,
But a certain fool obstructed him,
And boxed his ears.
Then Vasili cried out in a loud voice:
'Hearken, Kostya Novotorzhenin,   120
And Luke, Moses, boyar's sons,
They are beating Vasili here'.
The bold noble youths came hurrying up,
They soon made a clearance,
Many they beat to death,   125

---

[1] Spirits were regarded as a monopoly of the Crown in Russia and formed a part of the royal revenues. The inns bore the royal arms, the Russian eagle. Cf. p. 259 below.

They maimed them two and three at a time,
Breaking their arms and legs.
The burghers of the city screamed and roared,
Then Vasili Buslaevich spoke:
'Hearken, ye citizens of Novgorod,   130
I will lay a great wager with you,
I will attack all Novgorod,
Fighting and contending,
I and all my bold druzhina.
If you men of Novgorod should overcome me and my
      druzhina,   135
I will pay you tribute from now until my death,
Three thousand roubles every year;
But if I should overcome you
And you have to yield to me,
You must pay me the same tribute'.   140
And to this compact they set their hands.
Then a mighty onset took place between them...
Vasili went along the River Volkhov.
And as he came along the River Volkhov,
Along the Volkhov street,   145
The noble youths descried him,
Even his bold druzhina,—
They saw young Vasili Buslaev.
Wings grew on the bright falcons,[1]
Hope dawned for the youths.   150
Young Vasili Buslaevich,
He came to the rescue of the youths.
With those citizens of Novgorod
He fought and contended all day till evening,
And then the citizens yielded,   155
They yielded and made peace.
They took binding documents
To the venerable widow Amelfa Timofeevna,
They filled a bowl with pure silver,

---

[1] This is a figurative expression common in the *byliny*. The explanation follows in the next line.

And another bowl with red gold,   160
And went to the noble dwelling,
Beating the ground with their foreheads and bowing low.
'Venerable lady,
Accept our precious offerings,
And take away your dear son,   165
Young Vasili and his druzhina;
And we will gladly pay
Three thousand roubles every year,
And every year we will bring you
Bread from the bakers,   170
Rolls[1] from the confectioners
And offerings from the young married women,
From the unwed maidens,
From tradesmen and everybody
Except priests and deacons.'   175
Then the venerable widow
Amelfa Timofeevna
Despatched a serving-maid
To fetch Vasili and his druzhina,
                          etc.

[1] For these rolls (*kalachi,* sing. *kalach*), see p. 106 above.

MEDIEVAL BYLINY

XVII

The Princes of Tver

THE city of Tver, which had been founded at the beginning of the twelfth century, fell a victim to the Tartar hordes which swept over North Russia during the years 1237 and 1238. In 1238 Tver was sacked, and became a Mongol dependency. Early in the following century the city made a premature attempt to resist the Tartar yoke. Their leader and governor, Prince Michael, however, was murdered by Prince Yuri of Moscow in the Golden Horde in 1319. In revenge Prince Dimitri, Michael's son, killed Yuri of Moscow in 1325 in the Golden Horde and was executed by Khan Uzbeg ('Tsar Azvyak') for his act. His brother Alexander was appointed grand prince of Tver by Khan Uzbeg, but in 1327 he incited the citizens to murder the Tartar *bashkak* or tax-collector Chol Khan, a first cousin of Khan Uzbeg, in vengeance for the death of Dimitri. The citizens readily rose against the foreign oppressors, and, maddened as they were by the insolence and violence of the *bashkaks*, they burnt Chol Khan in the palace, killing all his followers. The following *bylina* has reference to this event, but the popular singer has forgotten the cruel consequences of the murder. Alexander, the prince of Tver, who had led the insurrection in person, was forced to flee for his life to Pskov, and Tver was cruelly ravaged by 50,000 Tartars in a punitive expedition led by Ivan of Moscow, the brother of the murdered Yuri. After many years Alexander succeeded in obtaining pardon from Uzbeg and was reinstated in Tver; but owing to Ivan's jealousy and his influence with Uzbeg the decision was reversed, and Alexander was killed.

THE PRINCES OF TVER

Recorded by Kirsha Danilov, from the miners in Perm

Kiréevski, *Pésni*, pt. v, p. 186 ff.

It happened in the Horde,
It came to pass in the Great Horde.—
On a golden throne,
On figured velvet,
On purple damask,   5
There sits Tsar Azvyak,
Azvyak Tavrulovich,
Holding tribunal,
Distributing rank,
Flourishing his sceptre,   10
Over the beardless ones,
Over the Tartars,
Over the black-pates.[1]
The Tsar was appointing his lieutenants,
He, Azvyak Tavrulovich,   15
To the royal cities:
Vasili to Pskov,
Gordei to Vologda,
Akhramei to Kostroma.
He made no appointment   20
To one honoured lieutenant:
Shchelkan Dyudentevich.[2]
Why did he not appoint him?
For this reason he did not appoint him:
He was away from home—   25
Young Shchelkan had gone away
Into the distant land of Lithuania,

---

[1] Probably a reference to the Kara Kalpacks (lit. 'Black-Caps')
settled in South Russia.

[2] The word translated 'lieutenant' in the text is *shurin*, lit. 'brother-in-law'. Shchelkan or Chol Khan, however, was not Uzbeg's brother-in-law, but his cousin. Probably the word (*shurin*) is used in a wider (military) sense throughout the poem for the leaders of Uzbeg's army. Rambaud translates 'capitaines'.

Beyond the blue sea;
Young Shchelkan was collecting
Tribute and arrears,   30
The royal revenues which had not been paid.
From princes he exacted a hundred roubles;
From boyars, fifty roubles;
From peasants, five roubles;
Whoever had no money   35
He deprived of his child;
Whoever had no child
He deprived of his wife;
Whoever had no wife
He carried off as a slave.[1]   40
Young Shchelkan seized
Tribute and arrears,
The royal revenues which had not been paid;
Young Shchelkan seized
A horse worth a hundred roubles,   45
A saddle worth a thousand roubles,
A bridle of priceless worth.
Not for this reason was the bridle precious—
Because the bridle was made of gold:
The bridle was precious for this reason—   50
It was a royal gift
From his sovereign lord.
And he would not, said he,
Either sell the bridle, or exchange it,
Or allow anyone else to use it,   55
Save only himself, Shchelkan Dyudentevich.[2]
Young Shchelkan spoke,
Young Shchelkan Dyudentevich:
'Greeting, Tsar Azvyak,
Azvyak Tavrulovich!   60

[1] Lit. carried off his head.
[2] The passage is obscure. Probably the reference is to some exaction made by Shchelkan in preparation for the return journey to Tsar Azvyak; but the account of his journey is omitted.

You have made grants to the youths,
Your dear lieutenants,
(The two bold Borisovichi)[1];
You have placed Vasili in Pskov,
Gordei in Vologda,   65
Akhramei in Kostroma:
Grant, Tsar Azvyak,
Grant to me
Tver the ancient,
Tver the wealthy,   70
And the two brothers,
The two bold Borisovichi'.
Tsar Azvyak replied,
Azvyak Tavrulovich:
'Hearken, my lieutenant,   75
Shchelkan Dyudentevich!
Stab your son,
Your beloved son,
Fill a bowl of his blood,
Drink up this blood,   80
This warm blood,
And then I will grant you
Tver the ancient,
Tver the wealthy,
And the two brothers,   85
The two bold Borisovichi'.
At once young Shchelkan
Stabbed his son,
Filled a bowl of his blood,
His warm blood,   90
And drank up the bowl of that warm blood;
And straightway Tsar Azvyak
Bestowed upon him

---

[1] So Bezsonov; but the line does not seem to belong here. It is omitted by Glazunov in his edition: *Byliny* (St Petersburg, 1912), p. 130. The two Borisovichi are Prince Dimitri and Prince Alexander Mikhailovich of Tver. See Introduction.

Tver the ancient,
Tver the wealthy,   95
And the two brothers,
The two bold Borisovichi.
So now young Shchelkan
Held tribunal
In Tver the ancient,   100
In Tver the wealthy,
But not much tribunal did he hold:
The widows were held in no regard,
Fair maidens were dishonoured,
He must needs insult everybody,   105
And make their families laughing-stocks.
Then the old men,
The wealthy men,
The men of the city,
They made complaint   110
To the two brothers,
The two bold Borisovichi.
On behalf of the people, they came and bowed,
With honourable presents,
And they brought honourable presents,   115
Gold and silver and round pearls.
They came to the house
Of Shchelkan Dyudentevich:
He accepted their presents,
But he did not requite them honourably.   120
Indeed young Shchelkan
Bore himself with hauteur, assumed an arrogant air;
And a quarrel sprang up between them.
One seized him by the hair,
Another by the legs,   125
And thus they rent him asunder.
Thus he met his death.
No one was made to answer for the deed.

XVIII

Prince Roman

THE hero is generally identified with Prince Roman, ruler of Galicia, who lived during the first half of the thirteenth century, the most brilliant period of Galician history. He was a fine soldier and conquered Galicia by the sword, vanquishing also Lithuania and parts of South-West Russia. According to a contemporary Polish writer he treated his enemies with great cruelty, quartering them or burying them alive. In Russian chronicles, however, he figures as a hero and a deliverer, no doubt on account of his victories over their enemies the Polovtsy. He appears to have been the centre of a Cycle of court poetry, most of which has perished, though a certain number of *byliny* relating to him still survive. They do not appear to have retained much historical tradition, though his reputation for savage cruelty has not been forgotten. Skill in magic and the power of shape-changing are attributed to him. His wife is known in the *byliny* as Marina, the White Swan.

PRINCE ROMAN

Recorded by Kirsha Danilov, from the miners in Perm

Kirêevski, *Pésni*, pt. v, p. 108 ff.

Prince Roman murdered his wife,
He murdered his wife, he rent her corpse,
He rent her corpse and threw it into the river,
Into the River Smorodina.
All the birds came flocking,   5
The beasts of the forest came running;
The little blue eagle carried away,

He carried away her little white hand,
Her right hand with its gold ring.
The young princess questioned him,   10
The young princess, Anna Romanovna:
'Oh, my noble father,
Prince Roman Vasilevich!
What have you done with my mother?'
Prince Roman answered her,   15
Prince Roman Vasilevich:
'Oh, my young princess,
My young maiden Anna Romanovna!
Your mother has gone to bathe herself,
To bathe herself and to blanch her skin,[1]   20
And to dress herself in a patterned dress'.
The young princess sped away,
The young maiden Anna Romanovna:
'Oh, my attendants and servants,
Oh, my pretty hand-maids,   25
Let us go to the high terem[2]
To gaze upon my lady mother,
And how she is washing and blanching her skin,
And dressing herself in a patterned dress'.
She went, the young princess,   30
With her attendants and servants,
She walked through all the upper rooms,
But she could not find her mother.
Again she approached her father:
'Oh, my noble father,   35
Prince Roman Vasilevich!
What have you done with my mother?
We could not find her in the upper rooms'.
Prince Roman made answer,

[1] For the profuse application of cosmetics by the Russian women of
the later Middle Ages and the Renaissance, see Rambaud, 'Les Tsarines
de Moscou', in *Revue des Deux Mondes* (Oct. 1873), p. 535 f.
[2] The women's apartments were always in the upper storey or
terem in ancient Russia.

Prince Roman Vasilevich: 40
'Ah, my young princess,
My young maiden Anna Romanovna,
With your attendants and servants,
Your pretty hand-maids!
Your dear mother has gone,   45
Has gone to walk in the green garden,
Among the cherry-trees and the hazels'.
Away went the young princess
With her attendants and her servants into the green garden:
They walked all over it, but no one did they find in the
         green garden.   50
But they descried in the green garden,
They descried something strange:
A little blue eagle carrying something,
Carrying in its talons a white hand,
A white hand with a gold ring.   55
The eagle let fall the white hand,
The white hand with the gold ring,
Into that green garden;
And at once the attendants and servants
Picked up the white hand,   60
And gave it to the young princess,
The young maiden Anna Romanovna;
And when Anna Romanovna
Looked upon the white hand,
She recognised the pure gold ring   65
Of her dear mother;
She fell to the damp earth,
She screamed like a white swan,
Thus did the young princess cry:
'Oh, my attendants and servants,   70
My pretty hand-maids!
Run quickly to the swift river,
To the swift River Smorodina,
And find out why the birds are flocking there,
Why the beasts of the forest are hastily mustering'.   75

The attendants and servants hurried away,
The pretty hand-maids:
At the edge of the River Smorodina
The beasts of the forest were sharing bones,
The magpies and crows were tugging at guts;   80
And there in the green garden
Walked the young maiden Anna Romanovna,
Carrying the white hand,
The white hand with its gold ring,
While her attendants   85
Found a hollow skull.
They took the hollow skull,
And with it all the bones and the ribs:
And they buried the hollow skull,
And the bones and the ribs with it,   90
And the white hand with the gold ring.

XIX

Prince Roman

THE personnel of the following *bylina* have not been identified with certainty, though it is generally thought that Prince Roman is the ruler of Galicia who lived during the first half of the thirteenth century. In spite of the wide divergence in details, the principal *motif* of this *bylina* is probably based on the same historical occurrence as that of the preceding one, and the two heroes are doubtless identical. A comparison of the two poems is of especial interest, as they probably represent not variant versions of a single original composition, but two independent compositions based on an identical occurrence and carried on for several centuries by oral tradition.

PRINCE ROMAN

Recorded from Archangel

Kirêevski, *Pêsni*, pt. v, p. 92 ff.

Once upon a time lived Prince Roman Mitrievich,
He slept with his wife and she dreamed in the night
That her ring fell from her right hand,
From the ring finger of her right hand, the middle finger,
And was shattered into tiny fragments.   5
'Let us publish it abroad throughout all lands,
Throughout all lands, throughout all hordes,
So that they may judge your dream,
So that they may interpret your dream.'
'I myself will judge my dream,   10
I myself will interpret my dream:
There will speed towards me from over the sea

Three ships, three black ships,
They will carry me, Marya, over the blue sea,
Over the blue salt sea,   15
To Yagailo, the son of Manuelo.'
Hardly had he heard her words
Ere he hurried away to the little quiet creeks,
Shooting geese, white swans,
And little feathered, grey ducks.   20
She sat by the window
And looked: there sped from over the sea,
From over the sea, the blue sea,
Three ships, three black ships
They made towards the haven,   25
And Marya saw them: 'They will carry me away
Over the blue salt sea!'
She closed the shutter,
And went into the palace of white stone,
From the white palace on to the new verandah,   30
From the new verandah on to the red staircase,
From the red staircase on to the oak floor,
From the oak floor on to the footpath,
And along the footpath Marya went into the open plain,
And sat under a blossoming apple-tree.   35
And the three black ships sped on
Straight into the haven;
They furled their linen sails,
And cast their steel anchors,
And played out the silken cable,   40
And lowered a light boat into the water,
And seated themselves in the little boat, and came
Straight into the haven,
And they went into the palace of white stone,
And sought for Marya; but they could not find her.   45
But one of them was a thief, a kitchen boy;
He tracked her with a blood-hound and found her tracks at once,
He found them and traced them:
Along the footpath he traced Marya's tracks,

The kitchen boy traced her,   50
And he found her under the blossoming apple-tree:
'Are you Marya Yurevna?'
'I am not Marya Yurevna,
I am Marina the maid-servant.'
'Tell me, are you not Marya Yurevna?'   55
'I am Marya Yurevna, the White Swan.'
He took her by the white hands,
By those same gold rings,
And led her away to the black ship
Over the blue salt sea.   60
And the kitchen boy went
To Manuelo Yagailovich.
He welcomed him with honour and gladness,
He took Marya by her white hands,
By her gold rings,   65
Thinking to kiss her on her sugar lips;
Marya Yurevna said to him:
'We must not kiss for three years,
We must not kiss, or embrace'.
And Manuelo Yagailovich went away   70
To the little quiet creeks,
Shooting geese, white swans,
And little feathered, grey ducks;
He went to his mother and charged her:
'Give her an attendant, a hand-maid,   75
In case she pines'.
She sat by the window,
She gazed through the glass pane;
Then his mother came and questioned her:
'Why do you sit by the window,   80
Why do you weep and shed tears?'
'To-day in my home, in Russia, it is the great holiday,
The great holiday of the resurrection of St Christopher.
Christian women walk abroad,
The womenfolk of the merchants, the ministers, and peasants,
And even the camp followers,   86

And the tavern wenches,
While I sit by the window,
And shed my bitter tears!'
His mother gave her an attendant, a hand-maid,   90
An attendant, a hand-maid, to walk with her in the garden;
She gave her drinks of every kind,
And gave her one of Manuelo's precious goats.
Marya plied her maid with drink until she was full,
So that she lay stupefied;   95
Then Marya took the goat and cut it up;
She went into a high mountain,
Laid aside her patterned robe,
Dressed herself as a forester,
And went down from the mountain   100
Towards the swift river:
And the swift river flowed
Like thunder rumbling.
And Marya prayed to the swift river:
'Oh, you river, mother Darya!   105
Grant me to ford you and go to my husband,
Make a little crossing, a tiny ford,
Help me to escape, me, Marya Yurevna!'
And the river gave ear to Marya.
It let her ford it and go to her husband.   110
She crossed the swift stream,
She went forward on her way.
And she came to a yet broader river,
She saw that she could not cross it;
She decided to float to the far bank,   115
To float on the trunk of an oak-tree.
And Marya prayed to the trunk of the oak-tree:
'Oh, you oak-tree trunk!
Bear me across the swift stream,
So that I may go to holy Russia,—   120
I will carve you into a little cross,
Into a little cross, into a wonder-working image,
And gild it with pure bright gold'.

And the tree trunk gave ear to her:
It bore her across the swift river.   125
And Marya Yurevna came
To Roman Mitrievich,
She spoke as follows:
'Greetings, Roman Mitrievich!
I have been carried on the trunk of an oak-tree   130
Into holy Russia.
Let us carve it into a little cross,
Into a wonder-working image,
And gild it with pure bright gold'.
And they took that oak-tree trunk   135
Into holy Russia;
They carved it into a little cross,
Into a wonder-working image,
And they gilded it with pure bright gold,
And sent it about throughout the churches.   140

XX

Prince Danilo

THE hero of this *bylina* is perhaps to be identified with Daniel, the ruler of Galicia, who succeeded his father Roman (cf. p. 164 above), and was crowned by the Pope in 1254 and died soon after 1260.[1] The *bylina* is interesting on account of the reference which it contains to the singing of popular narrative poetry (*pêsni*) by troops of girls. The poem may well represent historical conditions, if not an actual historical event. The cruelty of Prince Roman is proverbial, and his son Daniel was frequently troubled by revolts, of which the unpopularity of the Danilo of our *bylina* may be a reflection. But the identification is at best doubtful.

PRINCE DANILO

Recorded from Orlovsk

Kirêevski, *Pêsni*, pt. v, p. 183 f.

Prince Danilo was walking,
He was sauntering along the road,
Making eyes at the girls,
And staring after them,
And saying pretty things to them,   5
And promising them silken veils:
'Oh, pretty girls,
Oh, ye maidens!
Sing me a song[2]
About the poor fellow,   10

---

[1] According to Rambaud (*History of Russia*, Engl. transl. by L. B. Lang, vol. I, p. 125) Daniel died in 1264; according to Bain (*Slavonic Europe*, Cambridge, 1908, p. 7), in 1261.

[2] The word in the text is *pêsn*.

About the bold hero,
About Ilya of Murom,
About Egor Tsarevich,[1]
The hero and the son of a hero,
And how he fought the Turks,   15
How he took the Sultan captive,
How he tarred him,
How he cut up all the Turks'.
'We will not
Sing you a song   20
About the poor fellow,
About the bold hero,
About Ilya of Murom,
Or about Egor Tsarevich,
The hero and the son of a hero;   25
But we will sing you a song
About the scoundrel Danilo,
The robber, the pagan,
The villain, the heathen.'
Then Danilo grew pale,   30
And he ordered them all to be executed,
All their white heads to be struck off.
But all the people rose up,
And sent the guards packing,
They drove all the guards away   35
And so came at Danilo himself,
And forthwith slew him.

    [1] Svyatogor or Egor the Brave (Ed.).

XXI

Prince Mikhailo

LIKE the *bylina* which follows (XXII), this poem is classed in Kirêevski's collection among the 'Princely *byliny*' of the early Moscow Cycle. The person of the hero has not been identified, though he may be the same Prince Mikhailo whose death is narrated in the *bylina* below. For a brief note on these *byliny*, see p. 19 f. above.

PRINCE MIKHAILO

Recorded from Tulsk

Kirêevski, *Pêsni*, pt. v, p. 68 f.

When Prince Mikhailo went forth
On the tsar's service,
He commended his bride
To his dear mother:
'Take care of my bride,   5
And feed my bride
On rolls of white wheaten flour,
And give my bride drink
Of sweet mead'.
Hardly had Prince Mikhailo   10
Ridden away from the spacious court-yard
Ere his dear mother
Heated a hot bath,
Heated a hot bath,
And made hot a burning stone:[1]   15
'Let us go, my daughter-in-law,

---

[1] I.e. for the regular Russian steam bath. The steam is made by pouring cold water over red-hot stones heated for the purpose. The steam bath follows the 'washing' process. Reference is made to the steam bath in the *bylina* of Staver translated on p. 123 ff. above.

I will wash you in the bath,
I will wash you in the bath,
I will refresh your body'.
When his mother had placed her   20
On the white bench,[1]
She placed a burning stone
On her white bosom.
When she shrieked the first time
His good steed stumbled: 25
'Alas, friend, something is amiss:
Either your mother is dead
Or your young bride!'
When he rode up to the gateway
His serving-men met him: 30
'Oh, my trusty serving-men,
Is all well with the household?'
'Glory be to God, not wholly.'
He mounted the high staircase,
His attendants met him: 35
'Oh, my attendants, my serving-women,
Is all well with the household?'
'Glory be to God, not wholly.'
He entered the new hall,
The maids of the hall met him: 40
'Oh, my maids of the hall,
Is all well with the household?'
'Glory be to God, not wholly.'
He entered the lofty dwelling,
His mother met him: 45
'My lady mother!
Where, O where is my bride?'
'Your bride is in a well-lighted chamber—.
In an oaken coffin.'

---

[1] I.e. the bench on which a person lies during the steaming process, which is followed by a light birching. For an account of a Russian bathing process, see Hapgood, *Russian Rambles* (London, 1895), p. 266 ff.

His swift legs sank beneath him,   50
His white hands fell limp,
His white hands fell limp,
His bright eyes closed.
His dear mother
Walked around the green grave:[1]   55
'Alas, friends, I have sinned;
I have caused three souls to perish:
I have destroyed my son, and my daughter-in-law,
And her little unborn child'.

[1] Kirêevski wrote the word *požili* with a query; probably for *po želi*, lit. 'around the green', perhaps referring to the grass on the new grave. See editor's note *ad loc.*

XXII

Prince Dimitri

THIS *bylina*, together with the *byliny* on Prince Vasili and Prince Mikhailo, is classed in Kirêevski's collection among the 'Princely *byliny*' of the Moscow Cycle. Although attached to well-known historical names, however, they appear to have little connection with actual history. They belong, moreover, to the milieu of folk-tale and folk-song rather than to that of heroic poetry. The mutilation of a maiden by her suitor in revenge for her scornful mockery forms the *motif* of the Serbian poem *The Sister of Leka Kapetan*.[1] Curiously enough, a phrase not unlike that of Domna Faleleevna's mother regarding dreams also occurs in the Serbian poem of the *Marriage of King Vukasin*, l. 150 f.:

> 'Fear not, dear my lord,
> A good hero hath dreamt a good dream;
> Dreams are lies, God alone is truth'.[2]

The *motif* of the dream is very common in the Serbian *Narodne Pjesme*. The style of most of these 'Princely *byliny*' is very different from that of the old heroic tradition of Kiev, and has much in common with the condensation and directness of the *byliny* of Prince Roman, Prince Danilo, and the Princes of Tver.

---

[1] *The Ballads of Kraljević Marko*, transl. D. H. Low (Cambridge, 1922), p. 29 ff.　　　　[2] *Ibid.* p. 5.

PRINCE DIMITRI

Recorded from Simbirsk

Kirêevski, *Pêsni*, pt. v, p. 63 ff.

As Prince Dimitri was going to Matins,
Domna Faleleevna espied him through the window;
She cried out in a loud voice:
'Oh, my attendants and servants!
Is not that Prince Dimitri,   5
Is not that my betrothed?
He is going to Matins;
He is a crooked hunchback,
He has a snub nose and squint eyes,
He has teeth like bundles of straw,   10
And he shuffles with his feet,
And throws up all the snow in the street'.
When Prince Dimitri heard this—
This ridicule from his affianced bride, Domna Faleleevna—
He came home from Matins,   15
And went to his sister Olena Stepanovna:
'My sister Olenushka!
Make a feast for girls,
And invite to it Domna Faleleevna'.
'My own dear brother!   20
I can easily do that for you.'
His sister began to make preparations,
And sent messengers to invite her friends;
She sent a messenger to Domna Faleleevna.
Now when the first messenger entered the court-yard,   25
He did not remove his hat, or bow;
'Pray come, Domna Faleleevna,
To see Olena Stepanovna,
To eat bread and salt with her'.
'I will not go, I shall not go.   30
Olenushka has an unmarried brother.'
The second messenger came up to the window,

12-2

But he did not remove his hat, or bow:
'Pray come, Domna Faleleevna,
To see Olena Stepanovna,   35
To eat bread and salt with her'.
'I will not go, I shall not go:
Olenushka has an unmarried brother.'
Now when the third messenger arrived, he entered the room,
He took off his hat and he bowed: 40
'Pray come, Domna Faleleevna,
To see Olena Stepanovna,
To eat bread and salt with her.
She will not eat bread and salt without you,
Or carve the white swan on the table'.   45
'I will not go, I shall not go:
Olena has an unmarried brother.'
Her dear mother overheard her:
'Go, my child!
Go, my pretty child!'   50
'My dear lady mother!
Last night I dreamed an evil dream:
My velvet skirt was all torn,
And my gold ring lay broken.'
'Go child, my little child!   55
For no-one believes in dreams nowadays.'
And so Domna Faleleevna
Dressed herself and made herself ready,
And went to see Olena Stepanovna.
When Olena Stepanovna had greeted   60
Domna Faleleevna,
She seated the lady Faleleevna at the bottom of the table,
Below all her companions.
It was not the door opening of itself—
It is Prince Dimitri who has opened the door.   65
Then Domna Faleleevna cried:
'Oho! Prince Dimitri!
What a crooked hunchback you are!
You have a snub nose and squint eyes,

Your teeth are like bundles of straw,   70
You shuffle with your feet,
Dragging all the carpet into a heap!'
Then Prince Dimitri seized her—
Domna Faleleevna—by her right hand,
He took her to his bedroom,   75
And he beat the lady till she was half dead.
Then the lady sent a messenger to her mother,
To ask her mother for three garments:
Now the first garment was that of a maiden,
And the second was her wedding-dress,   80
But the third garment was her shroud.
Thus then did her mother speak:
'Now indeed will I have faith in dreams!'

XXIII

Prince Vasili

THE following *bylina* is classed in Kirêevski's collection among the 'Princely *byliny*' of the early Moscow Cycle, discussed on pp. 19 f., 178 above. The occurrence related has not been identified, however.

PRINCE VASILI

Recorded from Archangel

Kirêevski, *Pêsni*, pt. v, p. 66.

In the blue sea,
In the quiet bay,
Was Prince Vasili drowned
Through the weight of his gold crown.
The young princess was left alone: 5
'O, you boyars! boyars!
Turn your steeds
To my native land,
To my dear father,
To my lady mother'.   10
They came to the father;
There looked through the window
A young nun:
'Reverend Mother,
It is not a guest who has arrived,   15
It is a postulant who has come to us
To be a permanent inmate'.
'Hearken, you boyars!
Turn your steeds
To the holy convent,   20

To the great abbess herself':
'O, reverend abbess,
Shave me as a nun,
Build me a little cell,
Pierce three windows: 25
The first window
To look towards the Blessed Annunciation,[1]
The second window to look
Over my native land,
And the third window   30
Over the blue sea,
The quiet bay
Where sank my crowned husband,
My crowned husband, Prince Vasili!'

[1] I do not know whether a church of this name is referred to. Cf.
p. 264, l. 16 below.

XXIV

The Death of Prince Mikhailo

THIS poem is classed in Kirêevski's collection among
the 'Princely *byliny*' of the early Moscow Cycle,
discussed on pp. 19 f., 178 above. The hero has not
been identified, though it has been observed that the poem
may well have reference to an historical event. The style of
this *bylina* differs from those of the Princely Cycle already
discussed, being much nearer to the journalistic style of
the seventeenth-century *byliny* relating to Muscovite history.

THE DEATH OF PRINCE MIKHAILO

Recorded from Tulsk

Kirêevski, *Pésni*, pt. v, p. 77.

From the mountains, from the steep mountains,
From the forests, the dense forests,
As the red sun arose,
So rose also the Russian troops,
The Russian troops, the Cossacks of the Ukraine;   5
Prince Mikhailo was in command of the army.
Prince Mikhailo addressed his brave troops:
'O, my dear brothers, brave soldiers!
Do not lose courage, march against the wicked ones, the black
      Moldavians,
Cut them down, do not spare the wicked godless Tartars!'   10
They did not fight, or hew down, they were not able to vanquish
      their foes,
And Prince Mikhailo himself was taken prisoner.
They did not torture, or strike, they did not take his life:
And Prince Mikhailo died in his thirtieth year.

BYLINY RELATING TO
IVAN VASILEVICH

XXV

The Capture of Kazan

IN 1552 Ivan the Terrible captured the city of Kazan from the Tartars after a stubborn defence lasting six weeks. It is said to have been the first city taken by the Russians after a siege conducted on European lines. Ivan made entrenchments round the city and employed a German engineer who sank mines under the city walls. He is said to have had a hundred and fifty cannon. Ivan's call to surrender was treated with defiance by the garrison. In the contemporary account of Kurbski, we are told that the Tartars stood on the ramparts, their robes girt up to their waists, making, according to the popular poet, insulting gestures to the besiegers; but according to Kurbski making the enchantments which caused storms to rise, so that the tsar's transports were lost in the river. Gunpowder was employed to blow up the defences, and the Russians finally succeeded in entering the city. The garrison preferred death to surrender and died fighting with great courage, but the popular singer is mistaken in the fate of the Tartar khan, whose name was Ediger. He was voluntarily handed over to Ivan by his followers in order to ensure his safety, and he himself consented to become a Christian and was baptised under the name of Simeon—the name by which the poet remembers him—and subsequently lived in Moscow in attendance at Ivan's court. The *bylina* has, nevertheless, kept singularly close to historical fact for the most part. Of the spoils of Kazan Ivan consented only to accept those which rightfully belonged to the sovereign—the khan's crown and sceptre and the standard. The capture of Kazan broke the Tartar power in East Russia, and opened a free road for further conquests and for the occupation of Siberia.

THE CAPTURE OF KAZAN

Recorded from Varlam

Kirêevski, *Pêsni*, pt. VI, p. 1 f.

O ye guests, invited guests,
Invited guests, warrior guests!
Ye are to be told a wonderful thing, O guests,
A wonderful thing, and it is no trifle:
No less a thing than how the tsar captured Kazan.   5
He entrenched himself, and he lived on gruel,[1]
He entrenched himself in a second line, and again he lived on
      gruel;
He sank a mine under the River Kazanka,
He undermined the town of Kazan,
He rolled in barrels, barrels of oak,   10
Filled with violent, poisonous, black gunpowder,
And he lighted a fuse of pure wax.
The Tartars of Kazan were standing on the wall,
They were standing on the wall, and making insulting gestures:
'There's for you, sovereign tsar! and your taking of Kazan!'   15
The tsar's heart rose in anger,
He ordered his gunners to be executed, to be hanged.
Prudent men of the army came as deputies,
Prudent men, men of understanding:
'Hearken, our sovereign tsar, Ivan Vasilevich!   20
Do not order us to be executed, to be hanged,
Permit us, sovereign tsar, to speak a word:—
The fuse burns quickly in the open air,
But it burns slowly underground'.
The tsar had not time to speak a word   25
Before the town of Kazan began to give way,
To give way, to be rent asunder, to be hurled in every direction,

---

[1] Probably an allusion to the fact that the Russian ships and stores
had been sunk in the river. Kazan stands near the junction of the Volga
and the Kama.

The Capture of Kazan from the Tartars by
Ivan the Terrible in 1552

From an old Russian woodcut

And to fling all the Tartars of Kazan into the river.
The barrels of black gunpowder ignited,[1]   47
A high mountain was raised up,
And the white stone palace was blown to pieces.
Then the mighty Prince of Moscow ran   50
On to this high mountain,
Where the royal palaces stood.
When the Tsaritsa Elena perceived it,
She spread salt on bread,
She offered ready submission to the Prince of Moscow,   55
Our sovereign, Ivan Vasilevich, as he stood by and watched.
And he was gracious to the tsaritsa,
And converted her to the Christian faith,
And made her a nun in a cloister.
But for Tsar Simeon's pride   60
In not offering submission to the mighty prince,
He put out his bright eyes from their sockets,[2]
He deprived him of his royal crown,
He stripped him of his royal purple,
He took the royal sceptre from his hand.   65
And then the prince began to reign as a tsar,
And reigned in the kingdom of Moscow.
That was when Moscow was founded,
And since that time its glory has been great.

[1] The *bylina* ends at this point in the version which we have selected for translation. The following lines form the conclusion of a variant version recorded by Kirsha Danilov (Kirêevski, *Pêsni*, pt. VI, p. 8 ff.).

[2] Cf. p. 68, l. 73 above, and footnote.

XXVI

Fedor Ivanovich and Boris Godunov: the Failure of the Crimean Tsar

IN 1571 Devlét-Giréi, the khan of the Crimea, brought an army of 120,000 men, or, according to the account of the Englishman Fletcher, who went to Russia in 1588, 200,000 men from the Crimea against Moscow, and captured and burnt the suburbs of the city. In 1573 they again came, but were stopped some fifty miles from Moscow. According to the contemporary writer Kurbski, their leader was so sure of an easy victory that the streets of Moscow were allotted in advance to the *Murţas*, as their leaders were called. They are said to have left 100,000 men dead on the field.

The English colony in Moscow at this period has left us some vivid if slightly discrepant accounts of the first raid, which have been published in Hakluyt's *Voyages*. One or two extracts will serve to give an idea of how devastating an event was the Tartar raid of 1571.

Sir Giles Fletcher's account is as follows:

The Chrim Tartar...in the yeare 1571...came as farre as the cittie of Mosko, with an armie of 200,000 men, without any battaile or resistance at all; for that the Russe emperour (then Ivan Vasilowich) leading foorth his armie to encounter with him, marched a wrong way; but as it was thought of very purpose, as not daring to adventure the fielde, by reason that hee doubted his nobilitie and chiefe captaines of a meaning to betray him to the Tartar. The citie he tooke not, but fired the suburbs, which by reason of the buildinges (which is all of wood, without any stone, brick, or lime, save certein out roomes) kindled so quickly and went on with such rage, as that it consumed the greatest part of the citie almost within the space of foure houres, being of thirty miles or more of compasse.[1]

---

[1] Fletcher's *Russe Commonwealth* (publ. by the Hakluyt Society, London, 1856), p. 85 f.

Sir Jerome Horsey's account is more racy:

The enime approaching the great cittie of Musco, the Russ Emperor flies, with his two sonns, treasur, howshold, servants, and personall guard of 20 thowsand gonnors, towards a stronge monesterie, Troietts, 60 miells of, upon Assencion daye. The enyme fiers St Johns Church high steppll; at which instant happened a wounderfull stormye wynd, through which all the churches, howses and palaces, within the cittie and suberbs 30 miells compas, built most of firr and oak tymber, was set one fier and burnt within six howers space, with infinit thowsands men, weomen, and children, burnt and smothered to death by the fierie eyre, and likewise in the stone churches, monestaries, vaults, and sellors; verie fewe escapinge both without and within the three walled castells. The rever and ditches about Musco stopped and filled with the multitude of people, loaden with gold, silver, jewells, chains, ear-rings, braslets and treasur, that went for succer eaven to save their heads above water. Notwith-standinge, so many thowsands wear ther burnt and drowned, as the river could not be ridd nor clensed of the dead carcasses, with all the means and industrye could be used in twelve monneths after; but those alive, and many from other towns and places, every daie wear occupied within a great circuat to search, dregg, and fish, as it wear, for rings, jewells, plate, baggs of gold and silver, by which many wear inriched ever after. The streets of the cittie, churches, sellors and vauts, laye so thicke and full of dead and smothered carcasses as noe man could pass for the noisom smells and putrifection of the ear [air] longe after. The Emperowr of the Crimes and his armye beheld this goodly fier, lodged and solaced himself in a fare monuestarie by the river sied, fower miells of the cittie, called Symon monesterie; toke the wælth and riches they had, and of all such as fledd from the fier.[1]

These accounts help us to realise the relief from tension in which the following *bylina* was composed when, two years later, the same horde made another raid on Moscow which mercifully proved unsuccessful.

[1] Sir Jerome Horsey, *Travels* (publ. by the Hakluyt Society, London, 1856), p. 165 f.

FEDOR IVANOVICH AND BORIS GODUNOV:
THE FAILURE OF THE CRIMEAN TSAR

Recorded by Richard James in 1619

Kirêevski, *Pésni*, supplement to pt. VII, p. 56.

It is not a mighty cloud which has gathered,
Nor mighty thunder rumbling:
Whither goes the dog, the Crimean Tsar?—
To the mighty realm of Moscow:
'To-day we will go to stone-built Moscow,   5
And on our way back we will take Ryazan'.
And when they came to the River Oka,
They proceeded to pitch their white tents:
'Now reflect seriously with your full attention:
Which of us shall rule in stone-built Moscow,   10
And which of us in Vladimir,
And which of us shall guard ancient Ryazan,
And which of us shall rule in Zvenigorod,
And which of us in Novgorod?'   15
Up stood Divi-Murza Ulanovich:
'Hearken, our lord, Crimean Tsar!
You, our lord, shall rule over us in stone-built Moscow,
And your son in Vladimir,
And your nephew in Suzdal,   20
And your kinsman in Zvenigorod,
And let the equerry guard ancient Ryazan;
And to me, lord, grant Novgorod:
That is the place where my pleasure lies—
I will be their father, Divi-Murza Ulanovich'.   25
The voice of God called out from heaven:
'Hearken, you dog, Crimean Tsar!
Do you not know the realm of Moscow?
In Moscow there are still seventy apostles,
And besides them there are three bishops,   30
And moreover there is in Moscow the Orthodox Tsar!'
And you fled, you dog, Crimean Tsar,—
But not in marching order did you flee,
Not according to squadrons under your black ensign!

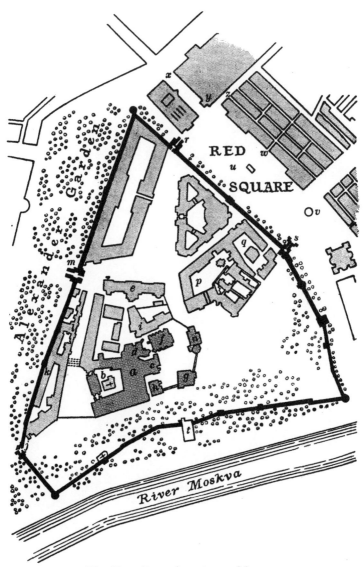

The Kremlin and environs, Moscow

ROUGH SKETCH PLAN

(a) Great Kremlin Palace.

(b) Church of the Redeemer in the Wood.

(c) Faceted Palace.

(d) Terem.

(e) Kremlin barracks, said to occupy part of the site of the old wooden palace of Boris Godunov.

(f) Uspenski Cathedral (Cathedral of the Assumption) where the tsars were crowned. Built in 1475–9 on the site of an earlier church, and repeatedly restored to its original plan.

(g) Arkhangelski Cathedral (Cathedral of Michael the Archangel) where the tsars were buried till the time of Peter the Great, and where their tombs are still preserved. Built in 1508 on the site of an earlier church.

(h) Blagovêshchenski Cathedral (Cathedral of the Annunciation) where the tsars were christened and married. Founded in 1397, rebuilt 1482–9.

(i) Synodal Building, completed in 1655, and originally the residence of the Patriarch.

(j) Borovitskÿa Gate, structure 62 ft. high, erected under Ivan III. Upper part restored in XVII century.

(k) Oruzheynaya Palace, or ancient armoury.

(l) Potêshnÿ Dvorets, or Pleasure Palace, came into possession of the Romanovs in 1648.

(m) Troitskÿa Gate.

(n) Ivan Veliki Tower, built by Boris Godunov in honour of Ivan the Terrible and completed in 1600. It rises in five stories to 320 ft. It contains over 30 bells, including the Bell of the Assumption, 65 tons in weight.

(p) Chudov Monastery, founded in 1358.

(q) Vosnesenski Convent (Convent of the Ascension), built in 1389 by Evdokhÿa, the wife of Dimitri of the Don. In the middle of the convent is the Vosnesenski Cathedral, built in 1519 and restored 1721. It contains the relics of 38 tsaritsas and grand-princesses, the last being the sister of Peter the Great.

(r) Nikolskÿa Gate.

(s) Spasskÿa Gate (Gate of the Redeemer).

(t) Tainitskÿa Gate.

(u) The Red Square.

(v) The Lobnoe Mêsto.

(w) The Trading Rows.

(x) Iberian Gate to the Inner City.

(y) Kazan Cathedral, built by Prince Pozharski in 1625 in gratitude for the deliverance of Moscow from the Poles.

(ẓ) Nikolskaya (street), leading towards Myasnitskaya (street).

XXVII

The Tsar resolves to slay his Son

IN 1581 Ivan IV, the 'Terrible Tsar', accidentally killed his eldest son and heir Ivan during an altercation. It was his habit to carry a wooden stick tipped with iron. One day he entered the room where his son's young wife was lying ill, and began to chide her in loud tones. His son Ivan rebuked him and the tsar dealt him an angry blow in momentary passion. He had no intention of killing him and was inconsolable. For three days he sat immovable beside the corpse and his reason was feared for. In the *bylina* the name Fedor, the second son of Ivan IV, has been substituted for that of Ivan, but there is no historical truth in the charge of treason made against him in the *bylina*. The dread of treason was well known to be almost a mania with Ivan IV, and the popular poet not unnaturally attributed this as a cause for the tsar's terrible deed. Rambaud suggests that the *motif* of the reprieve and the part played by Nikita Romanov may have been invented by the poet after Ivan's eldest son had been forgotten to account for the fact that Fedor, now looked upon as the victim, was still alive. The *motifs* of the rescue and restoration are very common in folk-tales, however, and it may be that they have been introduced into the historical narrative from popular stories in which a king or queen first orders the execution of a son or favourite, and subsequently regrets the deed, whereupon the victim is restored to them safe and sound, and his deliverer is richly rewarded. The mother of the tsarevich is Anastasya Romanovna, Ivan IV's first wife, and her brother is Nikita Romanov, the Mikita of the following poem. The family of the Romanovs was always dear to the people, and it is a curious fact that at the close of the Period of Troubles, when the anarchy was brought to an end in 1613 by the election of a new tsar, the crowd in the Red Square outside the Kremlin cried out for Mikhailo Romanov, Nikita's grandson.

THE TSAR RESOLVES TO SLAY HIS SON

Recorded from the Government of Vladimir

Kirêevski, *Pêsni*, pt. VI, p. 55 ff.

In mother Moscow, in stone-built Moscow,
Our tsar was reigning, Ivan Vasilevich,
And he gave an honourable feast,
He gave a magnificent banquet:
Princes and boyars assembled,   5
Powerful, mighty heroes,
And all bold women-warriors:
The feast was half over,
The banquet was half consumed,
The boyars had nearly eaten enough,   10
The boyars had nearly drunk their fill.
The terrible tsar Ivan Vasilevich was making merry,
He was walking through his apartments,
He was looking out through his glazed window,
He was combing his black curls with a small-toothed comb, 15
He spoke the following words,
He addressed his boyars: 'Drink and take your ease,
But you cannot boast about your own exploits.
It is I who have banished treason from my own country,
It is I who have brought the imperial purple from Tsargrad'. 20
Then they trembled before him,
His subjects were terrified,
They could not think of a reply.
The taller of them hid behind the lesser,
And the lesser for their part were speechless.   25
The mighty prince rose and stepped forward,
The young Ivan Ivanovich,
He spoke in the following terms:
'Hearken, my dear father,
My terrible tsar, Ivan Vasilevich!   30
Allow me to speak a word,
Do not bid them hang me for my speech,

Be not angry at my words.
Do you remember, do you call to mind
How we attacked the city of Pskov?   35
Greatly did we expend our forces,
But there was great treason in our midst
From your own son,
Young Fedor Ivanovich'.
The terrible tsar was incensed   40
Against his dear son Fedor Ivanovich:
'Have I no terrible executioners left?'
There were executioners there by tens,
There were executioners there by fifties,
But the executioners did not know what to say: 45
The taller hid behind the lesser,
And the lesser for their part were speechless.
Then arose and stepped forward young Malyutka, the
        son of Skuratin,[1]
And he spoke to this effect:
'If I must raise my hands   50
Against your royal line,
My hand will not falter with the sharp sword!'
He took Fedor Ivanovich by his white hands,
By his fingers with their gold rings,
Quickly he took him to the River Moskva,   55
To the Lobnoe Mêsto,[2]
To the lime-wood block,
Where terrible executions are carried out,
Where eyes are put out from their sockets,[3]
And tongues are torn from their roots.   60
Through the new palace of fine woodwork,
It is not the red sun rolling along the earth,

[1] A traditional enemy of the House of Romanov, and a character
hated by the popular singers. Cf. p. 233 below.
[2] I.e. the place of executions, a circular platform surrounded by a
stone balustrade in the Red Square outside the Kremlin, where the
archpriest stood to address the crowd, and from where Ivan the
Terrible harangued the Muscovites.
[3] Cf. p. 68, l. 73 above, and note.

It is the orthodox tsarina who has passed through
On her way to her dear brother,
Young Mikita Romanovich: 65
'O my sweet brother,
Mikita Romanovich!
Why do you sleep and wake not?
Do you not know what is happening?
How the terrestrial star has fallen,   70
How the torch of our earth is extinguished,
Our tsarevich is no more,
Fedor Ivanovich?
They have taken him this very hour to the River Moskva,
To the Lobnoe Mêsto,   75
To the lime-wood block,
Where terrible executions are carried out'.
Quickly he sprang to his nimble feet,
Thrust his shoes on to his bare feet,
Flung his coat over his shoulder with one arm in the sleeve, 80
Clapped his hat on his head quite flat,
Mounted his horse bare-back,
And hastily galloped to the River Moskva,
To the Lobnoe Mêsto,
To the lime-wood block;   85
He cried with a loud voice
And waved his hat:
'God has had mercy on him,
The sovereign tsar has pardoned him.
And as for you, my fine fellow Malyutka, Skuratin's son,   90
This morsel will not fall to your share,
With this morsel you will choke yourself!'
He dealt Malyutka a blow on the white breast,
And Malyutka was knocked off his legs,
And fell half dead.   95
He took Fedor Ivanovich by his white hands,
He took him into the spacious court-yard,
Into his palace of white stone,
And seated him on his gilded throne.

There was no long time to wait   100
Before they began to ring for early Mass.
There comes our father,
The terrible tsar, Ivan Vasilevich,
Wearing garments of mourning and in disorder;
He prays to God and bows down before Him,   105
Shedding burning tears.
There goes the illustrious prince,
The young Mikita Romanovich,
Wearing court dress;
He prays and bows down, and smiles,   110
And addresses the tsar direct:
'Hail to you, our sovereign,
Terrible tsar, Ivan Vasilevich!
I give you joy of your two sons:
Of the first—Ivan Ivanovich,   115
Of the second—Fedor Ivanovich!'
The terrible tsar was incensed
Against his brother-in-law, Mikita Romanovich:
'Do you mock me
Or do you not know, are you not aware   120
That the terrestrial star has fallen,
That the torch of our earth is extinguished,
The young tsarevich is no more,
Fedor Ivanovich?
Quickly they took him to the River Moskva,   125
To the Lobnoe Mêsto,
To the lime-wood block,
Where terrible executions are carried out,
Where eyes are put out from their sockets
And tongues are torn from their roots'.   130
The illustrious prince made answer;
The young Mikita Romanovich:
'Terrible tsar, Ivan Vasilevich!
Your son is sitting in my house,
In my palace of white stone;   135
He makes complaint against his beloved brother,

Against young Ivan Ivanovich, saying,
"He brought me to an unjust death"'.
The terrible tsar rejoiced:
'O illustrious prince!   140
What can I bestow upon you?
Shall I bestow upon you a third of my land,
Or gold treasure, or a city,
Or peasants, or Moscow itself?'
'I do not want a third of your land,   145
Or stone-built Moscow;
Grant me three streets:
The first street—the Arbatskaya,
The second street—the Nikitskaya,
The third street—the Myasnitskaya,[1]   150
Where I may rule
And be answerable to none'.

---

[1] The streets named are three of the great thoroughfares of Moscow.

XXVIII

Ermak the Cossack, Conqueror of Siberia

IN 1581 Ermak the Cossack, together with about a hundred and fifty companions, surprised and defeated Mahmetkoul (not Kuchum Khan as in the *bylina*) in his capital, the fortress of Sibir on the River Irtish, in what is now Western Siberia. Ermak was under sentence of death for rebellion against the Tsar of Muscovy, Ivan Vasilevich, 'the Terrible'. His companions likewise were adventurers who had incurred the tsar's displeasure. Following up their first advantage, by 1582 this handful of intrepid freebooters had made themselves masters of the Obi and the Irtish. They had conquered the only part of Siberia that concerned Russia at that time. They handed over their newly won territory to the tsar, who in return gave them a free pardon. Ermak was surprised and killed on the Irtish by Kuchum Khan in 1584. Many versions of the *bylina* relating his conquest of Siberia have been recorded in Russia, while among the Tartars of the valleys of the Obi and the Irtish, Radlov found prose sagas still current, relating both to his acquisition of land, and to his death, by drowning, as he was attempting to swim the Irtish during a battle with Kuchum.[1] It is interesting to note that in Tartar tradition Ermak owes his conquest not to valour but to cunning.

[1] See *Proben der Volkslitteratur der Türkischen Stämme Süd-Sibiriens*, pt. IV (St Petersburg, 1872), pp. 139 ff., 179 ff., etc.

ERMAK THE COSSACK, CONQUEROR OF SIBERIA

Recorded by Sakharov

Kirêevski, *Pêsni*, pt. vi, p. 39 ff.

On the glorious steppes of Saratov,
Below the town of Saratov,
And above the town of Kamÿshin,
The Cossacks assembled, my friends! those free men,
They assembled, the brothers, in a circle,   5
The Cossacks of the Don, the Greben, and the Yaïk.
For their Hetman they had Ermak Timofeevich,
For their captain they had Astafi Lavrentevich;
They planned a plan together:
'Summer, warm summer, is passing away,   10
And the cold winter draws near, my brothers.
Where then, brothers, shall we pass the winter?
If we go to the Yaïk, it is a great journey;
If we go to the Volga, we shall certainly be called robbers;
If we go to the town of Kazan—the tsar is there,   15
The terrible tsar, Ivan Vasilevich.
He has an army there of great size,
And hanging awaits you there, O Ermak,
And capture awaits us there, us Cossacks,
And in a strong prison we shall be confined'.   20
It is not a golden trumpet resounding,
Nor a trumpet of silver; it is someone speaking in a loud voice,
It is Ermak Timofeevich speaking:
'Hearken, my brothers, think, reflect,
Listen to me, my brothers, to Ermak.   25
Let us all spend the winter, brothers, in Astrakhan,
And during the winter, brothers, let us reform;
And when fair spring bursts forth,
Then, dear brothers, we will go on the march,
And offer compensation to the terrible tsar for our crimes;   30

For, my brothers, we have sailed the blue sea,[1]
The blue sea, the Caspian,
We have destroyed, my brothers, dark grey ships,
But those ships, my brothers, did not bear the Russian eagle.
We have slain a royal envoy[2] outright,   35
But he was an envoy of Persia'.
In the glorious town of Astrakhan,
In the broad, level square,
The Cossacks assembled, my friends, in a circle;
They were taking counsel together earnestly,   40
Taking counsel earnestly, and all of one mind:
'Now the bitter winter is disappearing,
And summer, warm summer, my brothers, draws near;
It is time, my brothers, to be on the march'.
Ermak Timofeevich began to speak: 45
'Hearken, my brothers, my brave hetmans!
Build boats and ships,
Drive in the thole-pins of pine-wood,
Lay to the oars of fir-wood;
Let us go, brothers, with God's help,   50
Let us row, brothers, up the River Volga,
Let us cross, brothers, the steep mountains,
Let us make our way to the Mussulman empire,
Let us conquer the empire of Siberia,
And subdue it, brothers, for the White Tsar,   55
And take Tsar Kuchum captive;
And in return our sovereign tsar will reward us.
Then I will go in person to the White Tsar,
I will put on a cloak of sable,
I will tuck my cap of marten-skin under my arm,   60
I will offer submission to the White Tsar:—
"O you are our hope, orthodox tsar!

---

[1] The particular exploits which follow have been transferred to Ermak from the later Cossack rebel, Stenka Razin, who was executed in 1676.

[2] In Sakharov's text the envoy is said to be *ne tsarskago*, 'not of the tsar'.

Do not bid them slay me, bid me speak a word,
For I am Ermak Timofeevich,
I am the robber Hetman of the Don;   65
It was I who sailed the blue sea,
The blue sea, the Caspian,
And I it was who destroyed the dark grey ships,
But the ships did not bear the Russian eagle.
But now, our hope, orthodox tsar,   70
I bring you my rebellious head,
And with my rebellious head I bring you the empire of Siberia"'.[1]
Then our hope, our orthodox tsar, begins to speak,
The terrible tsar, Ivan Vasilevich:
'Hearken, Ermak Timofeevich!   75
Hearken, you Hetman of the Cossacks of the Don!
I pardon you and your band;
I pardon you for your services,
For your trusty service to me,
And I grant you, Ermak, as an inheritance the glorious silent
        Don!'   80

[1] Our singer passes, by an abrupt transition, from Ermak's proposal to his arrival before the Tsar in Moscow. In some (longer) versions the intermediate events are narrated.

XXIX

The Tsar sends the Tsaritsa
into a Convent

THE occurrence of the name Marfa Matvêevna in the
following *bylina*, taken in connection with the re-
currence of the same name in the *Lament of the
Tsaritsa for the Dead Tsar* on p. 208 f., where the person
referred to is obviously Ivan's last wife, has led to the
belief that it has reference to Marya Fedorovna Nagoi, the
seventh wife of Ivan the Terrible, and the mother of the
Tsarevich Dimitri, who died or was murdered at the age
of nine at Uglich in 1591. After the murder of her son,
Marya entered a convent and became a nun, with the name
Marfa. There is no evidence, however, that she was enclosed
as a nun during the lifetime of Ivan IV, and the evidence
of the English contingent in Moscow suggests that this
was not the case,[1] though the Emperor had expressed his
willingness to enclose her, provided Queen Elizabeth would
grant him the hand of the Lady Mary Hastings in marriage.[2]
Compulsory banishment to a convent was the fate of
many of the Russian tsaritsas of the sixteenth and seventeenth
centuries. Ivan III, 'the Great', banished his wife Solo-
monÿa to a convent after twenty years of married life because
they had no heir. Ivan IV, 'the Terrible', also had his
fourth wife, Anna Koltovskaya, banished to a convent. His
niece Marya and her daughter were also thrust into a nunnery
by order of Boris Godunov. We shall find the first wife of
Peter the Great bewailing a similar fate. Sophia, the daughter
of the Tsar Alexis, and half-sister of Peter the Great, was

[1] *Fletcher's Russe Commonwealth: Horsey's Travels* (publ. by the
Hakluyt Society, London, 1856), p. 270.
[2] *Ibid.* p. xlix.

also forcibly immured by Peter on account of her ambitious disposition. The literary form of the *bylina* may therefore be older or, alternatively, more recent than the period of Marya Nagoi, and, like the *byliny* on the dead tsars, may have been adapted to fresh circumstances as occasion arose. The only Marfa Matvêevna mentioned by Solovev (*Istorÿa Rossi,* Kn. III, column 886, etc.) became the second wife of Fedor Alexêevich in 1682, but her husband died ten weeks later.

THE TSAR SENDS THE TSARITSA INTO A CONVENT

Recorded from Simbirsk

Kirêevski, *Pêsni,* pt. VI, p. 202 f.

Why is all so sad here in Moscow,
Why are they tolling the great bell?[1]
The tsar is displeased with the tsaritsa,
He is banishing the tsaritsa from his sight,
Away into the town of Suzdal,   5
Away into the Pokrovski convent.
As the tsaritsa wandered through the palace,
She lamented mournfully:
'Alas, you palace of stone,
Palace of white stone, and faceted![2]   10
Can it be that I shall no more wander about you, dear palace,
Shall I no longer sit at tables of cypress-wood,
Shall I no longer taste sugared foods,
And no more carve the white swan?'
Then the tsaritsa went out on to the staircase   15
And cried out at the top of her little voice:
'O you young squires,
You young squires, you grooms,

[1] For the great bell, see p. 207, footnote 1, below.
[2] I.e. the old *gridnya* or audience chamber in the Kremlin, known as the *Granovitaya Palata,* i.e. the 'faceted' or 'angular' palace, on account of the facets into which the outer face of the stone was cut on the façade.

Make ready the coach—but do not hurry;
Drive away from Moscow—but do not hurry;   20
Perchance the tsar may even yet relent,
Perchance he will order me to return!'
Then the young squires replied:
'Alas, our mother the tsaritsa,
Marfa Matvêevna!   25
Little hope is there that the tsar will relent!
Little hope is there that he will bid you return!'
They welcomed the tsaritsa with a peal of bells,
And the abbess approached,
Surrounded by her nuns,   30
She has taken her by her white hands,
She has conducted her into her cell.[1]
Then the orthodox tsaritsa addressed them:
'Away! Away! abbess and nuns!
It is not for an hour that I have come to visit you,   35
It is not for one dark night that I have come to lodge,
I have come to you to remain for ever!'

[1] Our version ends here. The concluding lines are translated from
the variant, also published by Kirêevski, *ibid.* p. 203 f.

XXX

The Death of the Terrible Tsar, Ivan Vasilevich

IVAN VASILEVICH, generally known as the Terrible (*Grozny*) Tsar, reigned 1533–84. Sir Jerome Horsey, the English ambassador from Queen Elizabeth to the Muscovite court, has left an account of the tsar's death in his diary, which concludes as follows:

He was a goodlie man of person and presence, wæll favored, high forehead, shrill voice; a right Sithian; full of readie wisdom, cruell, bloudye, merciles; his own experience mannaged by direction both his state and comonwælth affares. Was sumptuously intomed in Michall Archangell church, where he, though garded daye and night, remaines a fearfull spectacle to the memorie of such as pass by or heer his name spoken of [who] ar contented to cross and bless themselves from his resurrection againe.[1]

His tomb can still be seen in the Cathedral of the Archangel Michael (Arkhangelski Sobor) in the Cathedral Square of the Kremlin at Moscow.

THE DEATH OF THE TERRIBLE TSAR,
IVAN VASILEVICH

Recorded from Saratov

Kirêevski, *Pêsni*, pt. VI, p. 206 f.

Now, our father, bright moon!
Why do you not shine as of old,
Not as of old, not as in the past?
Why do you not rise from behind the cloud,
But hide yourself in a black mist?   5

[1] *Travels of Sir Jerome Horsey* (publ. by the Hakluyt Society, London, 1856), p. 209.

Portrait of the Tsar Ivan (IV) the Terrible

From a wood-engraving in the possession of Senator Rovinski

Here with us in holy Russia,
In holy Russia, in stone-built Moscow,
In stone-built Moscow, in the golden Kremlin,
In the Ivan Veliki Tower,
By the Cathedral of Michael the Archangel,   10
By the Uspenski Cathedral,
They have struck the great bell.[1]
The tolling has resounded over all damp mother earth:
All the princes and boyars are assembling,
All the men of the army are mustering,   15
To pray to God in the Uspenski Cathedral.
Inside the Uspenski Cathedral
There stands a new coffin of cypress-wood;
Inside this coffin lies the orthodox tsar,
The orthodox tsar, the terrible Ivan Vasilevich.   20
At his head stands the life-giving cross,
Beside the cross lies his royal crown,
At his feet his sharp, terrible sword.
To the life-giving cross each makes his prayer,
To the golden crown each makes his bow;   25
Each looks at the terrible sword, each feels dread.
Round the coffin burn wax candles,
Before the coffin stand all the priests and patriarchs.
They read the service and chant the dirge,
They chant the dirge to the memory of the orthodox tsar, 30
The terrible tsar, Ivan Vasilevich.

[1] The Ivan Veliki tower in the Kremlin was begun by Fedor Ivanovich and completed by Boris Godunov in 1600 in memory of Ivan the
Terrible. Boris also had the great bell cast and hung. Bell and tower
are thus described by Olearius, who was in Moscow in 1634: 'In the
midst of the Castle [sc. the Kremlin] are two steeples, one very high,
and covered with copper gilt, as all the other steeples of the Castle
are. This Steeple is called Juan Welike [i.e. Ivan Veliki], that is, the
Great John. The other is considerable only for the Bell within it,
made by the Great Duke Boris Gudenov, weighing 33,600 pounds.
It is not toll'd but upon great Festivals, or to honour the entrance and
audience of ambassadors: but to stir it there must be 24 men'. *Voyages
and Travells of the Ambassadors sent by Frederick Duke of Holstein to the
Great Duke of Muscovy*, transl. J. Davis (London, 1669), p. 43.

XXXI

The Lament of the Tsaritsa
for the Dead Tsar

FOR a discussion of the identity of Marfa Matvêevna, the tsaritsa whose lament is recorded in the following poem, see p. 203 above. The poet evidently identifies her with Marya Nagoi, the seventh and last wife of Ivan the Terrible, and the mother of the Tsarevich Dimitri, believed to have been murdered at the instigation of Boris Godunov (cf. p. 215 ff.). The minster is probably not the Cathedral of the Assumption (the Uspenski Sobor) referred to in the *bylina* of the *Lament of the Troops*, but the Cathedral of Michael the Archangel, also in the Kremlin at Moscow, where the remains of the 'Terrible Tsar' lay in state, and where they were ultimately entombed. The Streltsy were instituted as the Palace Guard by Ivan himself, and continued for two centuries to play an important part in state affairs as an armed unit. The fears of the tsaritsa were not groundless. Horsey tells us of the great panic which prevailed on the death of Ivan, and of the strong guard which had to be set at the doors and gates of the palace:

Cried owt to the captaines and gonnors to kepe their gard stronge and the gaetts shure aboute the pallace, with their peces and matches lighted: the gaetts of the castell presently shutt and wæll watched. I offered myself, men, powder and pistolls.... Yt was admirable what dispatch ther was in six or seaven howers: the treasories sealled up, and new officers added to the old of this famillie. Twelve thowsand gonners, and captaines over them, sett for a garison about the walls of the great cittie of Musquo.[1]

[1] Sir Jerome Horsey, *Travels, ed. cit.* p. 202.

THE LAMENT OF THE TSARITSA
FOR THE DEAD TSAR

Recorded from Moscow

Kirêevski, *Pêsni*, pt. VI, p. 207.

It is not from behind the forest, the dark forest,
It is not from behind the high mountains,
It is not the bright sun which has arisen,
It is the orthodox tsaritsa who has appeared,
The orthodox tsaritsa, Marfa Matvêevna.   5
On the floor, the floor of white hazel-wood,
On the carpet, the carpet of purple,
The orthodox tsaritsa has gone forth,
The orthodox tsaritsa, Marfa Matvêevna;
She has come to the cathedral   10
And cried in a loud voice:
'Are there any clergy in the church?
Open the cathedral
To admit the orthodox tsaritsa!'
When the tsaritsa entered the cathedral   15
She said her prayers, turning in three directions,
But on the fourth side she descried,
She caught sight of the coffin of white stone;
The tsaritsa cried in a loud voice:
'Alas, orthodox tsar,   20
Orthodox tsar, Ivan Vasilevich!
Why do you sleep so deeply and awake not?
Without you the whole realm will be in a turmoil;
All the Streltsy[1] will rise,
They will cut down all the princes and boyars in their ranks, 25
And me, the tsaritsa, they will not obey!'
'O, orthodox tsaritsa,
Orthodox tsaritsa, Marfa Matvêevna!
We will obey you indeed,
We will indeed offer you our submission.'   30

[1] The palace guard.

XXXII

Lament of the Troops on the
Death of Ivan the Terrible

THE opening lines constitute the *pripêvka*, a kind of overture, often wholly or almost wholly unconnected with what follows. The *pripêvka* is a common feature in Russian popular poetry. Cf. also p. 273 f. below.

The poem which follows is a very conventional type. Laments of the Troops on the deaths of subsequent sovereigns have also been recorded, notably on Peter the Great, Katharine II, and the Tsar Alexander. They differ only slightly in wording from the following one relating to Ivan the Terrible, and the formula recited by the young soldier is practically identical in all. Moreover it is also common in the popular elegies of folk-poetry in which no proper names have been preserved, and in which the milieu is that of peasants. Possibly it represents some ancient religious ritual for the dead.

LAMENT OF THE TROOPS ON THE DEATH
OF IVAN THE TERRIBLE

Recorded from Simbirsk

Kirêevski, *Pêsni*, pt. VI, p. 212.

O, our father, you bright moon!
You shine, moon, the whole dark night:
Shine out, moon, over stone-built Moscow!
In stone-built Moscow, in holy Russia,
Within the Uspenski Cathedral,   5
A young soldier was standing sentry,
Standing sentry, and praying to God,

Praying to God, and lamenting in tears:
'Rush down from the mountains, O fierce storms!
Scatter, O storms, all the golden sand;   10
Be rent asunder, damp mother earth,
Split open, coffin lid,
Fly apart, fine white shroud,
Stand forth, stand forth, orthodox tsàr,
Our orthodox tsar, Ivan Vasilevich!   15
All Moscow is in an uproar,
All the troops have mobilised!'[1]

[1] The text concludes with six additional lines which are believed to be spurious.

THE SUCCESSORS OF IVAN THE TERRIBLE AND THE PERIOD OF TROUBLES

XXXIII

The Murder of the Tsarevich Dimitri
by Boris Godunov

THE Tsarevich Dimitri was the youngest son of Ivan
the Terrible, by his seventh wife, Marya Nagoi. Ivan
had himself killed his eldest son. His second son Fedor
was feeble in mind and body, and seemed unlikely to live
to old age. Dimitri was the only remaining heir. Boris
Godunov, a Russian boyar, had held important office under
Ivan and acted as regent for Fedor. Able and statesmanlike,
he understood the art of governing, of which he had had much
experience, and he was well aware that should Dimitri die
he would probably himself succeed to the throne. The Tsarevich Dimitri, still a child, was living among his mother's
family, the Nagois, on his appanage at Uglich. Suddenly, in
1591, word came that he had been murdered, stabbed, as it
was believed at the time, and has generally been believed
since, at the instigation of the regent Boris. At the investigation which followed it was alleged by the regent's repre-
sentatives who conducted the enquiry that Dimitri had died
in a fit of apoplexy by falling upon a knife with which he had
been playing. The affair is still something of a mystery, and
there are historians who accept this explanation, but Godunov
was hated as a usurper, and appearances are certainly against
him. We may quote the contemporary diary of the Englishman Horsey who was in Moscow at the time. In June 1591
he addressed a letter from Yaroslav to Lord Burleigh in
which he states that

Upon the 19th of the same [month, i.e. May] a most unfortunate chaunce befell the yonge prince of ix yers adge, sone unto
the old Emperor and brother unto this; [who] was cruelly and
trecherously murdered; his throte cutt in the presence of his dere

mother the Emperis; with other suché lycke most prodigious
matter which I dare not wryt of.[1]

The same writer relates elsewhere in his own racy style
the manner in which he first received the news of the prince's
death:

One night I comended my soull to God above other, thinckinge
verily the tyme of my end was com. One rapt at my gate at
midnight. I was well furnished with pistolls and weapons. I and
my servants, some fifteen, went with these weapons to the gate.—
'O my good frend, Jerom innobled, lett me speak with yow.'—I
saw by moon shine the Emperis brother, Alphonassy Nagoie. . . .
'The Charowich Demetries is dead: his throate was cutt about
the sixth hower by the deaches [*diacks*]; some one of his pagis
confessed upon the racke by Boris his settinge one; and the
Emperis poysoned and upon pointe of death, her hear and naills
and skin falls of: hælp and geave some good thinge, for the
passion of Christ his sake!'—I ran up, fætched a littell bottell of
pure sallett oyell (that littel vial of balsam that the Quen gave
me) and a box of Venice treacle.—'Here is what I have, I praie
God it may do her good.'—Gave it over the wall; Who hied him
post awaie.[2]

THE MURDER OF THE TSAREVICH DIMITRI
BY BORIS GODUNOV

Recorded by Minyaev[3]

Kiréevski, *Pésni*, pt. VII, p. I.

It is not a whirlwind rolling along the valley,
It is not the grey feather-grass bending to the earth,
It is an eagle flying under the clouds,
Keenly he is eyeing the River Moskva,

[1] *Fletcher's Russe Commonwealth: Horsey's Travels* (publ. by the
Hakluyt Society, London, 1856), p. 365.
[2] *Ibid.* p. cix f.
[3] I do not know from what district Minyaev recorded his text.
A text differing only very slightly from Minyaev's was also recorded
by Dal. A variant *bylina* on the same theme was also written down
from the recitation of an old woman in Tulsk in 1834.

And the palace of white stone,   5
And its green garden,
And the golden palace of the royal city.
It is not a cruel serpent rearing itself up,
It is a caitiff dog raising a steel knife.
It has not fallen into the water, nor on to the earth,   10
It has fallen on to the white breast of the tsarevich,
None other than the Tsarevich Dimitri;
They have murdered the Tsarevich Dimitri,
They have murdered him in Uglich,
In Uglich at his play;   15
Then dark night fell upon the palace.
A kite built a nest for its nestlings!
Now this eagle is the Tsarevich Dimitri,
While the kite is Boris Godunov.
Having murdered the tsarevich, he seated himself on the throne,
And he reigned, the villain, for seven whole years.   21
It is not a whirlwind rolling along the valley,
It is not the grey feather-grass bending to the earth,
It is the terrible wrath of God sweeping
Over orthodox Russia.   25
And the kite has perished in his nest,
His plumage is wafted to the clouds,
His blood has been poured down the River Moskva.[1]

---

[1] Boris's wife and son were massacred by the adherents of the 'False Dimitri', and the opportuneness of his own death, which took place in 1605 as the usurper was approaching Moscow, was not without suspicion.

XXXIV

The Lament of Ksenÿa
(daughter of Boris Godunov)

O N the death of Ivan the Terrible the Russian throne
passed to his son Fedor, whose feeble intellect and
retiring disposition left the actual administrative
power largely in the hands of the boyars. Chief of these was
Boris Godunov who had played an important rôle in the
state during Ivan's last years, and whose sister Irene was
Fedor's wife. He is believed to have murdered Fedor's
younger brother in 1591 in the hope of himself succeeding to
the throne. In 1598, accordingly, on Fedor's death, Boris was
elected tsar. Shortly before his death a new claimant to the
throne appeared in the person of Grigori Otrepev—the
Grishka of popular song—who is believed to have been a
renegade priest, but who gave himself out as the Tsarevich
Dimitri, son of Ivan the Terrible. Even the mother of the
murdered tsarevich publicly recognised him as her son,
and King Sigismund of Poland lent him his support and
gave him his daughter in marriage. While the Pretender
was actually marching against Moscow Boris suddenly died
in 1605. It is to this crisis that the following little song, attributed to his daughter, the beautiful Ksenÿa, has reference. It
is no doubt absolutely contemporary. The song is one of the
six written down in a pocket-book by Richard James, who
was in Moscow as chaplain to the English merchants in
Russia during the spring of 1619. James's pocket-book is
preserved in the Bodleian Library at Oxford (cf. p. 7).

An interesting description of Ksenÿa is given by a contemporary writer, Sergius Kubasov, the son of a boyar of
Tobolsk, who during the first quarter of the seventeenth
century wrote a history or chronograph, as he calls it,

extending from the foundation of the world to the election of Mikhailo Romanov (cf. p. 241 below). His book is particularly valuable for its descriptions of the appearance of the members of the royal family and its account of events from the reign of Ivan the Terrible down to the accession of Tsar Mikhailo. He tells us that Ksenÿa was a girl of wonderful sense; of a fresh, healthy complexion; large, dark eyes, very bright, but especially when she shed tears.[1] She had been promised in marriage during her father's lifetime to a brother of the king of Denmark; but this unfortunate prince had died soon after his arrival in Moscow—apparently of hard drinking, though his end was regarded with suspicion in Denmark.[2] On the death of her father Boris, Ksenÿa was imprisoned till the conqueror, the 'False Dimitri', should arrive and make arrangements for her.[3] When he took possession of Moscow he had her made a novice perforce, with the name Olga,[4] while her mother and brother were massacred.

THE LAMENT OF KSENŸA
(DAUGHTER OF BORIS GODUNOV)

Recorded by Richard James

Kirêevski, *Pêsni*, pt. VII, p. 58 f.

The little bird laments,
The little white quail:
'Alas that I so young must mourn!
They will burn the green oak,
And destroy my little nest,   5
And kill my little fledgelings,
And capture me, the quail'.
The tsarevna laments in Moscow:

[1] See Morfill, *Slavonic Literature* (London, 1883), p. 91; Brodski, etc., *op. cit.* p. 134, footnote 2.

[2] See Rambaud, 'Les Tsarines de Moscou', in *Revue des Deux Mondes* (Oct. 1873), p. 526; cf. also Morfill, *Russia* (London, 1891), p. 108.

[3] Morfill, *Russia*, p. 101.   [4] Brodski, etc., *loc. cit.*

'Alas that I so young must mourn!
When the traitor comes to Moscow,   10
Grisha Otrepev, the unfrocked priest,
He will make me prisoner,
And having imprisoned me he will shave off my hair,
And impose monastic vows upon me.
But I do not wish to be shorn a nun,   15
Or to keep monastic vows.
The dark cell must be thrown open
So that I may gaze upon the fine youths.
Ah me, our pleasant corridors,
Who will walk along you,   20
After our royal life,
And after Boris Godunov?
Alas, our pleasant halls!
Who will dwell within you,
After our royal life,   25
And after Boris Godunov?'

XXXV

The Lament of Ksenÿa
(daughter of Boris Godunov)

THIS *bylina*, like the last, was recorded by Richard James in 1619 (see p. 218 above). It is possible that it forms a continuation of the last poem, and is, indeed, so printed in the translation of Wiener's *Anthology of Russian Literature*, vol. I, p. 132 f. I think it is more likely, however, that the poem is a variant version of the preceding, as printed by Bezsonov in his edition of Kirêevski.

THE LAMENT OF KSENÿA
(DAUGHTER OF BORIS GODUNOV)

Recorded by Richard James. See p. 218 above

Kirêevski, *Pésni*, supplement to pt. VII, p. 60 f.

The tsarevna laments in Moscow,
The daughter of Boris Godunov:
'O God, merciful Saviour!
Why have you overturned our throne?—
Is it for my father's sins,   5
Is it for my mother's lack of prayer?
O you dear ones, our lofty mansions!
Who will be your owners
After our living there as kings?
O you dear ones, you patterned towels!   10
Will they wind you round the birch-tree?
O you dear ones, you kerchiefs embroidered with gold!
Will they throw you into the forests?
O you dear ones, you jewelled ear-rings!
Will they clasp you on the branches,   15

After our living there as kings,
After the death of our father,
The illustrious Boris Godunov?
And when the unfrocked priest comes to Moscow,
He will destroy our halls,   20
He will seize me, the tsarevna,
And send me to Ustyuzhna Zhelêznaya;
He will shear me, the tsarevna, and make me a nun,
And enclose me in the cloister behind the grille:
Alas, alas, that I must mourn!   25
How can I pace the dark cell,
In the convent of the orthodox mother superior?'

XXXVI

Grigori Otrepev (the 'False Dimitri') and Marina

GRIGORI OTREPEV, the 'False Dimitri', succeeded to the throne of Moscow on the death of Boris Godunov in 1605 (cf. p. 218 f. above). He claimed to be Dimitri, the youngest son of Ivan the Terrible, believed to have been murdered (cf. p. 215 f. above). He was supported by King Sigismund of Poland who granted him his daughter Marina in marriage. He is said to have reigned for only thirty days, and in 1606 he was attacked in his palace by Vasili Shuyski and a party of boyars with their followers. He jumped from a window and was killed immediately afterwards. The poem is interesting as representing the hatred felt for the Pretender and his Polish wife. In reality Grigori seems to have been an enlightened and discreet ruler, hard-working and sensible. The popular singer has not remembered the political sympathies of the time as correctly as the narrative of occurrences. Actually it was the boyars who hated and opposed the Pretender, while the *streltsy* (cf. p. 208 above) gave him their support, and the Tsaritsa, Marya Nagoi, mother of the dead Tsarevich Dimitri, actually acknowledged him as her son, though she seems to have failed to make good her recognition of him when the tide set strongly against him.

GRIGORI OTREPEV (THE 'FALSE DIMITRI') AND MARINA

Recorded by Kirsha Danilov

Kirêevski, *Pêsni*, pt. VII, p. 5.

O God, God our merciful Saviour!
Why have you grown angry with us so soon?
You have sent to us, Lord, a seducer,
The wicked unfrocked priest, Grishka Otrepev.
Can it be that the unfrocked one actually ruled our realm?   5
The unfrocked priest claims to be the true tsar,
The Tsar Dimitri Ivanovich of Uglich.
Not long did the priest reign on the throne
Before he conceived a desire to marry;
He did not choose one of us in stone-built Moscow,   10
He brought from accursed Lithuania
The daughter of the Pan Yuri Sendomirski,
His daughter Marinka Yurêvna,
The wicked heretic, the godless woman.
It was at the time of the Spring feast of St Nikolai,   15
On the Thursday, that the unfrocked priest was married.
And on the Friday was the feast-day of St Nikolai.
Princes and boyars went to Matins,
But Grishka the priest went to the bath with his wife.[1]
Grishka was wearing a shirt of lawn;   20
Marinka, a mantle of rich damask.
When the second hour had passed
The princes and boyars came out of Matins,
And Grishka the unfrocked priest left the bath with his wife.
He went on to the Red Staircase,   25
He cried and bawled in a sonorous voice:
'O, my stewards and servants,
Serve food of all kinds,
Both lenten and flesh food;
To-morrow an honoured guest is coming,   30
The Pan Yuri with his lady'.

[1] For the Russian bathing process, see pp. 127, 175 above.

Then the Streltsy guessed,
From this speech they discovered the truth,
And they rushed off to the Bogolyubi monastery
To the Tsaritsa Marfa Matvêevna.   35
'Tsaritsa, Marfa Matvêevna!
Is this a child of yours who is reigning on the throne,
The Tsarevich Dimitri Ivanovich?'
Then the Tsaritsa Marfa Matvêevna began to weep:
And spoke through her tears these words: 40
'O you stupid and witless Streltsy!
How could a child of mine be reigning on the throne?
On your throne reigns
The unfrocked priest, Grishka Otrepev;
I lost my son, the Tsarevich Dimitri Ivanovich,   45
In Uglich, at the hands of the Godunov party;
His relics lie in stone-built Moscow,
In the church of the wondrous all-wise Sophia;
In the tower of Ivan the Mighty,
Every day they toll the great bell;   50
The Cathedral clergy assemble,
On all feast-days they say an office
For the memory of the Tsarevich Dimitri Ivanovich;
And they curse perpetually the Godunov party'.
Then the Streltsy understood;   55
They all assembled,
They rushed away to the royal Red Staircase,
And there in Moscow they rose in rebellion.
Grishka the unfrocked priest perceived what was happening;
He betook himself into a high attic,   60
And firmly shut himself up.
But his wicked wife, Marinka the godless,
Changed herself into a magpie,
And away she flew out of the palace.
And as soon as Grishka the unfrocked priest was aware of it, 65
He flung himself from the attic on to the sharp pikes,
The sharp pikes of the Streltsy, those bold youths;
And so in this way he met his death.

XXXVII

Vasili Shuyski

VASILI SHUYSKI, a member of one of the Russian princely families which had played a prominent part in Russian history since the middle of the sixteenth century, attacked and overcame the 'False Dimitri' in his palace in the Kremlin in 1606. Dimitri was assassinated, and Vasili reigned till 1610. His reign was stormy, and he lacked the ability to cope with the many dissentient parties in his own country, and their allies the Poles. In 1607 a new Pretender arose near the River Terek in South-Eastern Russia, a Cossack, Peter by name—the 'impostor Petrushka', and the 'Mussulman' of the *bylina*—who gave himself out to be a son of the Tsar Fedor, son of Ivan the Terrible, though it was well known that Fedor never had a son. In May 1607 Vasili marched against Tula to attack the Pretender who had taken refuge there with his allies, including certain of the boyars. The allusion to the 'impostor Petrushka', the 'Mussulman', as they called this Cossack of the South-East, leaves, I think, no room for doubt that it is to this incident that our *bylina* has reference. Peter was defeated and hanged almost immediately, and the *bylina* can hardly be later than May 1607. It must have served much the same purpose as a 'stop press' in a modern evening paper. It is interesting as representing contemporary popular opinion and popular ignorance. The people of Moscow appear loyal to the tsar, and suspicious of the boyars, and are aware of the disturbance at the palace, and the tsar's absence, but ignorant of the precise circumstances. Vasili, as a matter of fact, was never sent to Siberia, but three years after the events described above he was forced by the boyars and their Polish allies to abdicate, and was carried a prisoner to Warsaw where he died. Rambaud regards our *bylina* as having reference to this final enforced departure of Vasili from Moscow (*La Russie Épique*, p. 283); but the specific allusions in the poem make this less probable. It is worth noting, however, that when Vasili was called upon to abdicate on July 17, 1610, a large crowd, led by the boyars, met in the Red Square, and later at one of the gates of the Kremlin, to make the demand. The opening lines of the *bylina* perhaps look like an allusion to this circumstance; but the populace of Moscow always flocked into the Red Square on occasions of public disturbance.

VASILI SHUYSKI

Recorded from Ryazan

Kirêevski, *Pêsni*, pt. VII, p. 17.

Like crows flocking out of dense woods
The people of Moscow are meeting on the Red Square,[1]
On the Red Square of Ivan the Terrible.
Now in the lofty belfry[2]
They have struck the great bell.   5
'Alas, brothers, something is happening among us,
Is not something disastrous on foot?
In the palace all are strangely troubled,
All the lackeys, all the servants are running to and fro,
Are the boyars risen in mutiny?   10
Have the evil dogs gone mad?
Is our orthodox tsar still alive,
Our orthodox tsar, Vasili Ivanovich?
Why, brothers, is he no longer to be seen in his palace?
Why are the fretted windows all curtained?'   15
Now a bold youth addresses the people:
'Alas, brothers, do you not know the sad calamity?

---

[1] The negative comparative is employed here as elsewhere; lit. 'It is not a flock of crows', etc., 'it is the people', etc.

[2] I.e. the Ivan Veliki Tower. For this tower and the great bell, cf. p. 207, footnote 1, above.

The evil boyars have overthrown our Tsar Vasili,
The evil dogs have overthrown him, they have sent
    him to Siberia;
Now they have made tsar some Mussulman,   20
Some impostor Petrushka, an evil boyar!'
Now all the people have taken fright,
They have scattered in all directions.

XXXVIII

The Death of Skopin

P RINCE Mikhailo Skopin Shuyski was a nephew of the Tsar Vasili Shuyski. He was endowed with talent and character, and during the disorders of 1607 he played a distinguished part as leader of the Loyalist troops in their victory over the insurgent army of Bolotnikov and the Pretender Peter. In the two following years he took the lead against the supporters of yet a third Pretender, another 'false Dimitri', whose forces, composed of mixed troops of Cossacks, Poles and others, had encamped outside Moscow and occupied the Kremlin. Skopin made his way to Novgorod and obtained the help of the Swedes in return for the cession of Karelia. He gained some brilliant victories and marched to the relief of Moscow from the north, while another loyal force under Sheremetev converged from the east. Skopin made his way into Moscow in 1610, but his uncle Tsar Vasili Shuyski and his brother Dimitri Shuyski were jealous of their brilliant and popular young nephew to whom they owed so much. He was invited to a banquet where it is believed that he was poisoned. Two months later he died in 1610 at the age of twenty-four.

THE DEATH OF SKOPIN

Recorded by Kirsha Danilov

Kirêevski, *Pêsni*, pt. VII, p. 11.

Thus it happened in the 127th year,
In the seventh year and the eighth thousand,
Thus it happened, thus it took place:
The powerful kingdom of Moscow
Was besieged by the Lithuanians on all four sides;   5

And with them there was a force of long-skirted Saracens,
And therewith the Circassians of the Five Mountains,
And, further, Kalmuks and Tartars,
Tartars and Bashkirs,
Tchouds and Lutherans.   10
So numerous were the provisions,
Both for the royalties and the princes,
The boyars and the nobility,
That one could not pass through, either walking or riding,
Either on horseback or on foot,   15
Or even fly away as a falcon
From the powerful kingdom of Moscow
And the mighty realm of Russia.
But Prince Mikhailo Vasilevich Skopin,
The ruler of the kingdom of Moscow,   20
The defender of the Christian world,
And our whole land of holy Russia,
He flew away as a bright falcon,
Even as a white gerfalcon he took to his wings and away;
The governor of Moscow, Prince Skopin, rode forth,   25
Prince Mikhailo Vasilevich,
He made an expedition to Novgorod.
When he arrived in Novgorod,
He rode up to the assembly hall,
And entered the assembly room;   30
He seated himself on a leather chair,
And took a golden inkstand,
And in it a swan-quill pen,
And he took white note-paper,
And wrote letters in handwriting   35
To the land of Sweden, the land of the Saxons,
To his dear sworn brother,
To the Swedish king Charles.
And skilfully was the matter set down:
'Greetings, my sworn brother,   40
The Swedish king Charles!
Take pity upon us, incline your heart towards us,

Incline your heart towards us, be gracious unto us,
And give us troops for our assistance.
Our powerful kingdom of Moscow   45
Is beleaguered by Lithuanians on all four sides,
And hard pressed by long-skirted Saracens,
And also by the Circassians of the Five Mountains,
And by the Kalmuks with the Bashkirs,
And by the Tchouds with the Lutherans,   50
And we cannot get the upper hand of them:
I will pledge three Russian cities'.
And with these letters he sent a swift courier,
His dear brother-in-law,
Mitrofan Funtosov.   55
And when the courier arrived at the Polish Horde,
At the abode of the honourable king, the honourable Charles,
He rode at once into the royal court-yard,
To the Swedish king Charles.
In the middle of the royal court-yard   60
The courier leapt from his good steed,
Bound his steed to the oaken post,
Seized his wallet, and went into the palace;
For naught did the courier tarry;
He entered the palace of white stone,   65
He opened his wallet and took out the letters,
He laid them before the king on the round table.
The king received them and broke them open,
He broke them open and read them through,
And spoke words of sympathy: 70
'Skilfully is the matter set down
By my dear sworn brother,
Prince Mikhailo Vasilevich Skopin,
In which he asks for troops to assist him,
And pledges three Russian cities'.   75
And the honourable king, the honourable Charles,
Was exceedingly gracious to him,
He despatched troops from three countries;
The first troops were Swedish,

And the second troops were Saxon,   80
And the third troops were Shkolski—
A people drilled in warfare,
Forty thousand, neither more nor less.
The host arrived at Novgorod,
From Novgorod they went to stone-built Moscow.   85
Wings again grew on the bright falcon,
Hope dawned for Prince Skopin.
And in the morning early, very very early,
Skopin heard Matins in the Cathedral,
He heard Matins, and then he set off on his journey.   90
He hoisted the royal banner,
And on the banner was stamped
The miraculous Saviour and Redeemer;
And on the reverse side was stamped
Mikhailo and Gabriel the archangels,   95
With all the heavenly host.
They marched in an eastern direction,
They cut down the Tchouds with white eyes,
And the Saracens with long skirts;
They marched in a southern direction,   100
They cut up the Circassians of the Five Mountains,
They fought but little, and quickly they surrendered,
And so also the Little Russians;
And they marched on the northern side—
They cut down the Kalmuks with the Bashkirs,   105
And they went on the western side by night,
And destroyed the Tchouds with the Lutherans;
God's help be with him—
With Prince Mikhailo Vasilevich Skopin!
He purged the Muscovite kingdom,   110
And the mighty Russian realm.
In the great celebrations
Masses were said, and Te Deums,
And they marched round the city in stone-built Moscow;
And when they had completed the Masses and Te Deums, 115
And the whole of the great liturgy,

A feast was held as part of the great celebrations,—
A feast was held, a great banquet,
By Prince Mikhailo Vasilevich Skopin,
For the whole orthodox world;   120
And they sang a great paean in celebration,
To Prince Mikhailo Vasilevich Skopin.
When a short time had elapsed
In glorious stone-built Moscow,
It came to pass in the house of Prince Vorotinski,   125
That they were christening a little princeling,
And Prince Mikhailo Skopin was godfather,
And the daughter of Malyuta was godmother,
The daughter of Malyuta Skurlatov.[1]
In the house of Prince Vorotinski,   130
When the honourable banquet took place,
There were many princes and boyars and invited guests;
When the feast was half over,
And the princely banquet was half consumed,
Those who were drunk began to boast: 135
The strong boasted their strength,
The rich boasted their wealth.
Prince Mikhailo Vasilevich Skopin,
He did not drink green wine,
He only drank one draught of sweet mead,   140
It was not from dead drunkenness that he boasted;
'You foolish people, and senseless,
You are all boasting of mere trifles!
Now I, Prince Mikhailo Vasilevich Skopin,
I can indeed boast,   145
For I have purged the Muscovite kingdom,
And the mighty Russian realm;
Moreover they are singing a paean in my honour,
Both old and young,
Both old and young in my honour'.   150
And then, as evil would have it,
The boyars straightway did a deed;

[1] Cf. p. 195 above, and footnote 1.

They uprooted a deadly poison,
And sprinkled it in the glass of sweet mead,
They handed it to his godmother in the Cross,   155
Malyuta, the daughter of Skurlatov.
She was in the secret, his godmother in the Cross;
She handed the glass of sweet mead
To Prince Mikhailo Vasilevich Skopin.[1]
Skopin took it, he did not decline it,   160
He drank the glass of sweet mead,
And he spoke in these terms:
'I hear in my good belly all is not well!
You have destroyed me, godmother in the Cross,
Malyutka, the daughter of Skurlatov;   165
You knew that it was a glass of poison which you
        served me with—
You have destroyed me, you serpent under the stone!'
Her head rolled from her shoulders,
And Skopin quickly left the feast.
He mounted his good steed,   170
And rode away to his dear mother;
He could hardly manage to bid her farewell,
And his mother began to keen him:
'Alas, my darling child,
Prince Mikhailo Vasilevich Skopin!   175
I warned you,
I bade you not to go to Prince Vorotinski,
But you would not hearken to me.
She has deprived you of your life,
She, your fellow-godparent in the Cross,   180
Malyutina the daughter of Skurlatov!'
And Skopin died at evening.
This story and this geste
Are like the blue sea for comfort,
And a chant from a swift river flowing to the sea   185

[1] At Russian feasts it was the custom at this period for the lady of
the house to descend from her upper apartment and hand the cup to the
guests.

Is like good people for an audience,
Young men for capturing,
Even us 'joyous youths'[1] for amusing,
Seated in humble conversation,
Quaffing mead, and green wine;   190
Whose drink we drink, to him we pay honour,
To the mighty boyars
And our gracious hosts.[2]

[1] For the 'joyous folk', cf. pp. 27 f., 151, l. 29, above, and footnote.
[2] The concluding lines of the poem consist of a tag such as was commonly appended by the singers to their *byliny*. For parallels see Magnus, *Heroic Ballads of Russia*, p. 173 ff.

XXXIX

After the Death of Skopin

THE following *bylina*, recorded in 1619 by Richard James (cf. p. 7 above), has reference to the death in 1610 of Prince Mikhailo Vasilevich Skopin Shuyski, whose career is briefly sketched on p. 229 above. It will be remembered that the brilliant young prince made a journey to Novgorod in 1609 to obtain the help of Charles of Sweden. Here he collected Swedish and German auxiliaries, and then marched against the Poles who had command of Moscow. It was commonly believed at the time, and is still generally believed, that he was murdered by the jealousy of his uncles and their adherents. Skopin was the hero of the people, and the poet leaves us in no doubt as to his own sympathy and his suspicions of the crafty, smiling boyars.

Certain features of the *bylina*, notably the agitation and hasty preparations for departure from Moscow made by the foreigners, suggest a reminiscence of the *bylina*, also recorded by James, on the consternation and confusion which reigned in Moscow on the death of Ivan the Terrible. The interest of the poem lies in the fact that it was written down only nine years after the death of Skopin, and reflects the opposing tendencies and incompatible elements in Moscow during the Period of Troubles. Its political tone, the familiar manner in which allusion is made to current rumour, and the fidelity of its topical reference—its air of actuality—are in sharp contrast to the traditional heroic style of the longer poem (no. XXXVIII above) composed on the same event, and recorded more than two centuries later from the Urals.

AFTER THE DEATH OF PRINCE MIKHAILO VASILEVICH
SKOPIN SHUYSKI

Recorded by Richard James in 1619

Brodski, Mendelson and Sidorov, *Istoriko-
Literaturnaya Khrestomatÿa*, vol. I, p. 138.

Whatever is happening here in Moscow?
Ever since midnight they have been striking our great bell,
And the foreigners in Moscow are preparing to depart:
'Now we must bow our heads,
For our leader is no more,   5
Prince Mikhailo Vasilevich'.
And the princes and boyars have assembled before him,
Before Prince Mstislavski Vorotinski,[1]
And among themselves they have talked together,
They have talked together and smiled: 10
'Our swift hawk soared,
But he has bruised himself against damp mother earth'.
And the Swedes and the Germans are preparing to depart:
'For our leader is no more,
Prince Mikhailo Vasilevich'.   15
The Germans have fled to Novgorod,
And in Novgorod they have shut themselves up.
And many native Russians have been ruined,
And converted in the land of Poland.

---

[1] I.e. the president of the Duma of boyars which met on the death
of Skopin to establish a regency to elect a new tsar. It was at a feast
held in Vorotinski's house that Skopin is believed to have been
poisoned. Cf. p. 233 f. above.

XL

Prokop Lyapunov

PROKOFI LYAPUNOV, who was in charge of the troops in Moscow during the Period of Troubles, was descended from a princely family. In spite of the loyalty shown to him in the *bylina*, he is thought to have played a rather discreditable part in the disturbances following upon the death of Boris Godunov. He allied himself at the outset with the Pretender Peter and his associate Bolotnikov, but abandoned them shortly before their defeat, first by Prince Mikhailo Skopin, and, at the siege of Tula, by the Tsar Vasili himself. When Prince Skopin marched to the relief of Moscow, Lyapunov sent him a letter in which he addressed him as Tsar—a letter which the Prince had the good sense to tear up. In 1610, on the abdication of the Tsar Vasili, Lyapunov took the lead in an attempt to unite the Russian cities for the purpose of driving the Poles out of Russia, and besieged the Polish garrison in the Kremlin. He was murdered by the Cossacks in 1611 on account of a forged document in which he was represented as having ordered their massacre. He was looked upon as a champion of the Christian faith by the Russian cities who were anxious for a union with Moscow against the Poles; and it is not unlikely that contemporary opinion was right, and that his fumbling advances towards unity and nationalism have been misunderstood by modern writers. He seems to have felt strongly that a tsar was a necessary focus for the elements working towards liberty and national unity, though he showed little judgment in his choice. He is generally regarded by western historians as primarily a self-seeking adventurer. The statements in the *bylina* that Sigismund III of Poland had established his dwelling in Moscow, and was subsequently strangled there, are quite unhistorical. Sigismund was never in Moscow himself, and he lived till 1632.

PROKOP LYAPUNOV

Recorded from Tulsk

Kirêevski, *Pêsni*, pt. VII, p. 17.

This is what happened among us in holy Russia,
In holy Russia, in stone-built Moscow;
It was a period of wars, a period of dissensions;
The pagan Lithuanians had taken Moscow captive,
The pagan Lithuanians, the accursed Polish faction.   5
The impious Sigismund had established there his dwelling;
He had established himself in the holy places,
In the holy places, in the royal Russian halls.
His happy sojourn in Moscow was not of long duration,
Not of long duration; but many troubles did he stir up
    for us.   10
Many Russian boyars made a dishonourable surrender,
Made a dishonourable surrender, renounced the Christian faith;
But one boyar, the wise governor, sturdily defended the faith,
Sturdily defended the faith, and drove the traitors away:
Now this wise governor was Prokofi Lyapunov.   15
When this Prokofi Petrovich despatched his couriers,
He issued letters to them, and gave them injunctions:
'Go forth, couriers, into every part of Russia,
Into every part of Russia, into the chief cities!
Bid the governors come hither with their troops,   20
To free the city of Moscow, and defend the faith of Christ'.
When Sigismund knew from his traitorous boyars
That Lyapunov had despatched couriers to the cities,
Couriers to the cities, to bid the governors come hither with their
    troops,
He fell into a passion, the impious Sigismund became furious, 25
Became furious, and commanded the governor to be slain,
This same governor Prokofi Lyapunov:
And those accursed traitors slew our governor.
Then the wise governors set forth from the chief cities,

All the chief cities—Kazan, Nizhni—came hither with their
    troops;   30
Then the Russians took to hacking and hewing the pagan
    Lithuanians,
Hewing the pagan Lithuanians, and the impious Sigismund they
    strangled with a rope;
They strangled him to death, and all the impious race they drove
    out of Moscow.

XLI

Kuzma Minin and Prince Pozharski.
The Delivery of Moscow. The Election
of Mikhailo Fedorovich

AFTER the enforced abdication of Vasili Shuyski in 1610, a period of anarchy followed in which a second 'false Dimitri' appeared as claimant to the Russian throne. Again he was supported by the Poles. Marina, the daughter of Sigismund, who had been married to the first Pretender, accepted him as her husband, and the mother of the murdered tsarevich again recognised this second Pretender as her son. He was murdered at the end of the same year, but the Polish faction, which was uppermost in Moscow, continued to support the candidature of Sigismund or his son to the Russian throne, and a Polish army occupied the Kremlin. While negotiations dragged on between Sigismund of Poland and the boyars of Moscow the country had time to recover itself, and the Russian cities to organise the resistance to which the leaders of the Orthodox Church courageously incited them. The lead was taken by Nizhni-Novgorod, supported by Kazan and Perm. A leader of the Nizhni citizens, Kuzma Minin, a butcher by trade, roused his fellow-citizens to patriotic voluntary financial sacrifices for the re-establishment of the monarchy and Russian unity. At the same time he induced Prince Dimitri Pozharski, who was not yet recovered from wounds suffered in the national cause, to lead the new army. The movement was wholly successful. Moscow was attacked and won, and in 1612 the Kremlin was surrendered. In 1613 Mikhailo Romanov, the son of the Patriarch Filaret and grand-nephew of Ivan the Terrible by marriage, was chosen tsar by the unanimous election of the national assembly at Moscow, and the crowd in the Red Square shouted his name when asked for their assent. The election of Tsar Mikhailo Romanov was Russia's first serious step in the direction of democracy.

KUZMA MININ AND PRINCE POZHARSKI. THE DELIVERY OF MOSCOW. THE ELECTION OF MIKHAILO FEDOROVICH

Recorded from the recitation of an old woman of seventy in Kaluga

Kirèevski, *Pêsni*, pt. VII, p. 21 ff.

In the ancient city,
In glorious wealthy Nizhni,[1]
A wealthy citizen had established his abode,
The wealthy citizen Kuzma the son of Sukhoruk.
He collected around him an army of bold youths,   5
Of bold youths, of the tradesmen of the city of Nizhni;
And when he had collected them, he addressed a speech to them:
'Oh, hearken, you comrades, tradesmen of the city of Nizhni! Forsake your homes,
Abandon your wives and children,   10
Sell all your gold and silver,
Purchase for yourselves sharp lances,
Sharp lances, steel knives;
Choose for yourselves from the princes and boyars a bold youth,
A bold youth to be your ruler.   15
Let us go and fight
For the sake of our mother, our own land,
For our own land, for the glorious city of Moscow:
For those accursed people, the wicked Poles, have seized Moscow!
Let us break them in pieces, let us hang them in multitudes, 20
Let us take captive their king, Sigismund himself,
And deliver mother Moscow from the unclean Jews,
The unclean Jews, the wicked Poles!'
Thereupon they selected soldiers, young warriors,

[1] I.e. Nizhni-Novgorod.

Young warriors, tradesmen of the city of Nizhni;   25
They chose for themselves a bold youth,
A bold youth to be their ruler,
From the glorious royal stock—
Prince Dimitri, surnamed Pozharski.
Now the glorious Prince Pozharski led them   30
To fight for the glorious city of Moscow,
To make war upon the unclean Jews and Poles.
The glorious Prince Pozharski led his valiant warriors,
He led them to the walls of Moscow;
The glorious Prince Pozharski brought his noble warriors to a
    halt   35
At the strong walls of Moscow.
The glorious Prince Pozharski stepped forward in front of his
    army,
And so addressed his bold warriors:
'Ho, hearken, brave soldiers,
Brave soldiers, tradesmen of the city of Nizhni!   40
Let us pray at the holy gate of the Saviour
To the redeeming image of the Saviour!'
When they had prayed they set to work.
When they had smashed and broken in the holy gate,
And when our brave soldiers had entered the Kremlin of white
    stone,[1]   45
They began to hack and to hew the Poles,
To hack and to hew, and to heap them in great piles.
Sigismund himself they took prisoner,
They took him prisoner, and bound him hand and foot,
They bound him hand and foot and cut off his rebellious head.
All the princes and boyars of Moscow assembled,   51
They assembled and took counsel together,
And the oldest boyars, the governors of Moscow, addressed
    them:
'Say, you boyars, whom shall we have as tsar?'
And the boyars, the governors of Moscow, spoke: 55

---

[1] The Kremlin is the inner citadel of Moscow, surrounded by a wall
faced with stone and topped by battlements.

'We choose as tsar for ourselves
A glorious boyar from among the boyars;
Prince Dimitri the son of Pozharski'.
Then Prince Pozharski answered the boyars:
'Alas, you boyars, governors of Moscow!   60
I am not worthy of such honour at your hands,
I cannot accept the throne of Moscow from you.
My suggestion to you is this, you boyars, governors of Moscow:
Let us elect as our orthodox tsar
From the glorious, magnificent house of Romanov   65
Mikhailo the son of Fedor'.
And the boyars elected as their tsar Mikhailo the son of Fedor.

XLII

Prince Simeon Romanovich Pozharski

PRINCE Pozharski, the hero of the following *bylina*,
raised troops from the Russian cities with the help of
Kuzma Minin, and drove the Poles out of Moscow in
1612. He became a national hero. History has not recorded
the offer of the crown to him as stated in the *bylina* (p. 244
above), but the popular singer may nevertheless be right.
Many candidates were favoured by different parties in the
Period of Troubles preceding the election of Mikhailo
Romanov in 1613, and the hero who had been wounded in
the cause of Russia and who had banished the Polish heretics
may well have been approached. The *bylina* which follows,
however, appears to be wholly unhistorical. Pozharski is
believed to have died quietly in his bed. The popular singers
have attributed to their hero the adventures of the heroes of
ancient Kiev—perhaps of Vasili Kazimirovich—and have
transported him to the milieu of the *bogatyri* of Prince
Vladimir and their encounters with the Tartars of old.

PRINCE SIMEON ROMANOVICH POZHARSKI

Recorded by Kirsha Danilov

Kirêevski, *Pêsni*, pt. VII, p. 27 ff.

Beyond the river and the ferry, beyond the village of Sosnov,
At the city of Konotopa with its wall of white stone,
In the meadows, the green meadows,
The royal troops were stationed,
The troops were composed wholly of the nobility,   5
The squadrons were composed of gentry.
And from afar in the open plain,

From the free, wide plain,
Like black crows flocking together,
The Kalmuks and the Bashkirs assembled and thronged.   10
The Tartars fell upon the royal army;
The Tartars demanded of them
Someone from the royal opposing troops;
But from the royal opposing troops
None of the Streltsy were forthcoming, or of the bold soldiery.
Then Prince Pozharski rode forward,   16
Prince Simeon Romanovich;
The great boyar commends himself to God, he, Prince Pozharski.
He rode forth to the encounter,
Against a villainous Tartar horseman;   20
But the Tartar wielded in his hands a sharp lance,
While glorious Prince Pozharski
Had only a sharp sword in his right hand.
Like two bright falcons flying together in the open plain,
So encountered in the open plain   25
The boyar Pozharski and the Tartar.
God help Prince Simeon Romanovich Pozharski!
With his sharp sabre he parried the Tartar's sharp lance,
And cut off the head of that Tartar horseman.
And those accursed ones, the accursed pagan Tartars,   30
He slew their horseman—that was an inglorious Tartar!—
But those accursed Crimean Tartars, accursed and cunning,
They shot an arrow through the good steed of Simeon Pozharski;
His good steed fell hamstrung.
Prince Pozharski called out to the royal troops: 35
'Ho, you newly levied troops, you royal Streltsy:
Bring me a good steed, and take me away,
Take me away to the royal army'.
The accursed Crimean Tartars, accursed and cunning,
They flung themselves on his breast, they made Prince Pozharski
        prisoner;   40
They carried him off into their Crimean steppes,
To the Crimean khan himself—the boorish scoundrel.
He began to question him:

'Hearken, Prince Pozharski,
Prince Simeon Romanovich!   45
Serve me faithfully, faithfully and truly,
Staunchly behind my back;
Even as you have served your tsar, the White Tsar,
Serve me likewise, the Crimean khan himself;
Then will I bestow upon you gold and silver,   50
And charming wives, and gentle pretty maidens'.
Prince Pozharski answered the Crimean khan:
'Hearken, Crimean khan, you boorish scoundrel!
Gladly would I serve you, the Crimean khan himself;
If only my nimble feet were not fettered,   55
And my white hands were not bound with silken bonds,
And if I had my sharp sabre,
I would serve you truly on your rebellious head,
I would cut off your rebellious head'.
Then the Crimean khan, the boorish scoundrel, cried out: 60
'Ho, you pagan Tartars!
Take Pozharski away on to a high hill, and cut off his head,
Cut up his white body into tiny pieces,
Scatter Pozharski afar over the open plain'.
Like black crows shrieking, and cawing,   65
The Tartars seized upon Prince Simeon Pozharski,
The Tartars carried him off to a high hill,
The Tartars put Prince Simeon Pozharski to death,
They cut off his rebellious head,
They cut up his white body into tiny pieces,   70
They scattered Pozharski afar over the open plain;
They rode away to the Crimean khan,
They did not come back on the next day, and no one knew what
      had happened.
But from the royal troops there were two Cossacks who set forth;
Those two Cossack youths,   75
They went on foot to the hill,
And they arrived there at the lofty hill,
And those young men discovered the body of Pozharski:
His head lay apart, his hands and feet were dispersed,

And his white body was hacked to pieces,   80
And scattered in free space.
These young Cossacks collected his remains,
And laid them together in one place.
They gathered bast of the lime-tree,
And they laid him down upon it;   85
Firmly they fastened the lime-tree bast,
And carried Pozharski away to the city of Konotopa.
In the city of Konotopa a bishop officiated.
He assembled bishops, priests, and deacons,
And sextons of the church;   90
And to those bold young Cossacks
He gave orders to wash the body of Pozharski.
And they laid the remains of his body together in a reliquary of
    oak,
And covered it with a lid of white oak;
And then the people marvelled,   95
For his body grew together again.
When they had chanted through the requiem appointed,
They buried his white body in the damp earth,
And sang a Mass for the eternal welfare
Of the soul of Prince Pozharski.   100

XLIII

The Battle of Astrakhan

ON the accession of Mikhailo Romanov the country was still in a very disturbed condition. Many districts were still in the hands of the Poles, and powerful bands of Cossacks wandered about in the south on marauding expeditions. Their formidable nature may be gauged from the fact that in the town of Astrakhan their leader, Zarutski, still held out against the tsar. There also was Marina, the wife of both the false Dimitris, and her infant son by the second. In 1614 a Russian force marched against the city. The inhabitants, tired of Zarutski's cruelties, had imprisoned him in the Kremlin. He tried to escape, but was captured and impaled, while Marina was imprisoned for life and her infant son hanged. The Tsar Mikhailo was not more than sixteen years of age at the time of these events. The popular singer has not forgotten the non-Slavonic elements of which the Cossack forces were composed, and whom he calls *Burut*, i.e. no doubt Buryat, in reference to their Tartar (or rather Mongol) origin.

THE BATTLE OF ASTRAKHAN

Recorded from Tambov

Kirêevski, *Pêsni*, pt. VII, p. 24.

The orthodox tsar Mikhailo has equipped himself for a journey,
For a long journey to Astrakhan;
He has furnished himself with troops,
With the regiment of the Streltsy.
He has taken leave of the tsaritsa,   5
He has blessed his little children.
When she bade him farewell the tsaritsa wept bitterly,

And weeping she besought him:
'Come back soon, orthodox tsar!
Return safe and sound to your little children,   10
Return to live long with me, the tsaritsa!'
The tsar Mikhailo took leave of his boyars,
He took leave of all his retinue,
And the orthodox tsar Mikhailo set off to lead his army
To the great city of Astrakhan.   15
The tsar Mikhailo approached the strong walls of stone,
And descried a vast army;
The tsar Mikhailo despatched a scout to the hostile
    army:
'Go, scout, to the hostile army and ascertain
What that army on the stone wall amounts to.'   20
The messenger came back from the hostile area,
And addressed the orthodox tsar:
'That army is worthless—
They are all good-for-nothing Burut rebels'.
Then the orthodox army moved forward;   25
And they fought and slashed for three days and nights;
On the fourth day they entered the city,
They freed the glorious city from the evil insolent foes,
The evil insolent foes, from the Burut rebels.

XLIV

The Entry of the Patriarch Filaret
into Moscow

THE Patriarch Filaret, whose baptismal name was Fedor Nikitich Romanov, was the eldest son of Nikita Romanov, the brother of Anastasya, the first wife of Ivan the Terrible (cf. p. 193 above). The usurper Boris, jealous of the popularity and prestige of the Romanovs, deported the various members of the family to remote parts of the empire in 1601. Fedor was forced to become a monk, and assumed the name Filaret. His wife became a nun and their only son Mikhailo was exiled. The family were recalled by the Pretender, Grigori Otrepev, and Filaret was made Metropolitan of Rostov. During the Period of Troubles, following on the death of the Pretender, Filaret was seized by the Poles and imprisoned in 1611. In 1613 his son Mikhailo Fedorovich Romanov, a boy of 16, was elected tsar (cf. p. 244 above), and in July 1619 Filaret returned to Moscow from his captivity and was at once proclaimed patriarch. He acted as regent for his son and continued to take a leading part in the government till his death.

The chief interest attaching to the following poem is its complete contemporaneity. Richard James (cf. p. 7 above), who recorded the poem, left Moscow in August 1619. It was written down, therefore, within a month of its composition, and may safely be taken as a standard of the oral journalese of the time. In view of this evidence it becomes highly probable that the *bylina* on Vasili Shuyski (no. XXXVII), and other *byliny* similar in style, are also contemporary compositions, though they are not recorded till much later times.

THE ENTRY OF THE PATRIARCH FILARET
INTO MOSCOW, JULY 1619

Recorded by Richard James in 1619

Brodski, Mendelson and Sidorov, *Istoriko-Literaturnaya Khrestomatÿa*, vol. I, p. 135.

There is great rejoicing in the realm of Moscow,
And throughout the holy Russian land,
Our lord, the orthodox tsar, is happy,
The Grand Prince Mikhailo Fedorovich;
For they say our father has arrived,   5
Our lord Filaret Nikitich,
From the land of the heretics, from Lithuania.
With him he is bringing many princes and boyars,
And moreover he also brings the boyar of the tsar,
Prince Mikhailo Borisovich Shein.   10
Many princes, boyars, and many dignitaries have assembled
To the mighty realm of Moscow,
Anxious to welcome Filaret Nikitich.
From the glorious city of stone-built Moscow
It is not the red sun in its course;   15
Our lord, the orthodox tsar, has gone forth
To meet his father,
The lord Filaret Nikitich.
With the tsar has gone his uncle,
Ivan Nikitich the boyar: 20
'God grant that my noble father be well,
My noble father Filaret Nikitich'.
And now that they have come into stone-built Moscow,
They have not entered the royal palace,
They have gone to the sacred cathedral,[1]   25
To sing the appointed Mass.
He has blessed his beloved son:
'God grant that the orthodox tsar be well,
The mighty Prince Mikhailo Fedorovich,
And that he may rule the realm of Moscow,   30
And all the holy Russian land'.

[1] I.e. no doubt the Uspenski Sobor.

CYCLE OF PETER THE GREAT

XLV

The Birth of Peter the Great

PETER the Great, the 'first Emperor' of Russia, was born in 1672 and died in 1725. He was the son of the Tsar Alexis who reigned 1645–76, and the grandson of Mikhailo Romanov, who was elected tsar at the conclusion of the Period of Troubles (cf. p. 244 above). The impression conveyed by the following *bylina* of the gracious clemency and good-will of Alexis is true to history. The beauty and gentleness of his character has gained for him recognition among historians as 'Russia's most charming tsar'. The picture which the *bylina* gives of the splendour of his court is also entirely consistent with what we learn from contemporary records, such as that of Guy Miège, secretary to the embassy sent by Charles II of England to Moscow in 1664, who has left us an account of his reception at court. Rambaud also tells us that in Zabêlin's study of the *Childhood of Peter*, Alexis is seen sending in all directions to announce the glad tidings to the boyars, to the officers of the crown, and to the vassal princes and the patriarch and clergy, as well as to the Troitsa monastery. On the days following the bells were rung in all the churches of the Kremlin and a special service was held in the Cathedral of the Assumption. A grand festival was held in the palace, at which the tsar is said to have distributed rich food and drink to his subjects with his own hands. Rich gifts of silk and velvet and furs were made, honours were bestowed, and at the feast which followed magnificent architectural dishes were displayed in true Renaissance style. The little cradle was hung from the ceiling by cords, and surrounded with every luxury that could be devised.[1]

[1] *La Russie Épique*, p. 295.

THE BIRTH OF PETER THE GREAT

Recorded by Kirsha Danilov

Kirêevski, *Pésni*, pt. VIII, p. 1 f.

He is gracious and gay in Moscow,
The orthodox tsar Alexêy Mikhailovich;
For God has bestowed on him a son and heir,
The tsarevich Petr Alexêevich,
The first emperor in the land.   5
All the master carpenters in Russia,
The whole night long they have not slept—
They have been making a cradle, a little hammock,
For the baby tsarevich.
And the nursemaids and nurses,   10
And the pretty chamber-maids,
The whole night long they have not slept—
They have been embroidering a little cloth [1]
Of white velvet picked out in bright gold.   15
And the prisons with their prisoners—
They have all been emptied;
And the royal cellars—
They have all been thrown open.
In the tsar's palace   20
They are holding a feast, a joyous banquet,
The princes have assembled,
The boyars have met together from afar,
The nobles have met together from nearby;
And all God's people at the feast,   25
They are eating and drinking and taking their ease.
So happy are those celebrations
That they do not notice the passage of time—
Those celebrations for the little tsarevich,
Petr Alexêevich,   30
The first emperor.

[1] The cradle of Peter the Great, preserved in the museum of the Kremlin at Moscow, consists of a piece of cloth distended by poles, and suspended from the ceiling.

XLVI

The Sovereign wrestles with a Dragoon

THE reign of Peter the Great has furnished subjects for a large Cycle of popular songs. The *byliny* relating to the tsar and to his generals fill a whole volume of Kirêevski's collection. His enemies and the rebels who gave trouble from time to time during his reign are also celebrated in *byliny*. These *byliny* have been collected from all over Russia, and are by no means confined to the north, though the north is naturally especially rich in memories of the great tsar, and has retained a great wealth of tradition, both in prose and verse, relating to his remarkable character and habits, and to his early years. It is curious therefore that the historical value of these traditions should not be on a high level. Apparently what impressed the popular imagination was not so much Peter's greatness as his eccentricity. His strength of intellect is not realised, but his tall and powerful figure; his habit of associating with peasants; his foreign travel—Peter was the first tsar to venture on the sea; his love of foreign importations—folding tables, telescopes, embossed writing paper; his mechanical hobbies; all these things appear in the *byliny* in distorted and fantastic forms, transporting us into the atmosphere of folk-tale. Many of the adventures originating in the *byliny* of the Kiev Cycle have been attached to Peter, many of the features of the *bogatyri*, much of the supernatural power of the heroes of the 'Older Cycle', as well as their gigantic stature. Thus it comes about that while a large proportion of the *byliny* are quite unhistorical in their main facts, they yet reflect those spectacular features in Peter's life and character, especially in his early years, which impressed themselves on the people of Russia in his own time. We need not believe that Peter wrestled with a young dragoon; but it was the kind of thing he would be likely to do.

THE SOVEREIGN WRESTLES WITH A DRAGOON

Recorded from Ural

Kirêevski, *Pêsni*, pt. VIII, p. 37 ff.

In the palace, the royal palace,
Beside the Red Staircase[1],
There stood a folding table.
At the table sat the orthodox tsar,
The orthodox tsar, Petr Aleksêevich;   5
Before him stood the princes and boyars.
The orthodox tsar addressed them thus:
'Come now, you princes and boyars!
Is there no one among you who will volunteer
To wrestle with the White Tsar,   10
To pass the time and amuse the tsar?'
All the princes and boyars were scared,
They scattered to various parts of the palace;
But a young dragoon stood up before him,
A young dragoon, fifteen years old,   15
And addressed the White Tsar as follows:
'Hail, all hail, orthodox tsar,
Orthodox tsar, Petr Aleksêevich!
Do not order me to be executed, to be hanged,
Bid me speak a word,   20
Speak a word, and say my say:
I will volunteer to wrestle with you, White Tsar:
To pass the time and amuse the tsar'.
'If you overcome me, young dragoon, I will reward you;
But if I overcome you I will execute you.'   25
The young dragoon made answer:
'As God wills, and you the tsar!'
The orthodox tsar girded on his silk belt,
He went out with the young dragoon; they laid hold upon one
        another,

[1] The Red Staircase and other features relating to the tsars of
Moscow have been transferred from the earlier *byliny* to those of
Peter the Great and St Petersburg.

The young dragoon addressed him,   30
The White Tsar, Petr Aleksêevich:
'Behold, our father, orthodox tsar,
Orthodox tsar, Petr Aleksêevich!
I am going to overturn you'.
The young dragoon overturned him with his left hand,   35
The young dragoon caught him up with his right hand,
He did not let the tsar touch the damp earth,
And the orthodox tsar addressed him:
'Thanks to you, dragoon, for your wrestling!'
The young dragoon drew a little nearer to him: 40
'Hearken, pray hearken, our father, orthodox tsar,
Orthodox tsar, Petr Aleksêevich.
Do not be angry with me for my wrestling!'
'I give you thanks, young dragoon, for your wrestling!
What shall I bestow upon you, young dragoon, as a reward?   45
Shall it be villages or estates,
Or shall it be a chest of gold?'
'I do not want villages or estates,
Or a chest of pure gold.
Grant me to drink, free of charge,   50
Wine in the taverns of the Crown.'[1]

[1] Cf. p. 153, footnote 1, above.

XLVII

The Tsar's Voyage to Stockholm and his Return

IN 1697 Peter the Great set out on his travels to Western Europe, accompanied by a Swiss named Lefort, who had entered his service, and two Russian generals, Golovin and Vosnitsin. The tsar travelled *incognito*, and as he passed through Livonia the Swedish governor of Riga took advantage of the tsar's disguise to refrain from formally paying his respects to him. The tsar's visit was regarded with suspicion, and his movements were carefully watched. When he chanced to pass near the fortifications the garrison threatened to fire on him—an insult which he did not forget to avenge later. In the *bylina* the facts are completely distorted. The scene is shifted from Riga to Stockholm, and the governor Dalberg has become the Swedish queen. The atmosphere is that of folk-tale, to which also belongs the *motif* of the identification by means of the portraits.

THE TSAR'S VOYAGE TO STOCKHOLM
AND HIS RETURN

Kirêevski, *Pésni*, pt. VIII, p. 164 ff.

No one knows, no one can say
Whither our sovereign tsar is preparing to go.
He has loaded his ships with pure silver,
He has furnished his vessels with bright gold.
He is taking with him very few men—   5
No one except the Preobrazhenski grenadiers.[1]

[1] So called from the village of Preobrazhenskoe near Moscow, where Peter lived as a boy. The Preobrazhenski regiment developed out of the *druzhina* or body of personal followers which Peter collected

Our father, the White Tsar, has commanded us thus:
'Hearken, officers and soldiers!
Do not address me as your tsar or sovereign,
Address me as a merchant from overseas'.   10
Now our sovereign tsar has set off to amuse himself at sea.
When the White Tsar had been crossing the sea for a week,
He continued for a second week;
On the third week he reached the country of Stockholm,
The realm of Sweden.   15
Our merchant strolls about the town,
But no one will recognise that merchant,
Only the hetman of the Swedes recognised him.
In hot haste he rushed away to the king's daughter:
'O hearken, king's daughter, our mother!   20
That is not a merchant strolling about;
That person strolling about the town is the White Tsar!'
Then the king's daughter came forth on to her Red Staircase;[1]
She brought out the portraits of the tsars of seven lands,
She recognised the White Tsar from his portrait.   25
The king's daughter cried out in a loud voice:
'Hearken, my Swedish generals!
Shut the gates very securely,
Seize the White Tsar with all speed!'
Even then our father was not afraid;   30
He guessed all the intentions of the Swedes.
Hastily he rushed into a peasant's house:
'Take money, peasant, take as much as you want,
And take me to the shore of the blue sea'.

round him during his boyhood, as the tsars before him had done.
Many of these friends of his youth became his chief generals and
advisers in later life, and were known as Peter's 'Eagles'. When he
formed these personal followers into the Preobrazhenski regiment he
held a commission in it himself as captain of the gunners (cf. p. 273
below).

The famous Red Staircase of the Kremlin has been transferred by
the popular singer from Moscow to Stockholm. It led from the great
royal audience chamber known as the 'Faceted Palace' (cf. p. 204 above)
into the Cathedral Square in the east of the Kremlin.

Hurriedly the peasant took him to the shore of the blue sea,   35
And very hastily our sovereign tsar embarked on his ship.
He shouted to his sailors and soldiers:
'O, my children, pull together with a will.
Row and sail as fast as you can!'
First one pursuing party overtook the White Tsar;   40
Then a second came up with him.
And the pursuers addressed our sovereign tsar:
'Take us, White Tsar, take us away with you;
If you do not take us with you, our father,
None of us poor wretches will survive!'   45
But all the pursuers plunged into the blue sea,
And our sovereign tsar came back again to holy Russia.

XLVIII

The Song of the Tsaritsa, Evdokÿa Fedorovna Lopukhina

PETER the Great married Evdokÿa Fedorovna Lopukhina in 1689. By her he had two children, the unfortunate Alexis and a daughter. The latter died in
infancy. The marriage was not a happy one, and on Peter's
return from his travels in Europe he declared his decision to
repudiate his wife. She was sent to the Pokrovski monastery
in Suzdal, and in 1711 Peter married Marfa Skavronskaya, a
Livonian or Lithuanian peasant. Evdokÿa wrote pathetically
affectionate letters to the tsar; but her sympathies were reactionary and her cell became a centre for the discontented
elements of Church and State, and Peter had her removed to
stricter conditions in the nunnery of New Ladoga. She was
ultimately released and was present at the coronation of her
grandson, Peter II. The following *bylina*, in which she is
represented as bewailing her fate, is an interesting parallel
to that of Marfa Matvêevna, the wife of Ivan IV (cf. p. 203 f.
above). It is interesting to note that the singer never
alludes to her by name in the *bylina*. After her divorce
Peter issued a royal edict that her name was never to be
mentioned (cf. p. 22 above).

THE SONG OF THE TSARITSA, EVDOKŸA
FEDOROVNA LOPUKHINA

Recorded from Moscow

Kirêevski, *Pêsni*, pt. VIII,ˆp. 106 f.

I wander young beside the stream—
And like the stream my tears flow;
I stand, still young, beside the fire—
So burns my little flame within;

I sit, still young, beside my love—   5
My loved one chides and abuses me,
He chides and abuses me,
And orders me away to a nunnery.
'Go and get shorn a nun, you who are not dear to me,
Go and take the habit, you whom I abhor!   10
To be shorn a nun I will give you a hundred roubles;
To take the habit I will give you a thousand.
I will build you a new cell,
In a green garden under an apple-tree;
I will pierce three windows,   15
The first looking towards God's church,
The second on to the green garden,
The third on to the open country:
In God's church you shall say your prayers,
In the green garden you shall take your walks,   20
In the open country you shall look out upon the view'.[1]
The princes and boyars chanced to pass by,[2]
They asked: 'What is this cell,
What is this cell, this cell so new,
Who is this nun enclosed so young?   25
And why has she taken the veil?'
And the nun made answer to them:
'I have been made to take the veil by the tsar himself,
I have been made to take the habit by Peter the First,
With his cruel, vindictive heart'.   30

[1] From this point, with the rapid transition which is a striking
feature of these songs, the *bylina* passes to narrative.
[2] According to the version recorded from Samara (Kirêevski, *Pêsni*,
pt. VIII, p. 108 f.), it was the *kalêki* or wandering psalm-singers who
passed by.

XLIX

The Execution of the Prince,
the Great Boyar, Ataman of the Streltsy

DURING the foreign tour of Peter the Great in 1697–8, the discontented elements in the population had an admirable opportunity to assert themselves. One of the chief manifestations of this discontent was the revolt of the Streltsy, the old Muscovite palace guard, who belonged to the reactionary party. They favoured Peter's elder half-brother Ivan, and remained loyal to his elder half-sister Sophia, who had acted as regent for her two brothers during their minority. The Streltsy hated and distrusted the tsar's foreign tastes and innovations, and were discontented at the long military campaigns on which they were employed. The rising was easily quelled by the generals Shein and Gordon at the head of the regular troops, and the rebels were punished. Some were put to death at once, others were imprisoned till the tsar's return, when he meted out ghastly punishments. The following *bylina* is thought to have reference to the execution of the leader of the insurrection.

THE EXECUTION OF THE PRINCE, THE GREAT BOYAR, ATAMAN OF THE STRELTSY

From the collection of Chulkovski and Novikovski

Kirêevski, *Pésni*, pt. VIII, p. 22.

Out of the Kremlin, the strong city,
Out of the palace, the palace of the emperor,
There stretches to the Red Square,
There stretches a broad road.
And along this broad road   5

They are leading a fine youth to his execution,
A fine youth, a great boyar,
A great boyar, the ataman of the Streltsy,
For his treason against the royal majesty.
He marches, the youth—he does not falter—   10
Proudly he looks round on all the people,
Even now he will not humble himself before the tsar.
Before him marches the terrible executioner,
In his hands he carries the sharp axe;
And behind him walk his father and mother,   15
His father and mother, and his young wife;
They are weeping, as a river flows,
They are sobbing, as the brooks murmur,
Through their sobs they entreat him:
'Our darling child!   20
Humble yourself to the tsar,
Confess yourself in the wrong;
Perchance our sovereign tsar will pardon you,
And leave your rebellious head on your sturdy shoulders.'
But he hardens his brave heart to stone,   25
He defies the tsar and is obdurate;
His father and mother he will not hear,
He will not be moved by his young wife,
He will not have pity on his children.
They have taken him to the Red Square,[1]   30
They have struck off his rebellious head
From his sturdy shoulders.

[1] The *Krasnaya Ploshchad* immediately outside the Kremlin or fortified inner citadel of Moscow, on the north-east side. In the Red Square was the *Lobnoe Mêsto*, 'the place of execution' (cf. p .195 above).

L

The Boyar's Address to his Head

THE following *bylina* is probably a variant of the last, and may well have been composed for the same occasion. It is included by the editors of Kirêevski's collection among the *byliny* relating to the reign of Peter the Great.

THE BOYAR'S ADDRESS TO HIS HEAD

From the collection of Chulkovski and Novikovski

Kirêevski, *Pésni*, pt. VIII, p. 24.

'O my head, my dear head,
My useful head!
You have served me, my head,
For just thirty years and three,—
Without dismounting from my good steed,   5
Without drawing my feet from the stirrup.
Alas, dear head, you have not gained
Either profit or pleasure for yourself,
Nor any word of praise,
Nor exalted rank: 10
Only you have earned, dear head,
Two lofty posts,
And a cross-beam of maple-wood,
And one thing more—a silken noose.'
Along the famous Myasnitskaya,[1]   15
Through the Myasnitskaya Gateway,
They are leading a prince, a boyar.
Before him march the priests and clerks;

[1] One of the great thoroughfares of Moscow leading from the northeast towards the Kremlin.

In their hands they carry a great book;
And behind him marches a troop of soldiers,   20
Carrying unsheathed their sharp swords;
At his right side walks his terrible executioner,
Bearing in his hands a sharp sword.
At his left side   25
Walks his dear sister;
She weeps, as a river flows,
She sobs, as the brooks murmur.
Her dear brother tries to soothe her:
'Weep not, weep not, dear sister,   30
Do not bedim your bright eyes with tears,
Do not sully your fair face,
Do not let your gay heart be heavy.
What is it you long for?—
Is it for my lands or estates,   35
Is it for my possessions and wealth,
Is it for my gold or silver,
Or is it only for my life?'
'Alas, my darling, my precious brother!
None of those do I desire—   40
Neither your lands nor estates,
Neither your possessions nor your wealth,
Neither your gold nor your silver,
The only thing I would keep, brother,
Is your life.'   45
Her dear brother made answer:
'My darling, my precious sister!
You may weep, but it is in vain;
You may pray to God, but you will have no answer;
You may petition the tsar, but he will not yield.   50
Thus much mercy has God shown me—
Thus much grace has the sovereign tsar vouchsafed me:—
He has commanded them to hew off my rebellious head
From my sturdy shoulders'.
Then they took the prince on to the high scaffold,   55
To the spot appointed for him;

He prayed to the Saviour, to His wonder-working image;[1]
He bowed low on all sides:
'Alas and farewell, farewell, God's world and His people!
Pray for my sins,   60
For my heavy sins'.
The people had hardly time to look upon him,
Ere they struck off his rebellious head
From his sturdy shoulders.

[1] This was on the tower of the Saviour in the Red Square.

LI

Sheremetev and Shlippenbach, Major of the Swedes. The Battle of Ehresfer

IN 1700 Peter the Great declared war against Charles XII of Sweden. His aim was to obtain possession of the Baltic coastline which at this time was almost all in the hands of the Swedes. The first engagement, the Battle of Narva, fought in the same year, was a defeat for the Russians, in spite of their numerical superiority. In 1701, however, Sheremetev, the general who had commanded the cavalry at Narva, was victorious in a pitched battle fought against the Swedes at Ehresfer in Livonia. The *bylina* which celebrates this event is interesting for the singular fidelity of its details to historical fact. Rambaud, who was familiar with Ustryalov's narrative of the battle, has observed that one sees in the *bylina*, as in the historical account, the Russian general advancing from Pskov on Dorpat, the raising of 300 Esthonians commanded by the Swedish lieutenant-colonel Liven, the lakes and marshes of Kannapaeh which covered the Swedish army, the important rôle of the Russian artillery with their twenty-one cannon, and the final bayonet charge of the Russians. We have already noted the fidelity of much of the military detail of the *bylina* of the *Capture of Kazan* by Ivan the Terrible, of that of *The Conquest of Siberia* by Ermak the Cossack, and of the *Capture of Astrakhan* by Mikhailo Romanov. The Russian peasants have retained vivid recollections of the historical events in which they themselves have borne a part, and especially those in which they have borne the distasteful rôle of soldier.

SHEREMETEV AND SHLIPPENBACH, MAJOR OF THE
SWEDES. THE BATTLE OF EHRESFER

Recorded from the land of the Don Cossacks

Kirêevski, *Pêsni*, pt. VIII, p. 129.

It is not a threatening cloud which has come up,
Nor a heavy fall of sleet descending:
From the glorious town of Pskov
The great royal boyar has arisen,
Count Boris, the lord Petrovich Sheremetev,   5
With his cavalry and dragoons,
With all his Muscovite infantry.
As soon as he reached the Red Grange, he halted;
Well and smartly were the troops equipped;
Their cannon and mortars were all in position.   10
It is not a bright falcon flying through the air,
It is the boyar walking through our troops;
It is not a golden trumpet resounding,
It is the great royal boyar speaking,
Count Boris, lord Petrovich Sheremetev: 15
'My children, my dragoons and soldiers!
Can I count on you,
To stand firm against the foe?'
And the dragoons and soldiers replied:
'We will serve our sovereign,   20
Till we fall, one by one!'
At once the boyar arose
With his cavalry and his infantry.
They came upon the Swedish sentries,
They, the Swedish sentries, were relieving guard,   25
They took a major prisoner.
They took the major to the general,
The general ordered him to be questioned:
'Tell us, major of the land of Sweden,
Tell us the whole literal truth,   30
You cannot conceal it from the tsar:
Are your forces far off,
Are the forces numerous belonging to your general,

Belonging to your general, to Shlippenbach himself?'
Then the major of the land of Sweden made answer: 35
'Alas, great royal boyar,
Count Boris, lord Petrovich Sheremetev!
I cannot conceal it from the tsar,
I will tell you the whole literal truth:
Our forces are in the open plain,   40
Beyond those mosses and swamps,
Beyond the great ford,
Close to the shore of the Sea of the Norsemen;
And the forces with the general are forty thousand,
With the beloved General Shlippenbach'.   45
The boyar was not afraid at these words,
He arose at once with his troops.
It is not two thunder clouds appearing in the sky,
It is two great armies fighting:
The Muscovite army and the Swedish;   50
Then Sheremetev's infantry opened fire
From little guns and cannon.
It is not a thunder-clap bursting through a cloud,
Nor a booming cannon discharging,
It is the heart of the boyar which is enraged.   55
It is not damp mother earth rending asunder,
Nor the blue sea in agitation;
They have fixed their bayonets on their muskets,
They have fired their guns on their pursuers,
They have drawn their sharp sabres,   60
They have laid in rest their steel lances,
They have pursued the Swedish general
To the very town of Dorpat.
How the Swedish soldiers wept!
How painfully they spoke through their tears: 65
'O the accursed Muscovite infantry!
How constantly he comes on in the attack!
How cruelly has he conquered us!'
Then we gave the Swedes a thorough beating,
And took them prisoners three at a time;   70
And the tsar was the richer thereby.

LII

Lament of the Troops on the Death of Peter the Great

THE similarity of this *bylina* to the *Lament of the Troops for Ivan the Terrible* is very striking. There can be no doubt that the former served as a model for this and subsequent *byliny* of the same type, though it may not have been the first of its kind. Evidently such Laments are modelled on a well-established conventional type which has a long history, and which may be already ancient in the time of Ivan IV (cf. p. 210 above). We shall see similar Laments ascribed to the troops on the death of Katharine II and on that of the Tsar Alexander I. Morfill has published (*History of Russia*, p. 168) a translation of a variant version of the Lament for Peter which shows even closer verbal resemblance to that of Ivan, especially in the opening lines. The beautiful overture or *pripévka* which forms the opening of the following Lament for Peter is not found in the other Laments. Its connection with what follows is not obvious; but it leads by a delicate gradation to the tragedy of the dead tsar. The metaphor is that of the steppe blooms plucked early and cast away in their prime. The same delicacy of feeling is remarkable in the closing lines of the poem, in which the army is represented as standing to attention, drawn up in line and waiting for the word of command from their leader, the dead tsar. By an affectionate reminiscence he is referred to as captain of the gunners, the modest rank which he held in his youth during his military training among the soldiers of the little regiment which he had himself formed (cf. p. 260, footnote 1, above).

LAMENT OF THE TROOPS ON THE DEATH
OF PETER THE GREAT

Recorded from Saratov

Kirêevski, *Pêsni*, pt. VIII, p. 278 f.

'Alas, you native berry,
My beautiful sapling,
When did you sprout, when did you grow,
When did you bloom, when did you ripen?'
'In the springtime I sprouted, in summer I grew,   5
At dawn I bloomed, in the sunlight I ripened.'
'Alas, you native berry,
My beautiful sapling!
Why are you gathered so soon,
Tied into bunches,   10
And scattered over the wild steppe,
Perchance to the village of Sheremetev,
Perchance to the royal palace,
Perchance to the Red Staircase?'[1]
In this royal palace,   15
On this Red Staircase,
A young sergeant was standing sentry.
His nimble legs were frozen in his very boots,
His white hands to the very bone.
As he stood there he pondered,   20
He pondered and then began to weep;
And he weeps as a river flows,
His tears flow as the brooks trickle;
He sighs—it is like the forest murmuring,
He sobs—it is like the thunder rumbling,   25
And through his sobs he cried:
'Blow from the mountains, you rough winds,
Whirl away the white snow of heaven,
Scatter, you winds, the white, stinging hail,

[1] Cf. p. 258, footnote 1, above.

Shake damp mother earth, 30
In all four quarters;
Break in pieces, you winds, the coffin lid,
Unwrap the gold brocade,
Blow apart the fine white shroud!
Awake, stand up, orthodox tsar, 35
Orthodox tsar, Petr Alekseevich!
Lift up your head,
Look upon your army.
Your army stands drawn up in line,
Stands drawn up in line and does not waver; 40
They are trained in warfare,
They are going forth to battle![1]
All the troops stand drawn up in line,
And all the colonels before their troops;
The lieutenant-colonels are at their posts; 45
All the majors are on their good steeds;
The captains stand before their squadrons,
The officers before their platoons,
And the ensigns beneath their standards.
They are awaiting their colonel, 50
The colonel of the Preobrazhenski guard,
The captain of the bombardiers'.[2]

[1] The version which we have selected for translation concludes at this point. The passage which follows forms the conclusion of a variant version of the same poem, Kirêevski, *Pêsni*, pt. VIII, p. 280 f.

[2] I.e. the Tsar Peter himself; a touching allusion, as Rambaud observes, to the military comradeship which existed between Peter and his soldiers, and to his modest rank of captain of the bombardiers, with which he was content up to the time of the capture of Azov. For an account of Peter's institution of the Preobrazhenski regiment from the companions of his youth, cf. p. 260, footnote 1, above.

THE EIGHTEENTH CENTURY
AND THE MODERN PERIOD

LIII

Prince Vanya Dolgoruki and his young wife, the Boyarin Natalya Borisovna. The Execution of Prince Dolgoruki

ON the death of Peter II in 1730 the throne was offered to his niece, Anne Ivanovna, Duchess of Courland. The choice was made by the High Council, consisting of the old nobility and the marshals Dolgoruki and Golitsin, who drew up a set of liberal conditions, a kind of constitutional charter which has been likened to our Habeas Corpus, and which the new Empress was obliged to sign before her coronation. These conditions transformed the absolute monarchy into a constitutional monarchy, transferring the power of the Crown largely into the hands of the High Council. The measure was not popular with the country. The High Council consisted of only eight members, of which two belonged to the Golitsin family, and four to the Dolgorukis. It was felt that too much power was placed in the hands of two families, and the new Empress soon found that the constitution which she had been obliged to sign, and which had so greatly curtailed her prerogative, did not represent the wishes of the nation. She was not slow to profit by this discovery, and took cruel vengeance on those who had been responsible for the measure. The Golitsins and the Dolgorukis were executed or died in prison. Cruellest of all was the fate of Ivan Dolgoruki, the former favourite, who was first sent to Siberia, and then recalled to die on the rack at Novgorod. His sufferings were voluntarily shared by his young wife Natalya, daughter of Sheremetev, one of Peter the Great's generals, who married him, against the earnest entreaties of her family, after he was sentenced to banishment in Siberia. 'Just think', she writes in her memoirs, 'how little it would have been honourable for me to be willing to marry him when he was in prosperity, and to refuse him when he was unfortunate.' The reference to her ring in the following *bylina* may be a reminiscence of the jewel which she mentions in these memoirs as having been lost on the journey to Siberia. It is true that she had nothing left with which to bribe the executioner, and her husband died under torture. She has left a tragic picture of their last parting. 'I was the companion of my husband in all his sufferings', she writes, 'and now I speak the very truth when I say that, in the midst of my misfortunes, I never repented of my marriage nor murmured against God.'[1] Natalya became a nun in 1758.

PRINCE VANYA DOLGORUKI AND HIS YOUNG WIFE, THE BOYARIN NATALYA BORISOVNA. THE EXECUTION OF PRINCE DOLGORUKI

Recorded from Tulsk

Kirêevski, *Pésni*, pt. IX, p. 8 f.

Along the great road
It is not a merchant or a boyar whom they are leading,
It is Prince Dolgoruki himself.
On either side marches a troop of soldiers,
A troop of soldiers, each a thousand strong.   5
In front walks the terrible executioner,
Behind walks the boyar's wife,
Very pale and her eyes red.
She weeps as a river flows,
Her tears fall as the waves roll.   10
'Do not weep, my boyarin,
With face pale and eyes red!'
'How should I not weep?—
They have confiscated my peasants,
I have no gold treasure left to me,   15
Save one—my gold ring!'
'Give your ring, give it to the executioner,
That he may grant me a swifter death.'

[1] The text of the memoirs has not been accessible to me. The quotations are from Morfill, *Russia* (London, 1891), p. 358.

LIV

Krasnoshchokov and Frederick the Great

THE Seven Years' War, fought during the years 1756–63, is widely celebrated in Russian *byliny*, though some of its more important incidents are unrepresented. In 1757 the Empress Elizabeth joined the coalition of the principal European countries, which had for its object the curtailment of the growing power of Frederick II of Prussia. This increasing power, and the proximity of Frederick to the Russian frontier, were felt to be a menace to the country, and in 1757 the Russian troops took the offensive against Prussia, crossing the frontier, and winning an easy victory. The war continued, at first with varying fortunes, though with growing success for Russia. In 1760 a Russian force of Cossacks and Kalmuks even succeeded in raiding Berlin. This exploit forms the subject of the following *bylina*. The leader of the Don Cossacks was Krasnoshchokov, a Cossack general in the Russian regular army. He was greatly admired by his own followers, and enjoyed a reputation for magic.

True to their unswerving admiration for the Cossacks, the popular singers have celebrated Krasnoshchokov above all Elizabeth's generals. He is regarded in the *byliny* of the period as the principal hero of the war, and is credited with all the great deeds of courage and daring. He is represented as having disguised himself as a merchant and having an interview, unrecognised, with Frederick himself in his own palace in Berlin. Many of the deeds of the ancient Russian heroes have been attributed to him, and his name is sometimes substituted for theirs in the songs of the older Cycles. Curiously enough, in the following *bylina* it is not Kras-

noshchokov but Frederick himself to whom supernatural
power is attributed, and the Prussian Emperor figures as
assuming protean forms in order to escape from the relentless
Cossack. The naïveté of the popular singer is strangely at
variance with his theme in these songs of the Seven Years'
War and the greatest crowned head in Europe.

KRASNOSHCHOKOV AND FREDERICK THE GREAT.
KRASNOSHCHOKOV ENTERS BERLIN

Recorded from Moscow

Kirêevski, *Pêsni*, pt. IX, p. 154.

It is not a white birch-tree falling to the earth,
Or silky grass spreading over the plain:
The grass spread over the plain is bitter wormwood,
But bitterer than this to us soldiers is the tsar's service.
Our feet have stood long on the damp earth,   5
Our eyes are wearied with gazing on the fortress,
You, my fortress, my little fortress, city of Berlin!
Into whose hands, my little fortress, have you fallen?
You have fallen, my fortress, into the hands of the White Tsar,
Even of the General Krasnoshchokov.   10
Krasnoshchokov strolled along the merchants' row;
Krasnoshchokov purchased powder and lead,
Krasnoshchokov loaded forty cannon,
Krasnoshchokov discharged forty missiles;
Krasnoshchokov slew the Prussian queen,   15
He took prisoner the king's young daughter.
He does not beat her, he does not hang her, he only questions her:
'Tell me, king's daughter, whither has the Prussian king fled?'
'I called out to you, but you would not hearken,
I waved my silk kerchief, but you would not look: 20
He has perched on the window as a blue pigeon,
The Prussian king is sitting under the table as a grey cat,
He has flown from the hall as a free bird,

He has alighted on the black quagmire as a black crow,
He has plunged into the blue sea as a white fish,   25
He has swum to the islands as a grey duck,
He has embarked on his ship as a bold hero,
He has rolled about the ship as a white pearl.'

LV

Lament of the Troops on the Death of the Empress Katharine II (1796)

T HE following Lament is very closely modelled on the *Lament of the Troops on the Death of Ivan the Terrible* and the version of the *Lament of the Troops on the Death of Peter the Great* published by Morfill (cf. p. 273 above). The similarity is very striking, not only in the words of the sentry, which constitute a static formula of such poems, but also in the *pripêvka* or opening lines. Like these earlier Laments the following *bylina* ends on a note of melancholy and foreboding.

LAMENT OF THE TROOPS ON THE DEATH OF THE
EMPRESS KATHARINE II (1796)

Kirêevski, *Pêsni*, pt. IX, p. 264.

O our father, you bright moon,
Why do you hold your course so low,
Why has your light grown so dim,—
Not as of old, not as in the past?
In the new city, in the Uspenski Cathedral,   5
Stand pivoted doors,
Pivoted and painted;
By the door stands a young soldier,
A young soldier, a sergeant of a regiment.
As he stands he weeps—   10
He weeps as a river flows:
'Blow, you rough winds,
Whirl away all the golden sand,

Blow apart, silver brocade,
Break up, coffin lid,   15
Rise up, our mother,
Compassionate sovereign,
Katerina Aleksêevna!
Without you life will be very wretched for us.
The whole realm will be the poorer   20
Under your dear son,
Under Paul Petrovich:
He has worn out his army in Turkey,
He has starved them all to death with hunger,
He has frozen them with the cold of winter'.   25

LVI

The Cossacks before the French

THE following *bylina* records the protest of the Cossacks, the 'eagles' enrolled in the army of Alexander I, against the tsar's orders to abandon the traditional Cossack dress and conform to modern military standards. It is probably based on an earlier *bylina* of the time of Peter the Great, who issued an order to the Streltsy to shave the beard and abandon the long-skirted Russian costume. A Cossack song of that period concludes with the same words: 'Do not command us to lose our beards, but rather our heads'. The term 'eagles' was also applied by Peter the Great to his immediate followers. See p. 260, footnote 1, above.

THE COSSACKS BEFORE THE FRENCH

Recorded from the Government of Simbirsk

Kirêevski, *Pêsni*, pt. x, p. 83.

O my eagles with golden wings,
Our falcons flying in the clouds!
The eagles have come flying from very far away,
Into the city of Petersburg,
To our emperor, 5
To Alexander the son of Paul.
The sovereign is angry with them,
He has commanded them to take off their patterned robes,
Their patterned robes, their Cossack costume,
And to dress in civilian dress, and in soldiers' uniform; 10
He has commanded them all to shave off their beards,
But they have disobeyed him:
'O, hear us, our father,
Orthodox tsar, Alexander Pavlovich!
Do not bid us cut off our beards, 15
Bid us rather lose our heads!'

LVII

The Invasion by the French under Napoleon (1812)

THE invasion of Russia by the French in 1812 has been productive of surprisingly few *byliny*. Considering the magnitude of the issues, the brilliant and heroic character of the Emperor Alexander I, and the decisive discomfiture and final overthrow of the enemy, one would have expected a whole Cycle of *byliny*, such as we find on the wars of Peter the Great. The facts are quite contrary. No specific encounters are mentioned. The Battle of Borodino has been forgotten. Few of the Russian generals are remembered by name except the great Kutuzov, the hero of the people. The brilliant and courageous part which the Emperor played personally in the campaign of 1812 has left little impression. In the following naïve *bylina* he is represented as sitting inactive, wholly at a loss when he receives Napoleon's challenge. It is only when reassured by Kutuzov that he recovers his spirits and addresses encouraging words to his army. The principal facts, however, have not been forgotten. Napoleon presumed to covet Moscow; he hoped to rule in place of the Russian tsar; he was thwarted largely by the dogged determination and generalship of Kutuzov; Russia was saved by the loyalty and courage of her generals.

THE INVASION BY THE FRENCH
UNDER NAPOLEON (1812)

Recorded from the territory of the Don Cossacks

Kirêevski, *Pésni*, pt. x, p. 2.

It happened in the land of France,
Our dog of an enemy, King Napoleon, appeared.
He collected an army from various lands,
He loaded his galleys with various goods,
And these various goods were lead and powder;   5
And he wrote a dispatch to the Tsar Alexander:
'I beg you, Tsar Alexander, I beg you, do not be angry,
Prepare for me a lodging in the Kremlin of Moscow,
Prepare your royal palace for me, the French king'.
The Tsar Alexander sat down in his chair to think it over,   10
The expression of his royal countenance changed;
Before him stood a general—Prince Kutuzov himself:
'Fear not, fear not, Tsar Alexander, do not be dismayed!
We will welcome him half-way, that dog of a foe.
We will prepare him delicacies of bombs and bullets,   15
As an entrée we will offer him cannon-balls,
As a side-dish we will present him with deadly grapeshot,
So that his warriors will march home again under their banners'.
Then our Tsar Alexander rejoiced greatly,
The Tsar Alexander cried out and proclaimed in a loud voice:
'Exert yourselves to the utmost, you warrior Cossacks,   21
And I will richly reward your horsemen,
I will confer high rank upon your officers;
I will discharge you, my children, to the glorious silent Don'.

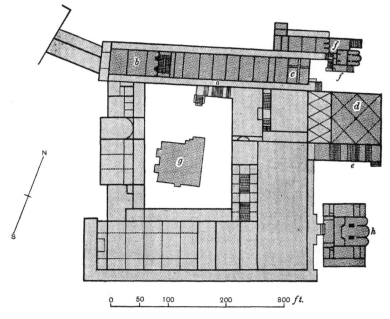

Great Kremlin Palace, Moscow, upper floor,
occupying the original site of the old wooden and
stone palaces of the tsars previous to 1737

Only the buildings of the north and east, notably the Terems, the Faceted Palace,
and the Red Staircase, retain their original structure

ROUGH SKETCH PLAN

(a) Terem gallery. Inner wall ancient.
(b) Church of the Nativity of the Virgin, formerly the domestic
chapel of the tsaritsas, founded 1393, rebuilt 1514.
(c) Golden chamber, audience chamber of the tsaritsas, dating
from the end of the XVI century.
(d) Faceted Palace, built 1473–91, restored 1882.
(e) Red Staircase, formerly roofed, but roofless since the fire
of 1696.
(f) Terem, built in 1636 by Mikhailo Fedorovich and Alexis.
It consists of five floors arranged in pyramidal form.
(g) Church of the Redeemer in the Wood, the original centre
of Moscow. Present structure built in 1330, restored in
1863.
(h) Blagovĕshchenski Cathedral. See key to plan of the Kremlin.

LVIII

The Death of the Tsar Alexander I

ALEXANDER I died in 1825 at Taganrog in South Russia, where he had gone for his health, and to visit his southern provinces. This picturesque little *bylina*, and those which follow, are interesting as showing the naïveté with which the old poetical diction and style was applied to modern conditions and events. Nevertheless the *bylina* has no predecessors as regards its form or framework, and so far as I know is original in theme.

THE DEATH OF THE TSAR ALEXANDER I

Recorded from Simbirsk

Kirêevski, *Pêsni*, pt. x, p. 197.

Our Tsar Alexander has gone to review his army;
Our Tsar Alexander has promised to come to the house of
    Rozhestov.
Everybody is out on holiday—Alexander is not at home.
'I will go,[1] I will climb the tower—the highest tower of all,
I will gaze in the direction where my Alexander has gone!'   5
Along the Piterski road the dust rises in columns,
The dust rises in columns—a young courier is running.
'I will go, I will question the courier: "Whither, courier, are you
    running?
Can you give us tidings, courier, of the Tsar Alexander?"'
'Throw off your crimson shawls, put on your black mourning-
    weeds,   10
I have tidings of the Tsar Alexander for all you loyal souls.
Our Tsar Alexander has died in Taganrog,
And twelve generals act as bearers to our tsar,
While two officers lead his raven steed,
And four guardsmen march with banners.'   15

[1] From the variants recorded by Kirêevski (*loc. cit.*) it appears that it is the tsar's mother who speaks.

LIX

Lament of the Troops for the
Tsar Alexander I

THE following *bylina* may be compared with the Laments ascribed to the troops on the death of Ivan the Terrible (p. 210), of Peter the Great (p. 273), and of Katharine II (p. 284). In its main outline it follows the traditional form, and the words of the sentry are practically identical with the preceding. The popular singer has not wholly lost the power of independent composition, however, and the opening lines and conclusion of the poem are independent of his predecessors and adapted to contemporary circumstances. The Emperor's body was embalmed and carried with ceremony to St Petersburg.

LAMENT OF THE TROOPS FOR THE TSAR ALEXANDER I

Recorded from Shenkursk

Kirêevski, *Pêsni*, pt. x, p. 201.

In the tower of Ivan the Mighty
They are beating and tolling the great bells,
Till the sound is heard throughout all Moscow,
Throughout all Moscow, through all the army;
That our orthodox tsar is dead,   5
Alexander Pavlovich;—not in his palace,
Not in his palace, but in a far city,
In a far city, at the hot springs,
At Taganrog, in a mild climate.[1]

[1] The tsar died at Taganrog on the Black Sea, a noted resort for invalids because of its warm springs and light air.

A young soldier is standing sentry,   10
Is standing sentry, mounting guard;
He has bowed his rebellious head to the damp earth,
He has struck his spear in the damp earth:
'Rend asunder, damp mother earth,
Unfold, gold brocade,   15
Split open, coffin lid,
Stand up, stand up, our orthodox tsar,
Look, look over the whole of Russia,
Over the whole of Russia, over your army,
Over your army, over your beloved horse-guards.—   20
But they are carrying you with ceremony,
With ceremony, with great ceremony,
They are carrying you to the cathedral church,
To the cathedral church, the church of God!'

LX

The Campaign of Nikolai I
against Warsaw

WE have seen with surprise how few *byliny* the wars of the eighteenth century and the Napoleonic War have produced, as compared with the Cycle of Peter the Great. The *byliny* of the period of Nicholas I with their variants occupy only thirty pages in the tenth volume of Bezsonov's edition of Kirêevski's great collection. It is believed that *byliny* were composed on the Siege of Sebastopol, but they have not gained a wide circulation, and had not been published at the time when Kirêevski's collection was made. We have no doubt that *byliny* would still be composed during the Great War, but they have not found their way to Western Europe, and it is doubtful if they will have survived the body of new popular poetry which has sprung to life in the Soviet State. The *byliny* of the reign of Nikolai (Nicholas I) all have reference to his military activities. The following *bylina* has reference to the suppression of the revolt in Poland in 1832. During the reign of Katharine II, in 1772, took place the first partition of Poland, by which the country was divided among the three European powers of Russia, Austria and Prussia. In 1791 the Poles asserted their independence; but internal dissensions ruined their efforts, the Prussians united with the Russians against them, and in 1793 a second partition of the country took place, by which Poland was divided between Russia and Prussia. Further attempts to regain her independence were crushed by the Russian general Suvarov who succeeded in capturing Warsaw. In 1795 the third partition of Poland put an end to the monarchy, and the country was again divided between Russia, Prussia and Austria. During the reign of the Tsar

Alexander I, in 1815, at the Congress of Vienna, a further rearrangement of territory took place. In 1830 an insurrection took place on account of the interference of the tsars with Polish constitutional rights. The grand duke withdrew from Warsaw, and the Poles awaited a war with Russia. A large Russian army entered the country in January 1831 and a series of battles took place in which the Poles were at first successful. In September, however, the Russian general Paskêvich succeeded in crossing the Vistula and taking Warsaw. The war was at an end, and in the following year Poland was declared an integral part of the Russian Empire.

THE CAMPAIGN FROM THE SOUTH AND EAST AGAINST WARSAW. THE EMPEROR NIKOLAI I

Recorded from Suzdal

Kirêevski, *Pésni*, pt. x, p. 472.

We stood at the frontier,
We thought of nothing else,
Save only we were thinking and devising
How to equip ourselves well,
To equip ourselves, and get ourselves ready,   5
To occupy the city.
We had scarcely had time to equip ourselves
Before they sent us our orders;
We read through the orders,
And at once we set off on our march.   10
We went forward on our march
Till we came to the River Danube.
Quickly we made the crossing;
It was a crossing full of woe!
Two enemies did we meet,   15
In broad daylight.
When we discharged our cannon,
It was like thunder-clouds bursting;

When we fired off our muskets,
Mother earth groaned.[1]   20
All the summer we remained in camp.
The sovereign presented himself to us;
He passed before us,
Before us grenadiers,
And spoke a gracious word: 25
'Salutations to you, you grenadiers,
Long may you live, my glorious heroes!
Tell me, you grenadiers,
How you have fared on the way?'
We marched forth on our campaign,   30
We marched over the steppe,
We poured out our blood
On the bayonets at Warsaw,
In the fourth and fifth platoons,
With our banners before us,   35
In the sixth and seventh platoons
We all cried 'Hurrah,
Honour and glory to our sovereign!'

[1] Our version concludes at this point. What follows forms the concluding portion of a variant version of the same poem recorded by
Kirêevski, *Pêsni*, pt. x, p. 474 f.

For EU product safety concerns, contact us at Calle de José Abascal, 56–1°,
28003 Madrid, Spain or eugpsr@cambridge.org.

www.ingramcontent.com/pod-product-compliance
Ingram Content Group UK Ltd.
Pitfield, Milton Keynes, MK11 3LW, UK
UKHW010349140625
459647UK00010B/946